"Reading D.W. Brown's lovely and miraculous book, and seeing acting through his brilliant eyes, I found myself again passionate for the nuts and bolts of craft and the simple beauty of expression he so gorgeously clarifies. *You Can Act* proves the theatrical endeavor to be a brave act of pure being and soul."
— Jeff Goldblum (*Jurassic Park, Independence Day*)

"If you're serious about being an actor, read this book. D.W. Brown knows what he's talking about and he communicates it with inspiration, humor and simplicity."
— Leslie Mann (*The 40-Year-Old Virgin, Knocked Up*)

"D.W. has a way of communicating complex actions with such simplicity and clarity that the heartbeat of the scene suddenly appears thrillingly within you. He guides you to the tools you are already holding, and then reminds you how exciting it can be to really use them. Under his direction I felt inspired, safe, and capable of anything."
— Olivia Wilde (*House, Alpha Dog*)

"I remember feeling a sense of security from D.W. He provided an atmosphere within which the insecure, novice actor could safely strive, explore, and even fail."
— Robin Wright-Penn (*The Princess Bride, Forrest Gump*)

"D.W.'s commitment to push his students to achieve the absolute best they possibly can, was a major factor in helping me understand the level of dedication, perseverance and effort it takes to succeed in this business at any level. D.W. has an uncanny ability to make one feel comfortable and safe, while at the same time pushing for excellence and creativity. It is an experience that undoubtedly helped me find work, and keep working in this unpredictable industry, instilling in me a sense of pride and confidence that I otherwise lacked!"
— Michael Vartan (*Alias, Never Been Kissed*)

"I owe D.W. Brown so many thanks for teaching me the craft of acting. The work I did with him changed my life and my career."
— Jamie Kennedy, actor, writer, producer
(*Three Kings, The Jamie Kennedy Experiment*)

"D.W. Brown's manner as a film director captures the essence and class of Old Hollywood directors. When giving input to his actors, he gracefully tackles the most complex issues with the utmost simplicity, and always with his signature charming smile."
— Shoreh Aghdashloo (Academy Award® nominee,
Best Supporting Actress for *House of Sand and Fog*)

"D.W. Brown guided me in how to work with actors. I've incorporated the basic premises he works under and he gave me a lot of tips. We've spent time talking about character and he raises interesting questions and suggests approaches we might take in pulling off certain scenes. He has really helped me a lot."
— Sam Raimi, director (*Spider-Man* 1, 2 & 3)

"D.W. Brown is one of the world's foremost experts in the craft of acting and the school where he teaches is the finest in Los Angeles. I always look to cast his well-trained actors in my films."
— Martha Coolidge (*Real Genius*), President of the Directors Guild of America

"D.W. Brown trains beginning actors and makes them working actors, and he takes working actors and makes them stars."
— Valerie McCaffrey, Head of Casting for New Line Cinema

"Working with D.W. Brown is the most important thing I have done for my career. He has a gentle, disarming way about him which helped me break down my social veneers and limitations, and allowed me to expand my capabilities as an actress. This method gave me a road map to follow and all of the tools I needed to continue to develop my instincts so I could take on any role and feel confident about it."
— Sharon Case (six-time nominee and winner of the Daytime Emmy for Outstanding Actress, *The Young and the Restless*)

"DW directs with much skill and an intuitive knowledge of character. He seems to excel at various creative forms. He's a fine actor, writer, and director. These are all forms of storytelling, and, above all that's what I would call D.W. — a great storyteller."
— Nick Stahl, Actor (*Terminator 3, Carnivale*)

"I am amazed by just how much my training with D. W. has impacted my work as a host/journalist during the past 14 years. Whether sitting for an in-depth interview or delivering copy directly into camera, the tools and skill set I established years ago while studying Meisner with him continue to serve me today. Listening, being curious, staying in the moment, and reacting have helped me develop into the best interviewer I can be. I approach my on-camera reads with an open heart so I can allow the story I am communicating to my audience to effect me and flow through me, allowing an emotional reaction the audience can connect with."
— Mark Steines, host of *Entertainment Tonight*

YOU CAN ACT!

A COMPLETE GUIDE FOR ACTORS

D.W. BROWN

Published by Michael Wiese Productions
3940 Laurel Canyon Blvd. # 1111
Studio City, CA 91604
tel. 818.379.8799
fax 818.986.3408
mw@mwp.com
www.mwp.com

Cover Design: MWP
Interior Book Design: Gina Mansfield Design
Editor: Paul Norlen

Printed by McNaughton & Gunn, Inc., Saline, Michigan
Manufactured in the United States of America

Library of Congress Cataloging-in-Publication Data

Brown, D. W., 1956–
 You can act / D. W. Brown.
   p. cm.
 Includes bibliographical references and index.
 ISBN 978-1-932907-56-8 (alk. paper)
 1. Acting. I. Title.
 PN2061.B765 2009
 792.02'8—dc22

                                        2008051689

This book is dedicated to my dad,
Richard Brown

&

my wife,
Joanne Baron-Brown.
Together they made a man of me.

Table of Contents

Acknowledgments

It all started when, at the age of six, I saw my father, a pediatric cardiologist, perform in a community theater production of *The Diary of Anne Frank*. With the blessings of this wonderful man, I have pursued a life in the arts. At fourteen, having bounced around children's theater in Tucson, Arizona, I joined a group lead by Andy Quirk, out of the Actor's Studio in New York, and he showed me that acting wasn't fun — it was everything. I also owe thanks to the many actors, directors and writers, good and not so good, from whom I have learned over the years, and to the passion and beauty of the many students it has been my good fortune to join for a time on their journey. I've had great friends who egged me on in my madness, Mike, Robin and Eric, but far and away the greatest influence on my life and my craft has been my wife of twenty-two years, Joanne Baron, one of the acknowledged master teachers of acting of this age. And lastly, the publisher of this book, Michael Wiese, who encouraged me to write in my own voice, and who, along with assistance from Ken Lee, Paul Norlen and others at MWP, maintains a catalog I am ever so proud to join.

Introduction

I've put everything I know about the craft of acting into this book. My dad was a doctor, and he told me his job was to try and eliminate the need for his services. So it is I've aspired to be a teacher of acting whose students eventually wouldn't need me. I never wanted to run one of those acting classes where the instructor enters and the students are expected to stand and applaud; or like the guy with lights, not just for the stage, but one directed at the chair where he sat. It's easy for an acting teacher to take on the aspect of a cult leader. You don't need credentials. All you have to do is put some poor soul on a stage and ask them to confess what their issue is with the same-gender parent, or their weight, or the reason they're holding themselves back, and the tears will flow and, lo, power shall be conferred upon whoever is asking all these personal questions. I never had time for that. I had enough to do trying to get my students ready to act so well they could get cast in a part instead of the producer's kid.

That's not to say I haven't pushed for personal truth, volcanic emotion or primitive recklessness in the actors I've worked with. I just wanted it clear I wasn't running psychological experiments and that we were always in the service of something besides our own acting out. That we were supposed to be about "holding a mirror up to nature."

Acting is an art, and, like all arts, it will ultimately be beyond intellectual understanding. Yet, while the spark of life within a seed may be an unfathomable miracle, we have real, no-nonsense ways of bringing forth the fruit. Likewise, the cultivation of an actor's talent and the process of their doing a decent job playing a part doesn't have to be treated like voodoo. In these pages I will hopefully convey my profound reverence for the nature of beauty, and the romantic adventure that is acting in particular, but I intend to give you straightforward techniques you can use to create an effective performance, under all circumstances, whether it's a comedy or a drama, a classic stage production or a TV commercial.

This book is meant to provide a detailed, comprehensive system that will help you do what you've been charged to do as an actor: perform an entertaining character that serves the fiction of which it is are a part. The technique I advocate is, first and foremost, what is referred to as internal acting, with the major influences being those of Konstantin Stanislavski, Sanford Meisner, William Esper and my brilliant wife, Joanne Baron. By internal I mean that you will be asked to live through your performance, utilizing your true emotions at their most vivid, with a priority placed on an active participation with moment-to-moment events and your genuine effort to attain objectives. This is in contrast to external acting, which has its priority on the clarity of a performance that can be followed from the back of a large theater, where emotions are demonstrated, rather than truly felt, and what is done is pretended to be done in a controlled fashion. In my opinion, the vast majority of good acting arrives at the same place, regardless of the emphasis of the school. Whether it's someone trained in an external school who then comes to value the aspects of connecting emotionally to their circumstances, and leaps in with a spirit of improvisation by really doing what they're doing with a sense that it could go any way this time, or the internal actor who respects the demands of representing themselves in a particular way, as when there is a need for performing specific Actions, doing the proper accent or projecting to the back of a large theater. My feeling is simply that the horse of real connection should always be in front of the cart of theatrical obligation.

The heart of this book is represented in the first three chapters: Breaking Down the Material, Working Toward Performance and Doing the Performance. Beyond this, I've included a description of fundamental principles for your development and work habits, and offered information that you can apply to specific parts and situations. I even threw in a chapter for our sister profession with Advice for Commentators.

Breaking Down the Material is a guide for you in how to analyze your text so you fully appreciate what will be necessary to craft a clear and moving portrayal. This is the deep science of character interpretation that takes into consideration the style of a piece, its theme, and the specific way each scene might be played. The next section, Working Toward Performance, gives you instruction for putting those determinations into practice so that the desired responses and behaviors become, for the most part, unconscious in the playing. This is a process that allows you to dedicate yourself with such intensity to the preparation that you achieve maximum freedom and ease during the performance. Then, in Doing the Performance, I specify where you should have your attention while you're acting, what pitfalls to avoid, and how you can use attention to detail and an embrace of the unexpected to optimize the release of your preparation and encourage your intuition. I'm getting excited just writing about it.

The procedure for Breaking Down the Material will address first the Whole Piece, then the Specific Character, then the Specific Scenes. While the process is put forth in this way, going from an examination of the big picture to isolate the small detail, it certainly isn't meant to be a one-way street. Assessments ought to be made continuously from every angle. Perhaps only after intensive work has been done within a specific scene, within a specific moment, will a new understanding reflect back on a larger truth about the theme or your character's part in the story, and you'll have to reexamine and readjust accordingly.

By the same token, in analyzing your specific character, we'll look at the behavior explicitly described in the text first — your character's demonstrated behavior — before we examine the underlying psychology that creates that behavior. Without question, the work you do on the psychology of the character will result in behavior not explicitly referred to. For example, while a nervous gesture would obviously need to be applied if it is described in the text, it's also possible that, although such a gesture is never mentioned, you will choose to have one after you've explored the character's internal life.

I love actors and acting. Such brave, passionate people. Such an opportunity to taste so many aspects of life. As an actor you go into a wild realm, and, although you're given a map by the playwright and maybe some instruction from a director, ultimately you go it alone. I hope this book will be of some aid for you on your journey. I want this so that you achieve greater heights and deeper insights for the benefit of us all.

Teaching class.

SECTION

ACTING A ROLE

chapter 1

Breaking Down the Material

The first thing you need to do if you're going to act in something is to find out what needs to be worked on so you can do justice to the part and make every possible appeal to your artistic sensibilities. Great performances aren't an accident. You may be talented and you may be cute, but a real actor is called upon to assay material written by some of the finest minds humanity has ever produced and, I'm sorry, that's probably going to take a little work.

You're like an architect who's been given a set of constraints: the particular type of building to create (your role), the exact dimensions of the lot (this production), and the demands of a perfectionist client (the director). While intuition must be respected and flexibility encouraged, before you start buying lumber and hammering nails, it's nice to have some idea of what the hell you're doing.

The Emotional Bridge. Having said this, depending on the part, some issues may be more important to consciously examine than others. There may be roles that don't require a great deal of deliberate analysis because, by way of your own natural make up, you'll supply the necessary details. If you're a socially shy, Italian-American boxer from Brooklyn, you won't have to do a lot of planned character work to play a character like Rocky. The most innate situation for you is going to be playing someone exactly like yourself right now in a contemporary, naturalistic setting.

If the values and basic behaviors of the character are the same as yours, and you feel an affinity for the piece, then just about all the analysis you'll need to do can be gotten by using the Emotional Bridge (using your own emotional sensitivities to "bridge" you to the part). You simply ask yourself: *If I were in this situation, how would I feel about it, and what would I do?* This is the most basic use of what's called the "Magic If."

But come on now, don't be lazy. Be an actor. Maybe you can pull it off doing the part straight from yourself, but seriously assess what's in front of you before you decide to go that way. There's a much greater chance that the Emotional Bridge by itself won't be enough and you're going to have to pursue a deeper examination of the character and the piece. Also, a case can be made that the only way to deliver a truly great acting performance is as a result of willful, aesthetic choices. Stella Adler said: "The talent is in the choices." What makes a performance transcendent is that there's been an approach decided upon that then, in the actual presentation, adapts itself to the moment. A plan brought to life. Or, as "greatness" is defined by Fast Eddie Felson (in Robert Rossen's *The Hustler*): "If a guy knows what he's doing and he can make it come off."

THE PIECE AS A WHOLE

Did I say you're like an architect? Forget that. You're a detective. There may be explicit information in the text about things like what's happened or what your character wants, but often it won't be openly disclosed and you'll have to sift through clues and make inferences. Whether your character, or even the playwright who created them, consciously knows the exact details underlying this story, it'll be up to you to establish a working theory for the specifics.

Before getting started on an explanation of how to break down the material as a whole piece, let it be said that, if you're going to be performing in a play that's been done before, you can probably get a leg up by researching reviews and other sources that will tell you what experts have had to say about the plot, style, theme and character dynamics of the piece you're going to undertake. This is, of course, no substitute for doing your own investigative work, but if the information is out there, why not take advantage of it?

How does it strike you? You should be especially sensitive to your first impression when exposed to the material, and read the entire piece with an open heart. Suppress the desire to go right to your part so you can count how many lines you have and imagine how wonderful you'll be when momma comes to see it. Easy, Tiger. Right now you need to get a sense for the piece as a whole. How it hangs together as a work of art. This means you might also have to leave aside, as much as possible, preconceived ideas about who's involved in the production, how it might have been done before, or how it would have been better if it had been written in a different way. Let it play upon you new, just as it is; there'll be time enough for that other stuff.

It should be read repeatedly.

What happens? You want to get a handle on the plot so that you could tell somebody the basic story. It should be felt as an experience that is lived through with a vivid and specific life.

What is the style of the piece? Try and imagine what the overall tone and spirit of this presentation might be. Style is the form that's been used to transmit this particular artistic vision, and it's intimately connected with the genre. There should be consistency to the natural law and the phenomenon within this fictional world: the atmosphere, the design and decor, the motifs, should all be harmonious.

Every time you take on a part you're like a musician entering a new band who needs to get a feel for the type of the music they'll be playing. Often you see an actor whom you've previously liked totally tank in a part because they don't play the qualities of this different kind of style.

Maybe you have a favorite style you prefer and it suits you and, hell, maybe you'll get on a successful television show and make a handsome living never having to deviate from it. That's fine. But every role you take on has to be performed in the particular style required. It's your job.

To ascertain the style of the piece, it's probably best to visualize how this kind of thing has been done in the past. Ask yourself: *What does this remind me of?* Unless it's from a completely different culture, you've almost certainly been exposed to something similar to this. Authors will tend to write in a favorite style, so maybe it's possible to compare it to their other works.

You can look at this issue of style from the point of view of genre. Certain types of subject matter have particular styles associated with them and will tend to similar points of view and common qualities among the characters. A gritty crime story will feature characters with raw emotional lives, whereas, in the sunnier world of Light Comedy, no one is savagely enraged or catastrophically grief stricken; those qualities will be limited for the most part to irritation and sentimentality.

A character in a Light Comedy who discovers their spouse is cheating on them relates to this event probably more the way you would if you were to find out that they'd ruined your credit. The feelings should be real, but they're going to be lightened in their intensity for the style. Light Comedies don't feature acts of real depravity: pirates are fun pirates. As these values start to increase in their gravity and realism, the style gets darker, until it passes through Naturalism and into the portrayal of a ridiculously grim world, referred to as a Black Comedy. In Black Comedy you may have to adjust your character's responses in the other direction, and be over-the-top awful, as in *There Will Be Blood* where Daniel Plainview pledges to cut a business rival's throat because he innocently asks him about his son.

The style will very much affect the way actors conduct themselves vocally and physically. If it's a naturalistic drama, or what's been called a "kitchen sink" drama, you can mumble and, if you itch, scratch away; but if it's a glossy High Drama, I don't care how much that costume pinches or that wig is bugging you — no touchy, Desdemona.

Style Value Ranges

You can evaluate the tone of a piece in relation to where it falls on a scale of values.

- ▶ Realistic *vs.* Bizarre (Broad)
- ▶ Gloomy *vs.* Sparkling
- ▶ Chaotic *vs.* Orderly
- ▶ Brash *vs.* Tranquil
- ▶ Dangerous *vs.* Leisurely
- ▶ Raw *vs.* Poised
- ▶ Grim *vs.* Silly
- ▶ Stark Patina *vs.* Glossy Patina

Some Style Labels

- ▶ Absurd: odd people in completely unrealistic, painful situations. (*Waiting for Godot, Eraserhead*)

- Action: the heroic and the eccentric in a flamboyant, tough world.
  (*Die Hard, Goldfinger*)
- Black Comedy: desperate people in a grim, eccentric world.
  (*Fargo, Dr. Strangelove*)
- Camp: a skewed period setting with dark, adult, but safe, silliness.
  (*Pirates of the Caribbean, Blazing Saddles*)
- Fantasy: a romantic, elegant world of heroes and monsters.
  (*Lord of the Rings, Harry Potter*)
- Farce: goofy and scheming people in fanciful situations.
  (*There's Something About Mary, Some Like It Hot*)
- High Drama/Comedy: formal, elevated lives of suppressed passion.
  (*Atonement, Shakespeare in Love*)
- Historical: an orderly stage where definitive, romantic actions unfold.
  (*Patton, Glory*)
- Horror: an orderly, naturalistic world with ghastly phenomena.
  (*The Exorcist, The Ring*)
- Light Comedy: silly, good-hearted folk in an unthreatening world.
  (*Little Miss Sunshine, Notting Hill*)
- Mystery: innocence and meanness in a glossy, shadowy world.
  (*Casablanca, Chinatown*)
- Naturalistic Drama/Comedy: realistic, human stories.
  (*Kramer vs. Kramer, The Goodbye Girl*)
- Surreal: a bleak, beautiful world on a precipitous slant.
  (*Blue Velvet, The Cabinet of Dr. Caligari*)
- Thriller: a sleek jungle of ruthless survival.
  (*Seven, The Bourne Identity*)
- Zany Comedy: fun outrageousness in a free-form universe.
  (*Airplane, Austin Powers*)

All these styles can overlap and blend, as when Horror mixes with Black Comedy so that the subject is both genuinely frightening and funny (as with *The Shining* or *Psycho*), or as Zany Comedy blends the melodrama of Light Comedy and is able to generate sentimental feeling (*Liar, Liar* or *Mrs. Doubtfire*).

▶▶ *Note:* **Talking about style is like describing cuisine. It's clumsy. And, just as saying a meal is "Northern Italian" is a long way from**

7

conveying the actual experience of the dish, calling something a "Mystery" doesn't give more than a vague sense for how it's going to be experienced. But don't let anybody kid you, everything has a style. It may be an inconsistent mess that no one can get comfortable with because the tones keep changing; or there's an intense effort made to make it look like reality, with ad-libbed dialog and inexperienced, unveneered actors and all, but everything that's created has its style.

In determining the style of a piece, as with all elements of Breaking Down the Material, using precedent isn't meant to be a substitute for your personal vision. The artist's creative invention should be working at all times and it may be worthwhile to revisit a work with a stylistic approach very different from what is the convention — it just shouldn't be done arbitrarily.

What is the setting? The environment in which the piece takes place must be examined for its Culture and Location, and all of this will have to be taken into account and later brought to life in your performance.

The Culture is where and when it takes place:
- ▶ The History
- ▶ Current Events
- ▶ System of Government
- ▶ Values of the Society
     Formal Religion
- ▶ Fashion
- ▶ Technology
- ▶ Economics (Standard of Living)
     Jobs

Values and economics may be interrelated in so far as there are class levels and different moral standards for people of different social standings. It's a scandal if the son of the mayor is seen intoxicated in public, but not so much when he's a boy from a family of ordinary construction workers. That construction worker's son, however, will probably receive more condemnation when he crashes his car than the rich kid who's more likely to receive sympathy because of "the disease" of his addiction.

The Location:
- ▸ Terrain
- ▸ Weather
- ▸ Architecture
   Furniture
- ▸ Lighting
- ▸ Sounds
- ▸ Smells

How do the characters interact? Think about the dynamics of the relationships in the piece, whether it is a family (literal or non-literal), a group organized to further a purpose, or different types of people who find themselves together and are currently sorting themselves out. The basic systems of human interaction repeat themselves in every culture: Collaborative Romantic Couple, Hierarchical Group with established responsibilities, Non-Coercive Adviser, and Willing Student(s).

People will tend to gravitate toward the model of the nuclear family. In a military squad, the leader will become like the dad, the sergeant something like a mother, and the privates take on the various roles of the children. In prison, it'll happen that an older, hardened criminal and his softer "wife" will assume the role of parents to young inmates.

Also, there are classic groupings that reoccur as entertaining models in the world of literature: Combative Romantic Couple, the Fool and the Bigshot, Flawed Leader and Idealist.

More rarely, the characters symbolize abstract concepts or entities, and just as with human systems, there are classic cosmic dynamics as well: Chaos/Order, Greed/Fellowship, Idealism/Humility.

What is the piece saying? You have to consider the Theme. The Theme is the message underlying the work, its unifying idea, the issue implied by the events and their conclusion. It can be identified through the central conflict and how the details of the story are connected to it: what the people are either embracing or denying. The title will usually speak to the Theme. As with style, authors tend to favor certain themes and there may be a trend within their work. Biographical information about the author might reveal clues to their point of view.

Actors can sometimes feel uncomfortable with the topic of Theme and avoid it for fear of being seen as ignorant or pretentious, but a purist would say it's essential to have an appreciation for the message of the piece, and that you have no right to take on the part if you have no idea why it exists in the first place. Silly purists. You can always tell them you like to operate on a deeper, intuitive level when it comes to the Theme — then just appreciate for yourself the subject as yet another helpful tool for creating a satisfying performance.

You needn't feel the Theme has to be some grand concept that if declared at a dinner table would bring everyone to reverent silence. Maybe it's just a simple fact of life. Or there can be multiple, overlapping Themes. Arthur Miller said almost all themes in literature were basically variations on "how the birds come home to roost." Also known as: "What goes around, comes around."

I do recommend you eventually get some kind of feeling for your Theme. Beyond giving you a way of breaking down the material effectively, if you understand the theme of your piece, you can connect to your purpose for presenting this work of art, and having that sense of mission will infuse your performance with extra passion.

Possible Themes

▶ Fate cannot be changed.
▶ Life must express itself.
▶ A person must live by a code.
▶ Know your limitations or face ruin.
▶ You have to risk big to live big.
▶ A sin/truth cannot be buried.
▶ Unchecked Greed/Pride/Lust/Vanity/Wrath/Idealism brings ruin.
▶ Greed/Pride/Lust/Vanity/Wrath/Idealism will make you look foolish.
▶ Virtue (charity, hard work, moderation, etc.) will be rewarded.
▶ There are monsters in the world that must be dealt with.
▶ You must do what it takes to get yourself home.
▶ What is attractive can be harmful.

- Innocence must be left behind.
- A person must take responsibility for/forgive/let go of what's past.
- Pursuing a romantic idea brings unhappiness.
- Society/technology/business is heartless.
- Evil cannot crush the human spirit.
- A person/a couple/a social order must withstand a trial.
- One person can make a difference.
- Unity is strength.
- Family is a war to be survived.
- Family is a crazy mess, but will sustain you.
- People find a way to get what they need from each other.
- People are never satisfied.
- We must struggle for Truth without ever knowing absolute Truth.
- The fragile will be crushed by an uncaring world.
- We must deal with Death in order to live.
- Life is to be embraced, not understood.
- God/Life is playing a joke on us.
- Love is all that matters.

It's extremely rare in the material you will be working with as an actor, but there may be esoteric productions where the Theme is impossible to describe as an idea, just as it may be impossible to describe the message of an instrumental piece of music or an abstract painting. It's possible the presentation is intended only to have an emotional impact; and the theme may be perceived simply as a distinctive reoccurring form or motif. Maybe it's only saying: "You are please-able" or "You are alarmable." This kind of material tends toward what you might think of as "performance art," and perhaps is less likely to be presented on a stage than it would be, say, a museum or a mental institution.

THE SPECIFIC CHARACTER

Who am I in this? When you start to concentrate on your specific character, you have to give attention to the part you play in the story. Your character should be considered for the contribution they make to furthering the plot: *as the bad guy's fresh and innocent first victim you show how evil he is and the need for him to be stopped, or, by acting foolish, you show how some people like you bring trouble on themselves. As the bad guy's henchman you show, through encouraging his misdeeds, the power of this particular confederacy of evil*, or, through signs of true friendship with him you show that, regardless of how evil someone is, they still need companionship.

Ask yourself: What would be missing from the story if my part were removed?

Weigh how your part reflects on the theme. Do you affirm the theme: as a fragile person you are crushed by an uncaring world, or, even though your body is fragile, your human spirit cannot be crushed. On the other hand, maybe your part is meant to apply tension against the theme: the message is "one must forgive what is past to move on," but it's difficult when the crime committed against you was so terrible, or, "one must live by a code," but the justice that is brought as a function of that code is questioned by your decent character advocating the enlightened position of due process or forgiveness.

▶▶ **Note: It's going to be difficult for you to do justice to your part if you have an overweening desire is to show yourself off and stand out as a distinctive voice when your role is that of a supporting player. In this case, you must get yourself to accept that you are, literally, a role-player. If you'll allow me my musician analogy again: you're not doing your job as the rhythm guitarist if you're noodling away when you should be playing solid chords. My suggestion is to seek perfection in, and take joy from, striving for greater and greater purity in doing just the simple thing that is required. You may be surprised at how embracing profound simplicity can make you stand out and get you noticed.**

What would I be called? I'm a _____. Envision how your character's most remarkable qualities and basic essence might create a single entity. This is called the "Character Handle." It is a concise, meaningful description, expressed from a universal point of view. It may be a stock character. (*See* Table of Characters.)

A character's most important qualities may be singular, big things (*an alcoholic prostitute*), or a collection of small attributes that create something

12

pronounced (*an innocent farm boy*), but whatever the extent of the complexity, the Character Handle should be concise and it should have bite. It's preferable to have a succinct description that will effectively drive to the essence of the character, rather than a long, analytic pronouncement that might impress your fellow intellectuals over drinks, but do nothing toward getting you closer to the part. The best Character Handle to inspire you may even be more of an image than a description: *a wounded lion, a spark of light, a little boy looking out a window.*

Your character's basic qualities will fall somewhere on the many scales of descriptions for people, for example:

- Introverted *vs.* Extroverted
- Carefree *vs.* Severe
- Anxious *vs.* Depressed
- Chaotic *vs.* Orderly
- Adventurous *vs.* Timid
- Submissive *vs.* Authoritative
- Sensitive *vs.* Blunt
- Volatile *vs.* Even-Tempered
- Tactile *vs.* Physically Isolated
- Funny *vs.* Serious
- Romantic *vs.* Pragmatic
- Profane *vs.* Pious
- Tasteless *vs.* Stylish
- Clumsy *vs.* Nimble

And on and on I could go with this two-pole smorgasbord, I suppose. Please remember, though, that all the naming and categorizing in the world might shed less, true light on your character, and provide less tangible results in your performance, than the way you, for instance, equate them with the feeling you get from a pair of boots, or four bars of music, or the smell of a hospital. I personally felt something happen for me when I approached my role as a pediatric oncologist in *A Haunting in Connecticut*, simply by saying to myself: "I am the knife."

What's made me this way? It's essential in your analysis of your character to consider the details of their history: the environment in which they were raised and the specific, vivid events of their life. This history may be openly described in the text, or inferred from it, or maybe you'll want to use your imagination and fill it in yourself.

A person's prominent characteristics are usually observable very early in life. Parents will tell you they knew what kind of person their child was going to be before the age of three. It's quite possible, however, that a major aspect of someone's character has been defined by something that happened later in life: *falling in love, suffering a debilitating injury, trying an addictive drug, being traumatized by witnessing something terrible.*

It's worth making the point that you don't necessarily have to come up with any history at all to explain why your character is the way they are. Maybe they were simply born this way. They came into the world a wolf, or a beagle. Yes, you absolutely have to have a sense of context for your character, and a specific past may be a crucial factor in determining how your part should be played, but as long as you're creating specific behavior that hangs together and serves the piece, no one really cares where it comes from.

How do I speak, move, and perceive? You have to get a feel for how your Character carries themselves, their basic mental and physical attributes, including their speech, faculties, and the functioning of the five senses. If these factors vary from your normal way of being, they are referred to here as Character Additions, and they run the gamut of true human conditions and idiosyncrasies: *intoxication, brain damage, a Southern accent, the bearing of having been raised in military schools,* but also include the fantastical behaviors of theatrical presentations, as well: *demonic possession, love potion intoxication.*

A fundamental characteristic of your character is their Class: their refinement, intellect and charm. This isn't meant to describe your character's social standing, although it's likely it will be related. For the most part, Class is a result of your education and the amount of culture you've been exposed to. It probably influences your occupation and economic situation, although not always, as with a poet laborer who's turned his back on polite society, or an impoverished doctor. You may also have occasion to play someone whose Class has changed: *a lower class criminal who's become a lawyer in prison,* or *formerly of the upper class, they're now, as a junkie, living a life on the streets.*

The intellect is made up of both IQ and one's cleverness. These are distinct in that someone with a high IQ can be brilliant within certain fields, but nonetheless socially ignorant and easily confused by common concerns, while someone who is clever might be far more quick-witted and socially astute, even though they have less raw intelligence.

The charm someone possesses, their charisma, is an evaluation made by the present culture as to what their interesting qualities are and how they correspond to a universal type. Charm may come in part from a character's virtue and the amount of empathy they have, but with respect to theatrical presentations, more than anything charm is a factor of how passionately a character engages with the world. The necessity for a character to have "goodness" in order to be charismatic is refuted by the allure of such characters as Richard III and Count Dracula. These villains charm us because of their keen pursuit of Objectives and the interesting slant they take in getting them. Still, this kind of charisma without compassion, while fun to watch, doesn't empathetically connect us with the character, and we will shed no tears as the stake or sword pierces their black heart.

▸▸ *Note:* Class is one of the most difficult qualities for an actor to represent as different from their own, and casting is especially prone to being done to type in this area. It's possible that the style of the piece is formal enough that it allows for a performer to have more refinement as that character than if it were taking place in a naturalistic world: as with the glossy, stylized world of *Oh, Brother Where Art Thou* that forgives George Clooney's lack of true, hillbilly grit. If George Clooney showed up alongside the backwoods rapists in *Deliverance* it would be jarring, to say the least. Costume and makeup may help in this area a little, and, of course, taking on an accent consistent with the class level desired, as well as having a way of carrying yourself, perhaps related to years of a particular physical profession: Helen Hunt in *As Good As It Gets* made an effort to have the heavy feet of a career waitress. Another technique to bridge this discrepancy of refinement might be to adopt an addiction or some personality disorder to justify how someone of your innately higher Class level has come to find themselves in a lower class situation: *if not for the alcoholism, this character might be working as a professor instead of as a janitor, or, poor impulse control or attention deficit prevents them from holding a normal job, so they have resorted to a life of a petty crime.* In this way it seemed perfectly acceptable that someone as brilliant as David Thewlis' character in *Naked* would be nonetheless homeless, because, given how angry and misanthropic he was, you doubted he could hold any kind of job for more than half a day.

A character's speech consists of their voice and their diction. Voice is the way the sound is generated, resulting in timbre and resonance; diction is elocution and regionalisms, or how words are formulated, called by some specialists "the point of resonance."

The physical life of the character involves their bearing, where and how they place their energy and tension, influencing their balance and the way they walk. It also incorporates the character's overall movements, mannerisms, and the way they use personal objects and costume. A character's physical life will be influenced by their culture, occupation, individual psychology, physical afflictions or impairment of their faculties due to damage, psychosis or drugs.

It may be the total behaviors of your character represent a *Personification*. A Personification may be a Stock Character (*see* Table of Characters), an Incarnation or an Impersonation, or a combination of these.

A Stock Character is a character whose combined behaviors are recognized by the audience as a character they already know: the Miser, the Sweet Fool, the Casanova. Certain Stock Characters are associated with certain styles of presentation, and may be part of conventional pairings, "Scalawag" against "Stern Boss" in Broad Comedy, "Adventure Hero" against "Elegant Evil" in Adventure.

Personifications may also involve Incarnations. These are characters that resemble a specific animal (or, say, breed of dog) or, much less commonly, a specific object. To play the Incarnation of an animal, you study the particular qualities of a species of animal and then apply them to the behaviors of a human being. The animal may be sensuous, like a cat; or they might emphasize the sense of smell, like a dog, or they could have precise, sudden movements like a bird.

Many very successful performances have been based on animals: Dustin Hoffman took on some of the qualities of a rat in *Midnight Cowboy*, Lawrence

Olivier imitated a weasel when playing the title role in *Titus Andronicus*. Creating a character that is a composite of an animal is particularly effective for several reasons. For one, it presents a pattern of behaviors that hangs together and, even if the audience never consciously knows that you're working from an animal (which, unless the material is particularly stylized, should more often than not be the case), it carries with it the authenticity that somehow nature is capable of creating such a thing. Also, it inclines you to stay out of your head, because, in portraying an animal, you will also tend to take on their pure, beautiful spontaneity.

Note: I had an actress do a scene for me and completely blow it open, far and away better than anything she'd ever done before; so I asked her what happened. It was the scene was from *The Owl and the Pussycat* where her character comes in and confronts a man who has had her evicted. She said that, when I was giving her partner his notes, I told him that he was being too reasonable with her, and that he should relate to her character as if dealing with a crazed raccoon in his house. She said that this struck a chord in her because she'd grown up in an area with raccoons, and she knew them, and that she then imagined herself as one, dealing with a threat. All I knew was she was fantastic.

To perform an Incarnation of an object is more esoteric; but it is a viable way to tap into something intuitive and bring about specific character behavior. You could be, for instance, the spirit of a thorny rose, or an electrical storm, or a small creak in the woods. Of course, it's beyond exceedingly unlikely anyone will ever guess you're doing such an Incarnation; and if you do find yourself in a situation where your audience is suppose to know you're playing, say, "The Wind" or "An AK47," well, all I can say is I suggest you think long and hard before you insist Nana come see that particular show.

Another approach to character is an Impersonation. An Impersonation is when you choose to imitate a specific famous person who the audience knows. If the behaviors resemble the distinct characteristics of a definite person the audience recognizes, this will usually have the same effect as a Stock Character because the audience associates that celebrity with a Stock Character: Groucho Marx as "Scalawag," Jerry Lewis as

"Sweet Fool." Whether a given style will accommodate this celebrity impersonation or not typically requires that it be a good distance from naturalism, but the use of Impersonations is a completely legitimate way to portray a character, and the incongruity of the known person to the place may provide a nice jolt of camp.

What do I wish for most in life? Now we enter the realm of psychology and the internal motivations of your character. It can be immensely helpful in the portrayal of your character if you can pin down what is referred to as their Super-Objective or Life Drive: their dominant wish for their life, their overall longing, their heart's aspiration. Looked at from the other direction, ask yourself: *What situation would your character most hate to be in?*

One way of thinking about your Life Drive is in how it is your character wants to be praised. Everyone wants to be praised. The only difference is by whom and for what. One person wants all good-hearted people to praise them for being thoughtful, while another wants to be praised by a few superior minds for being effective; one wants to be praised for causing so little disturbance, another for the excitement they bring, pleasant or not. A person carries with them an internal spectator who is always judging their actions as praiseworthy or condemnable, and the people we encounter in life simply reflect back at us how we're doing at this job.

You can either work from the fact that there has been some event that put your character on the path toward this particular Life Drive, or you can simply say you were born moving on this course. It may be that your Life Drive is set and something happened to coax it toward a particular direction. For instance, a person might have been prone to adventure, and could have either found that adventure in mountain climbing, experimental medicine, or the exciting lifestyle of a heroin addict.

While it's actually rare for a person to themselves give much conscious thought to what their Life Drive is, it'll be helpful for you to think of the character's Life Drive as a definite vision for what would be their ideal state, or conversely, their worst. An awareness of your character's Super-Objective offers you an excellent tool in helping align a clear portrayal and can serve as the spine that connects the ways you'll react as a character to events, and the scene by scene, moment by moment, individual Objectives you seek.

There are nine major Life Drives and, although a person may combine aspects of any three groups, given the archetypal quality of storytelling, there's nothing wrong with your zeroing in on one.

Possible Life Drives

- Acceptance: *to be embraced, to be felt necessary.*
- Adventure: *to be at the most exciting spot, to see what's over the horizon.*
- Exchange: *to get people together, to see that justice is done.*
- Expression: *to be creative, to share oneself.*
- Freedom: *to defy authority, to be unrestrained.*
- Community: *to do what is honorable, to be of help.*
- Conquest: *to possess what is valuable, to be the first to get there.*
- Power: *to be seen as important, to create paradise.*
- Security: *to be protected from poverty, to be with someone protective.*

Of course, these Life Drives are described in general here and you'll want to make the details of these desires specific. Examples:

Acceptance: *to get your mother's approval or to be a good doctor.*

Adventure: *to be in the championship game or explore cutting-edge particle physics.*

Exchange: *to build a community center or to solve your brother's murder.*

Expression: *to paint the perfect painting or to get that man to marry you so can become your true self.*

Freedom: *to upset your father or to be able to move on without looking back.*

Community: *to help your family or to be a great cop.*

Conquest: *to get that beautiful woman or diagnosis that disease.*

Power: *to have your name on an imposing building or a lovely restaurant.*

Security: *to have a fortune as a safety net or to keep that scary man on your side.*

Note: **Many actors won't play what they think of as unlikeable**

▸▸ characters without unconsciously doing them in bad quality, "commenting on the character," so the audience is clear that they themselves aren't actually like this. One actor may be willing to fully inhabit an ineffectual type, but then be unwilling to be seen as an aggressive bully; others, vice versa. I asked Sean Penn how it was that he was able to play in good quality such a wide variety of characters who have what's generally thought of as repellant characteristics. He said: "As much as I might get angry at an individual who's being a problem for me in a moment, I think I'm basically non-judgmental about the human condition. We're all in this together." Terence expressed this sentiment over two thousand years before him: "I am a human being, and nothing human is alien to me."

A person's Life Drive is the expression of their "life force," what Nietzsche called "the will to power," one might even say, Love. It can be judged as distorted or misguided, and in particular cases evil, but it is an effort by life to thrive and express its nature. Lifting a rock you can find a plant that is yellowed and twisted, but all that tangle was its valiant effort to get to the sun.

What do I crave? Hang in here with me now, because words can be a problem in this area. In examining the motivations of a character, I'm going to try to distinguish between two types of desires: wishes (Life Drives) and cravings. Wishes are what someone wants as an ideal, a striving for bliss; cravings are pathological urges and compulsions, and they are made up of both universal needs and particular quirks only certain people have. Cravings would include: water, a cigarette, food, a lucky charm, a safe place to live, to talk with someone about common interests, to be around horses, a meaningful job, a gamble in play, a child close and happy, a garden to sit in, sleep, dangerous sex, demeaning sex, romantic sex, to get out of the cold… did I mention sex?

So you see, you can say a character wants to go on vacation, but you as the actor will want to make a distinction between them wanting it because it fulfills their desire to see what's over the hill, or to be thought of as affluent, or to be around people of a common heritage (all wishes for one's Life Drive), or do they want to go because they need to relieve built-up stress (a universal craving). And yes, it can be both.

The flipside aspect of someone's cravings are their repulsions

20

(phobias) and you should ask: What do I find revolting? These include things commonly detested (spiders, sewage smell, fingernails on a blackboard, cannibalism, incest), things somewhat common (fishy smell, crinkling plastic, mice), and things repulsive only to particular individuals, made up of a bizarre, almost infinite array (clowns, polka music, the smell of old people). You probably know someone with one of these freaky idiosyncrasies.

The gratification of a Life Drive wish, by itself, will fill a person with a sense of harmony; the gratification of a craving, or the avoidance of a repulsion, provides a release of tension, an itch that is scratched. What a person wishes for they usually embrace as their identity, proudly claiming it as such with an intention for future behavior: "I throw great parties" or "I love adventure" or "I was born to play music." What they crave, on the other hand, is either accepted with a shrug, actively despised as a weakness, or, at best, thought wonderful only for how much delight it brings them. Rare is the person who thinks of a craving or revulsion as conferring any special talent on themselves, and you don't often hear anyone boast, "I'm great at enjoying cheesecake" or "I love having a safe place to sleep" or "I was born to avoid bats."

Bearing in mind the author's intent, you can visualize what would most satiate your character, *what would directly neutralize their elemental urges.* Whether or not it's what the character wants to want, imagine what would give them the greatest release. This isn't to say, by any means, that your character is choosing to move towards the gratification of what they crave; on the contrary, they might even take pride in punishing their appetites. But ask yourself if they have a craving or a repulsion that is currently pressing for relief.

The psychologist Abraham Maslow was first to list a universal hierarchy of these cravings, which he called "needs," putting forth that only when a priority level need is gratified will the next level express itself. A person must first have air before they will worry about food.

Maslow's Hierarchy of Needs

> ▷ 1st Level: Physiological Needs: the demands necessary for sustaining the body (may include things the body thinks it needs to sustain itself, e.g. drugs).

▶ 2nd Level: Safety Needs: shelter and protection from imminent physical threat.

▶ 3rd Level: Social Needs: intimacy with others.

▶ 4th Level: Esteem Needs: to feel meaningful.

▶ 5th Level: Aesthetic Needs: to have beauty.

▶ 6th Level: Understanding Needs: to have a sense of one's context.

▶ 7th Level: Self-Actualization Needs: to realize one's highest purpose as a being.

▶ 8th Level: Transcendence: to join with all things.

Without laboring the point overmuch, these psychological systems are continuously debated and it's worth noting that there is some question as to the rigidity of the hierarchal nature of these needs and how the fulfilling of a higher need will abate the desire for a lower one. While addictive substances can operate at such a deep level that the brain says, "Get more of this or you will die!", recovery programs suggest a reliance on community and spirituality, higher level values, to help quell the craving. Viktor Frankl wrote brilliantly of how he and others in a concentration camp survived extreme physical deprivation through a search for meaning in life. Also, in a theatrical presentation, the death of a character for a good cause, such as rescuing a stranger, can be felt to be a kind of victory, even though this is obviously a failure for their biological needs.

What is the dynamic between what I wish for and what I crave? Some wishes drive a person to pursue an objective that overlaps with what they crave in that moment, and this character, moving directly on the path of their Life Drive, as they gratify their craving at the same time, will probably feel themselves in a state of true contentment: *a thrill seeker working as a missionary fulfills both the wish for adventure and the need for meaning; a justice seeker hearing the harsh sentence given the man who injured them fulfills both the wish for justice and the craving for revenge; a lover of power taking a hit of cocaine gets both the substance they crave and the demonstration that they are indulging in an expensive luxury; a good Samaritan helping their child tie their shoe both relishes doing good and bonds with family.* This is why sexual relations can be so powerful because they not only fulfill the universal and specialized cravings associated with sex, but they also work to satisfy Life Drives such as Adventure, Expression, Conquest.

It's also possible that a character's Life Drive can be at odds with an essential craving (or repulsion) of their nature, and so this character will experience the ache of being torn: *a girl wishes to have the approval of her parent, but craves a lover who her parent rejects; a prisoner escapes and beats the system, but feels insecure without the stability of institutional life, a man wishes to do what is honorable, but is obsessed with a new stepdaughter.* In this way, there are characters who will have a constant, internal conflict: *they want to be impressively powerful, but crave the embrace of their unimpressive family, they want safety, but crave companionship that can only be achieved through risk; they want freedom of expression, but live in a society that only embraces conformity.*

It's possible to have a character who lives without internal conflict, and the subject of the presentation is an external conflict, or to have a situation where an otherwise deeply conflicted character, when faced with an external conflict, such as being trapped in a burning building, becomes completely unconflicted in wanting and craving the same thing, namely to survive the fire.

The conflict may be caused by something mundane: *wanting to be helpful by listening to the troubles of a friend, but desperately having to go to the bathroom; wanting to camp out, but fearing snakes, or the tension may be on a larger scale: wanting to land the airplane, but losing consciousness from exhaustion; wishing to be with the rich girl, but craving the poor one.*

Cravings operate independent of a person's judgments or society's values, and the craving itself cares not at all that an addiction to heroin is considered shameful while the desire to protect one's offspring is thought admirable, or that a sexual attraction on a honeymoon is considered romantic, but at a funeral for one's wife it's obscene. Even so, an audience will as likely as not favor your character's pursuing the gratification of their particular craving over their quest for their Life Drive: *better to have intimacy than to prove power over someone, better to go it alone than to have a creep as a dependant; better to find meaning in what's near than to chase what's over the hill.* An audience usually finds it preferable if your character pursues what they truly crave instead of the conventional niceties and poses we assume to come off a certain way as part of our Life Drive schemes; *the boy should take care of his mentally challenged brother instead of trying to fit in with a hip crowd; the starving man should just eat and not worry about his table manners; the girl should go with the boy she loves instead of trying to please her selfish father.*

Regardless the relative goodness value of a craving or whether it's thought the right thing to do, an audience will feel a release of tension when your character gives over to gratifying these more elemental urges in preference of the ego-based Wishes. And, while this feeling of release may not be an overall pleasant one, filled as it can be with sadness that your character is giving in to a self-destructive addiction or a behavior that victimizes someone else, there will nonetheless probably be an empathetic feeling for the satisfying of this impulse.

Having said all this, because cravings and repulsions are most often a universal value and what your character responds to we would likely all crave or find repulsive in that situation, the entire issue may not require much pointed examination in Breaking Down a Character. Our basic urges are, for the most part, constant and the same for everyone; so unless it's distinctly germane to the dynamic or special to the character, like heroin addiction, obsession for a particular person or repulsion to polka music, the craving can be thought of as a given in the same way it's taken for granted that your character needs to breathe, eventually requires food, likes companionship, and dislikes the smell of sewage. The smart actor will, however, always be on the lookout for the dramatic effect these cravings and repulsions provide as obstacles on their character's path.

How do things affect me? It's worthwhile in defining your character to evaluate how they typically react to things. The question is: *Do they respond with a greater, lesser or nearly ideal sensitivity to an event?* These responses relate directly to your character's Life Drive and cravings, and they may be detected in the text as described or responded to by other characters, as when someone says of your character, "Are you just going to sit there?" or "You don't have to raise your voice."

A large part of what makes a character definable is the nature of their responses. It may be the extremity of their response or relative lack thereof: *someone who wants to be revered may react violently to a perceived humiliation, while someone who is a peacemaker will enjoy the joke on themselves as a tension reliever; a hardened soldier who just wants to survive will eat his lunch next to a dead body, while a character more driven to do what is honorable will want to give the body a proper burial; career criminals and people in law enforcement are sensitized to the proximity of each other and desensitized to all kinds of bad behavior.*

24

You must weigh what this person cares about and what, if anything, they are desensitized to. Some deep part of the human psyche is always relating to things at the height of their personal meaning: "What does this mean to me?"

Psychologist Jonathon Haidt has parsed five, basic ethical pillars, and determined that all of our deepest reactions are born of how, with varying emphasis, we respond in relation to these five values.

The Moral Spheres

Safety: no harm being done.
Justice: fairness being done.
Loyalty: the good of the group being maintained.
Deference: authority and the pecking order being honored.
Purity: cleanliness, wholesomeness and sanctity being maintained.

Not only can this list aid in breaking down your character and determining how they react to an event, but later, as you look for things that will bring you alive emotionally and help connect you to your Circumstances (Working Toward Performance), you can use it to pinpoint what makes you tick, and find that precise preparation that brings your sensitivities most vividly to life.

How do I go about getting what I want? You might want to give thought to the ways your character does the things they do. In criminology this is referred to as "modus operandi," a person's method of operating. Some behaviors are more natural for people than others, and, usually, they simply can't conceive of doing things any other way. A character's basic methodology results in distinct habits out of which are born their mannerisms, their dress and the way they use objects. Some individuals may be extremely narrow in the variety of approaches in life: *always blunt* or *always gracious*; others may have greater range in their methodologies, applying certain ways of doing things to certain situations and people: *playful with children, suave with women* and *matter of fact with men*; but everyone has tremendous consistency in how they do what they do, and the number of ways in which they do things is limited.

A methodology can be thought of as an adverb: *plainly, sincerely, casually, elegantly, flamboyantly, properly, flirtatiously* (see List of Adverbs), and in the doing, you're always trying to achieve a greater superlative of that quality, a simpler, more quintessential version of that adverb.

It is supremely rare for a character to change their basic approach to things and perhaps only brain damage will cause a person to adopt an entirely new approach as their own. While any other life-altering event may give someone a new understanding of the world and dramatically change the way they relate to things, even causing them to abandon a particular, previous methodology so that they, for instance, cease being harsh or silly, they will almost never embrace completely new means. A plain-speaking mercenary will become a plain-speaking missionary; an outspoken sourpuss will become an outspoken do-gooder.

On the other hand, it is possible for your character to do something "out of character" at a telling moment. This can happen when your character is "acting" something as a deception. Often this takes the form of behaviors that indicate innocence, such as casualness, earnestness, flirtatiousness or silliness. In *Goodfellas*, Robert De Niro's character is always direct and absolute, whether congratulating a young boy on his first arrest or threatening someone with death for risking his freedom, but in the scene where he knows he's soon going to kill a mobster for insulting his friend, when the mobster asks his opinion if he was being insulting or not, De Niro's character acts offhand and wishy-washy, saying, "A little bit."

Just as a character can be in an unhappy state because they are constantly torn between what they wish for and what they crave, it's possible for a character to be stuck consistently using a faulty methodology to get their objectives, and so always be in a losing struggle: *they crave companionship, but their attempts to be liked by being a know-it-all only alienate; they wish to be useful, but their gentleness is ineffective in the tough environment of law enforcement; they crave romance, but their harshness estranges; they wish for expression, but their formality keeps them from being able to perform in the arts.*

▶▶ *Note:* **Using a consistent methodology is one of the clearest ways to carve out a character, and usually the most challenging. Because a particular methodology might be totally foreign to you yourself, it will be uncomfortable and you will tend not to trust it. Like everyone, you are strongly inclined to do things the way you personally** tend to do them, especially under pressure when the desire for competence is high. A right-handed person doing a difficult job naturally wants to use their right hand, and in the intense environment you're in while acting, you aren't going to want to throw a ball with your off hand and risk looking like a sissy. Additionally, there is the confused belief that, because something is deeply felt, it will have to alter the way a character does what they do, and this is simply not true. A straight-laced sergeant will toast his victories straightforwardly and, even though he is internally jubilant, things are done with proper decorum; although gripped in anguish, a good mother will keep trying to be cheerful and act confidently so as to better reassure her frightened child. Only performers who think in terms of demonstrating their feelings, mistakenly believing that this is what makes for a successful performance, allow their emotional life to freely disrupt the strong line of their character's methodology.

From who do I want what I want? With information drawn from the Piece as a Whole and how the characters interact, and with what is known about the Specific Character's Life Drive and their cravings, it may be possible to infer how this person you're playing relates to other characters. *Determining Relationships and how they are rendered is one of the most important aspects in the overall quality of a performance.*

A Relationship might express itself in your character because they relate to all such people in a given way: *maternal feelings for young children, someone of superior rank revered, an attractive person sexualized*, or the feelings for the person come from specific, past experience: *a life saver worshipped, an injury giver feared and hated*. It may be that the Relationship is created from the current Objective wanted from this individual (as will be addressed in Specific Scenes). It's also possible your character will feel strongly about another character for no good reason at all. Maybe it's chemical, maybe something from, who knows, a past life; but, certainly in the rich world of the stage, whether it's love, hate, or friendship at first sight, it's acceptable that that's just the way it is.

The Seven Primary Relationships

- ▶ Child: someone to nurture.
- ▶ Enemy: someone to push away.
- ▶ Friend: someone to be nurtured by.
- ▶ Idol: someone to submit to.
- ▶ Lover: someone to have sex with.
- ▶ Monster: someone to run away from.
- ▶ Stranger: no connection.

Just as the human eye has molecules for registering the primary colors of yellow, blue and red, and these blend in an infinite number of shadings, our psychological system recognizes these primary Relationships, and they also mix in an infinite variety. How a Relationship is felt is influenced by its Objectives in a particular context: *the experience of a lover is different at a family gathering than it is in the bedroom; a child is responded to differently when they are sick in bed than when running late for school.*

Relationship values are in a constant state of flux, played upon by new events: the "Lover/Friend" romantic partner who is discovered in an affair becomes an "Enemy;" the "Monster" with the gun who then identifies himself as a policeman becomes an "Idol" and the "Idol" who shows himself wounded needs to be nurtured as "Child."

There also may be an association of people with events, in the same way as can happen with locations, objects, music, and so forth. A person will elicit a particular feeling because they are reminders of those feelings: *the mother of a tragically killed fiancé is painful to be around; the waitress at a favorite restaurant gets a warmer response than the one working where the meal caused food poisoning.*

An important factor in Relationships is personal boundaries. There are levels of intimacy that people feel for each other, both physical and emotional, and there are different kinds of intimacy. These intimacies are influenced by age, gender, culture, context and, of course, the specific Relationship itself. Physical contact involves the pressure and placement of touches and nearness to the body. There may be a feeling of emotional intimacy that because of other factors prohibits physical intimacy: *a couple breaking up cannot express their still vivid physical attraction; a close family member nonetheless avoids the taboo of touching sexual areas; soldiers who are best friends don't feel comfortable touching each other the way they would if they weren't wearing their uniforms of different rank.* The issue of emotional intimacy involves the types of subject matter felt to be appropriate for a particular Relationship: *a loving brother feels embarrassed to hear of his sister's romantic encounter; a man who is uncomfortable with his mother in front of an obscene drunk finds this same drunk funny when he is in the company of his brother.*

How do I relate to my body, clothing and the objects around me? Your character will deal with costumes, props, and parts of their own body in a particular way, and, as part of your development of the character, you'll have to work out your orientation to these things, both physically and emotionally. They are often associated with Character Additions, habits and mannerisms, and may be connected to the time period, your profession, leisure pursuits, a disability or special situations. It is essential that you decide which of the ways your character does things, those superlative adverbs, they apply to these individual areas of the physical world.

This vast array of potential objects you have to personalize might include, for instance: a wallet, a throbbing temple, a shirt, a sidearm, a strand of hair, a wheelchair, a watch, a remote control, a chalice, a bowling ball, an earlobe, a lamp, a syringe, a bridle, a sword, a pillow, a glockenspiel, whatever a glockenspiel is! Okay, look — it's everything your character touches. Get it? Oh, and everything they hear, too. And look at. And smell and taste. You have to figure out how you feel about each of these things, your history with it, and what you use it for and how you use it. All of that.

▶ *Story:* **My wife and I are driving back with Jeff Goldblum after seeing a play that had someone we know in it, and we talked and talked about the play and the problems in the performance, and then there's one of those pauses that will happen in a conversation in a car on a freeway, and, finally, Jeff breaks the silence, flatly stating: "Acting is hard."**

THE SPECIFIC SCENES

All right, my fine, ambitious actor, this is where an examination of the material gets down to brass tacks. It's the specific scenes, after all, that are actually going to be presented; all the rest of it only serves to make informed decisions about what's to be played.

A. Before the First Moment

What has happened before the scene begins? The first questions you ask yourself are with regards to what happened before the scene begins, and what has put your character on this path, at this location, in this condition. It may be something important: *trying to solve a murder*, or it may be something simple: *going to your job at the grocery*, but every character has a Circumstance that first brings them into view. The central question has traditionally been phrased: "What is the Circumstance without which this scene would not exist?" This is called the Prior Circumstance, the first of all the considered events that are called the Given Circumstances. If it weren't for this event your character would be doing something else.

It may be your character is doing something directly related to the most important circumstance they are presently living with: *rushing to the emergency room after a call about your child being in an accident*, or *attending your daughter's wedding*. Or it may be that you are experiencing a major circumstance in your life, and yet you're engaged in a secondary circumstance and you're currently doing something unrelated to it: *you go to your grocery store job (where the scene takes place) knowing that later that day you will be signing your divorce papers*, or, *attending your daughter's wedding (where the scene takes place), you know that two days later you will be having life-threatening surgery.*

How do I feel about it? You need to imagine to how your character might relate to an event and ask: What emotional condition is created because of this Circumstance? The response may be the same as yours would be, and you can use the Emotional Bridge, or, because of the Type of Character (which would include the Style of the Piece), it's different from how you would react, and you have to take into account the character interpretation work you've done.

Every event is related to in terms of two values: how significant it is and how strange it is. The significance of something is how consequential it is and will continue to be, to a person's life and psyche. Its strangeness is a function of how dissimilar it is from their norm. Things can be significant, but not strange: *the death of an ill grandparent*, or strange, but not significant: *a drop of water out of nowhere*, or they can be both: *a*

30

child disappears without explanation. If something is strange, however, that by itself brings in a measure of significance that your world isn't what you thought it was.

An event begins to be processed immediately and will be assimilated with a connection to the best and worst case scenarios. This is a rush toward the essential, bottom-line truth: *What does this mean?* A person will try to process all the possible outcomes of an event, good and bad, with whatever information they have: *if it's only known that the plane is missing, it may have crashed; if it's only known that it has crashed, the loved one may have survived.*

Everything gets assimilated, and the strangeness of an event affects how quickly it is assimilated: the stranger it is, the more difficult to process. Curiosity is generated by an event's strangeness in order to gather information that will reduce the strangeness and aid in assimilation.

The Primary Responses

- Fear: a threat is present.
- Joy: what is desired is being achieved.
- Grief: loss has occurred.
- Anger: something is being taken away.
- Upset: something important is taking place.
- Shame: being judged as bad.
- Pride: being judged as good.

Both Fear and Joy have extra shadings: Fear is experienced differently if the threat is physical or if it's psychic (felt as spooky); and the quality of Joy is different if it's a wish or if it's a craving that is being gratified (a wish fulfilled creates happiness, a craving fulfilled creates pleasure).

▸▸ *Note:* Upset shouldn't be thought as only a response to loss or threat. There is also joyous upset, even though, from appearances, it might be mistaken for grieving upset. This quality was used to clever effect in Quentin Tarantino's script *True Romance*, wherein Christian Slater's character mistakes Patricia Arquette's upset as grief over her dead pimp, only to have it revealed that she is joyously upset that he is "so cool" to have killed to protect her.

Just as with Relationships, these responses blend and are experienced as part of a context, especially influenced by excitation, and are constantly evolving based on new events. Some emotional combinations have names: Triumph is Joy and Anger, Thrill is Joy and Fear. A wedding could be a rich blend: Joy for the wonderful new union, Upset at the significance of the event, Grief and Anger for the loss of old conditions and a relationship being taken away, and Fear that the marriage may not succeed.

Every event will include all the feelings related to that event in its entirety. This means that, while the main significance of an event dominates, every association with that Circumstance should be represented as well: *the joyous release from an unfair imprisonment includes the sadness and anger for each day that was lost.* While, on first hearing news, the feelings associated with its dominant factor will usually be pronounced, over time the fullness of the response may develop and there can be subsequent waves of emotion as assimilation continues and releases new relatedness to different aspects of an event: *first hearing of a death brings only immediate sadness and upset, and not until the time of the funeral do the joys of having known the person become felt, or, when told of being promoted, the joy for the new salary is the big response, but later, feelings arise for the guy who was passed over for the job and a fear for the responsibility it will now require.*

An event will generate the entire string of history related to that event. I mean, isn't this really why it's so difficult to have a long-term relationship? Every time the person does something wrong, the entire list of their crimes against you lights up, and, in trying to address the latest thing they've done, you end up angrier than you started because you can't help reliving all the awful things they've done to you in the past. Gad.

The point is, assimilation never stops and our mechanism is always moving to fully process an experience. A classic example of assimilation is the five stages a person moves through when they learn they have a terminal illness: anger, denial, bargaining, grief, and acceptance.

As an actor, you must never hold off assimilation of an event by using the human talent (or curse) for disassociation. For an audience it's not important where your character is in the assimilation process, only that they are actively assimilating. Even if you're in denial, you should be intensely in denial, forcefully pushing away the magnitude of what's happened. In large part it is the intention of your character as they process their experiences that causes an audience to connect with that character.

What do I want? What is the Objective? The Circumstance and the Response creates a trajectory that leads to an Objective. That Response to the Circumstance is crucial because, given a different Response, the Objective could be very different: *a spouse leaves, the person is devastated, they want to get them back,* as opposed to: *they leave, the person is relieved and joyous, they want to celebrate with their lover.* The Objective should be consistent with a character's Life Drive or their cravings.

The Objective should be as near as possible to addressing the maximum value of the Circumstance for your character: *getting married, joy, they want the most wonderful wedding or honeymoon possible; someone dies, upset, they want to attend the funeral or fulfill the dead person's last wish.* By the same token, you should strive to have the Objective be as significant as possible to a greater purpose, perhaps seeing yourself as a representative of an entire cause: *having been betrayed by someone powerful, seek revenge for all those who have been abused by the powerful; given a chance at a wonderful job, seek to take advantage of it for all those who provided this opportunity.* In this way it's very good if you can connect this higher purpose to the Theme of the piece.

While the Circumstance will create a Main Objective, there may be lesser Objectives, Mini-Objectives, requiring attention first. These will either be Objectives that relate to the Circumstance, but are not the Main Objective: *having to break the news of a death to someone before attending to the funeral,* or they might be routines of life: *eating, going to work.*

▶▶ *Note:* **Watch for the Mystery Objective. I call it a mystery because people who are after it almost never know it's what they're really after. The Mystery Objective is:** *To get someone to register the type and magnitude of your feelings.* **Your character may look on paper like they're doing a lot of explaining about why they have a right to feel the way they do, but they really just want to get someone to get what their experience is like. By the way, this Objective does not require you to be especially emotional while doing it. The Objective is for someone to get what you're feeling, not to demonstrate for them that you're feeling it. It's entirely possible to pursue this objective with a flat demeanor as you lay out what's going on with you.**

By far the most common Objective you'll encounter, and the most common source of conflict between two people in a scene, will be the desire of one of them to get the other to appreciate how important something is, while the other one is trying to get them to not make such a big deal out of it.

Something like:

She: Slow down.
He: I'm going the speed limit.
She: But there's ice on the road.
He: I've driven on ice my whole life.
She: It doesn't matter if we're a little late.
He: They said they're starting exactly on time.
She: They always say that.
He: I don't want to walk in after everyone's already sitting.
She: You don't have to prove anything to them.

What is the obstacle? Often the only obstacle to a character attaining their objective is time and space, and your approach will be a straight line from you to it: *crossing the room to pick up a ringing phone, waiting for the doctor to enter and give you the test results.* At other times, there is a definite obstacle that has to be surmounted in order to get what you want. That obstacle might be a distracting demand of everyday life: *getting the ringing phone out from under the bed where it's fallen, getting the distracted receptionist to register that you are here to get your results,* or the obstacle will be something or someone directly oppositional to achieving this particular objective: *the criminal you're trying to apprehend is trying to kill you, the father you want to hear how badly you feel betrayed by is drunk and argumentative.* It is in the nature of drama that these obstacles are usually people. This is why it's been said: "Every scene is an argument."

How do I get what I want? You now determine: What are my Actions? Once you've figured out the Objective, you can make a choice for how your character will go about getting this thing they want, choosing from that group of adverbs that your character will use to do things: *forcefully, flirtatiously, casually, earnestly.* This creates the Action. Actions are the things the character does: *What do I want and how am I going to get it?* An Action will always be a basic, human doing, recognizable through history and different cultures — hell, almost all our Actions are recognizable in dogs.

Hey, pay attention here now, because this is really important! Knowing your Actions is huge. Almost all this stuff I've been going on and on about until now has been so you could distill it down to finding out what your Actions should be. The more I'm around acting, the more I come to value a basic Action well done. If you can find the right Action, and then, simply and personally play the hell out of it — you're golden.

The first Action creates the first Through Line. This is the path that the character is on before the scene begins.

Actions

- ▶ Assure (pledge, warn)
- ▶ Connect (share, reminisce)
- ▶ Deceive (masquerade, blend in)
- ▶ Effectuate (employ, maneuver)
- ▶ Entice (lure, charm)
- ▶ Establish (confirm, testify)
- ▶ Explore (detect, test)
- ▶ Insist (command, press)
- ▶ Inspire (encourage, exhort)
- ▶ Proclaim (herald, boast)
- ▶ Provoke (tease, challenge)
- ▶ Punish (destroy, hurt))
- ▶ Revel (relish, luxuriate)
- ▶ Share (confide, present)
- ▶ Solicit (implore, coax)
- ▶ Soothe (pacify, console)
- ▶ Surrender (confess, exhibit)

The words used here to describe the Actions may be misleading because the behavior used to get an Objective may be different from what is conventionally suggested by that Action. Someone may wish to console, but not want to use the Action of soothing because it would come off as patronizing, so they console by establishing the facts: "*You are being fired through no fault of your own, and only because of economic necessity.*" A person can seek to hurt a spouse not only with blatant punishment, but by how coldly effective they are in how they pack; the best seduction might not be an obvious enticement or a direct solicitation, but to show oneself a sensualist by luxuriating or a free spirit by reveling.

Also, these listed Actions do not specify the underlying emotional condition, nor the adverb used to attain them, and this difference can give a completely different tone to the thing being done. A person can "entice" by being flirtatious or by being crude, and whether because of a genuine attraction or to get back at a betraying spouse; they could "insist" by being blunt or by being officious, and it might be to stop someone's rudeness or to close a lucrative deal. All these variations create a different tone for the Action.

Watch for new Actions. An Objective will be pursued by your character until it is either gotten, replaced by a more important Objective, or found to be either impossible to get, or not worth the effort (the difficulty of getting it is greater than the desire to attain it).

Most of the time it's going to be fairly obvious when your Action ought to change. Something will clearly happen to change your character's pursuit of what they want. Maybe you get your Objective; and as the comedian David Brenner pointed out: "People will say: 'It's always the last place you look.' Of course, it's the last place you look. Once you've found it, you don't keep looking for it!" As soon as you get an Objective you will immediately have a new Objective. Maybe something happens that takes priority over your previous Objective; *a man trying to seduce a woman in the woods notices that a bear is watching him.* Maybe something happens that proves it can't be gotten: *the man who's been attempting the seduction is told by the woman that she's just become engaged to his brother.* In these instances, it should be plain that the Action will have to change. Perhaps the irritation from trying to get it builds to a breaking point, and the Objective is abandoned, in which case your character will probably, but not necessarily, give a vocalization of some kind indicating their frustration.

At times, however, it can be tough to spot where the changes are actually happening, and you have to detect them by backtracking to find out how it is that you used to be going for one thing in one way, and now you seem to be doing something else. Sometimes, but not always, you're given the clue in stage directions.

Here's an example, from *Mademoiselle Colombe* by Jean Anouilh: A girl waits to deliver flowers to a famous actress in the same room with a boy she doesn't know.

Colombe: Isn't she beautiful?

Julian: Oh, sure. Like an old building.

Colombe: She isn't old. I saw her in the play.

Julian: Don't be ridiculous. That's makeup and good lighting.

Colombe: That's mean of you. What if she heard you?

Julian: She has. I'm her son.

Colombe: You're her son?

Julian: Uh huh. Not that we brag about it.

Colombe: So she isn't old.

Julian: Why?

Colombe: Because you're so young.

Julian: I'm not one for compliments, but you're very pretty.

As you look at this exchange you see that it starts with dialog indicating he's impatient and rude with her, and then somehow he's telling her she's pretty. Where does the change happen? It's more obvious to spot a change with her character because he's added information she didn't know when he reveals to her that he's the son of the actress she idolizes. That's where you would logically place the change of Action for her. But why would he change?

You really would have two choices and both would be based on the same event: her beauty. He could possibly change as a result of continuous exposure to her, until he can't avoid mentioning it and he comes clean with "you're very pretty." In that case, it would be a change that occurs because one Objective is overtaken by another, his desire to slander his mother overtaken by his desire that she know of his appreciation for her looks. The problem with that being the way the change occurs is that, while it's true you can put all kinds of crazy subtext under anything, at the point where she calls him mean, it seems unlikely that she's sensing any attraction he's having for her. You could possibly justify her missing it because she's so angry that he's attacking her idol, but that would be risky because she's meant to be our leading lady, and she should therefore be prone to maximum sensitivity for the emotional lives of others. The solution, and the change I would recommend, would be that an entirely new event occurs when he looks at her. This requires that he not be looking at her at the beginning of the scene; at least not in the eyes, so that he can continue to freely slander his mother. If you're playing the part you might choose to be distracted by a physical activity (something petty, irritating and revelatory to the character perhaps) until, irritated by her contradicting him, he turns to her and says: "I'm her son." At which point he makes eye contact, the anvil drops on his head and he's in love.

What specific behaviors do I bring into the scene? You will have to address the particular Character Additions you will be performing at the first moment, whether speech patterns, the character's style of movement or their faculties. Character Additions may also include mannerisms and the way you handle some specific objects, although these things remain very much impacted by the character's methodology and orientation toward those objects. For instance, if your Character Addition is a limp and you use a cane, the cane will need to be handled appropriately with respect to the influence of the debility, but still very much as the character carries himself, whether with flamboyance or in a business-like manner, and how the cane is related to, whether as a trusted friend or a despised necessity.

The Character Additions might have been determined because they are clearly spoken of in the text, or the director has given input as to what is expected; but it could be they'll be a product of your personal, creative choices; and may even be born less out of a deliberate choice you make than as a natural, perhaps even unconscious, outgrowth of work that is done on the psychology of the character. Playing someone blunt, you may take on lower class speech or some other vocal quality; playing someone nervous, you might develop an organic tick or a stammer.

In evaluating the playing of the Specific Scene, you'll need to settle on how exactly a Character Addition will be executed. This decision should be affected, of course, by how the condition actually exists in life, and you'll have to do research. A condition should be explored for its range of possibilities and investigated for its specific details. Many observable symptoms of a condition are adopted because they are useful compensations, and so you ask yourself: What is the usefulness of this behavior?

What's important is that you isolate the reasons for the behavior, and not just attempt to ape the resulting behavior. A schizophrenic may be described as having bizarre behavior with poor concentration, but you would too, if you were coping with a hallucinatory snake coiled around your neck at the same time as you smelled burning sulfur and were hearing three different demons tell you how your landlord wanted to kill you.

In any case, the final Character Additions chosen must be theatrically viable. You want to create the clearest possible portrait, and this usually means establishing a pattern of behavior. The simplest and truest thing done that will bespeak the character.

Everything has to have a theatrical purpose and prudence needs to be exercised so that the audience is never taken out of their involvement with the imaginative experience because you've drawn attention to your technique ("Look at me, everybody, I'm playing a funny drunk person!").

There's also a warning for prudence, especially when playing for a live audience, that they not fear for your personal safety. This is true whether the stunt is actually dangerous or merely perceived to be so. An audience can be gripped with dread that the character in the fiction they are watching will be killed, only to be jerked out of it and made aware of the real world with a petty fear that you're going to bump your head on the corner of a table.

There are times when you'll need to bring in Character Additions special to a given scene: *cold*, *fatigued*, and these then must be attended to at the appropriate level. It may be that the new condition is in fact directly related to the Circumstance of the scene: *injured attempting a rescue*, or *having gotten drunk because of the emotional pain of a breakup*.

If it's an ongoing condition that is always present with your character, it must be nonetheless evaluated for its present degree of extremity: What stage is the condition now? In creating a portrait of a deteriorating or improving condition, you must attend to where it presently is on the scale of severity. An emotional state or certain new Character Additions may influence other Character Additions; *tired, drunk or upset, an accent that has been covered becomes more pronounced, or a stammer more frequent.*

When the Character Additions brought into a scene are those that the audience will be seeing for the first time, there is usually an advantage in demonstrating the catalog of symptoms as quickly as possible, so you get the audience on board sooner rather than later. Once a Character Addition is established with an audience, they will typically become less critical of its details and execution, and more involved with the story.

On the other hand, it's possible to delay an audience's understanding of the exact Character Addition in order to heighten a tension that can then be released with a gratifying revelation: *a man is strangely tentative and awkward in his movement, finally his coat opens and a bloody gunshot wound is exposed; a girl is oblivious to vivid sights in front of her and overly precise in her behaviors, her book falls open, the pages are blank, it's Braille!* Keeping an audience in the dark is a tricky maneuver, however, because confusion can turn to disinterest, and then resentment and resistance to ever becoming involved. Someone attempting the technique of suspending an audience's understanding does well to reflect on the amount of favorable involvement the audience has already invested, how inherently interesting these mysterious behaviors are, and how much your target audience will tolerate and enjoy the enigmatic.

There is another special theatrical approach that might be considered when applying Character Additions, although it's so dangerous I hesitate to even bring it up. I'll called it "The Addition Slide." This is when you choose to perform a Character Addition in a more conspicuous way at the beginning of a scene or piece, and then gradually lighten it once the condition has been firmly established in the mind of the audience: *a thick accent lightened, the severity of the cerebral palsy lessened.* You would do this so that the condition doesn't detract from your clarity, and so you avoid potential distraction or tedium. If attempted, the Addition Slide must be executed with great virtuosity, because if you don't pull it off with finesse, you run the risk of being caught out by an audience that rightfully interprets inconsistency as a mark of shoddy craftsmanship ("Did you see how he suddenly lost his limp?").

Debra Winger gave a deep and nuanced performance in *Shadowlands*, and yet it seemed every reviewer felt compelled to slam her on doing a bad New York accent. The truth is it wasn't so much a bad accent; it was fine while she was doing it, it just varied in thickness from scene to scene. Not good.

What props, costume or special associations with my body parts do I bring into the scene? This is that vast array of potential objects I mentioned earlier (please don't make me go through another list). Items your character enters the scene handling, wearing, hearing, seeing, smelling or tasting. It might be that they are objects that are dealt with this way routinely, or maybe they are being newly manipulated for this particular circumstance.

What is the first stage direction? You'll need to learn the Stage Directions and familiarize yourself with them in the same way as Character Additions, and they require your consideration from entrance to exit. Every Stage Direction is a definite choice, whether the character is entering as they would normally, and it's just a matter of what door they use, or if there is some special factor involved: *climbing through a window, finishing dressing.*

▶▶ *Note:* By "Stage Directions" I don't necessarily mean those things that are written in parenthesis in your text. In plays those are often merely written by the stage managers of the first production so that a reader can have a better idea of what is taking place. Why should you have to follow the poorly chosen physical things performed by that less-talented actor who was cast in the part? I mean really, watch out. There are some truly terrible stage directions floating around out there. By Stage Directions I mean here the blocking and the business that you and your director have decided works for the piece, that may or may not be what's written as Stage Directions in your book.

B. During the Scene

What happens during the scene and what do I do? Just as you broke down what's necessary to know before the first moment of the scene, you will need to go through the same process and examine each moment in the scene itself: What happens? How do I feel about it? What do I want because of it? How do I go about getting it?

Each moment should be examined for its impact on your character, their particular response, their particular Objective, and their precise methodology for attaining the Objective of this moment. Events will either be of benefit to achieving your character's objective: *discovery of a witness, food left in the trash*, or they will be obstacles: *a stubbed toe, a girlfriend who's made other plans on the night you've planned to propose*. A mixed message toward getting your Objective will nonetheless always fall out as either a plus in total or a minus in total; and a completely unclear message will be responded to as a bad message.

Every moment is an event. Every reference has a meaning. Upon hearing that his sister is about to marry someone a man knows, all his feelings about his sister, all his feelings about this man, and all his feelings about marriage will be called upon.

All Character Additions, Stage Directions and uses of costume, props and body parts must be taken into account for every moment of the scene; each passing moment may cause a condition to deteriorate or improve, maybe a new physical object that must be dealt with. The new moment might bring an event that will require addressing new behaviors: *a pulled muscle, a stiff drink, a spotlight*.

How do I feel about each person I encounter? Having broken down your character's Relationships and Objectives, you now have some idea of the emotional response your character might have to the other people with whom you interact.

What is said? Very simply: What is the sense of what's being said? If the character you're playing expresses their thoughts in language, you should understand this language, and, beyond this, truly own it. To own the language it will be necessary for you to paraphrase all your dialog into your own words, with the exception of the pronouns and proper names.

A dictionary should be used in developing this paraphrase because it might reveal definitions or nuances of definitions that you either don't know or don't fully appreciate. You shouldn't use the exact wording of a dictionary definition in creating your paraphrase, however; this would only be substituting one set of foreign words for another. The meanings in your paraphrase need to be fully understood by you, and you will only get to this by using language you yourself would use. There's no concept so grand, nor terminology so technical that anyone cannot convey its meaning using their own mode of speech. It may take you many common words to express the meaning of a single, technical term, but it can be done, and it must be done if you intend to work from a connection to the language.

"She was asphyxiated" becomes perhaps "She couldn't get enough oxygen into her system so her brain died." The paraphrase should adhere to exactly what is spoken in the text and not embellish or express additional values, such as: "In desperate terror she struggled to breathe." You can do that kind of embellishing all you want, I suppose, as long as you first have a hard-core, word-by-exact-word paraphrase first.

While the dialog others speak in a scene needn't be paraphrased in the same meticulous way as your own dialog, your understanding should nonetheless extend to everything that's spoken to, and in the presence of, your character and how well they would understand those words as well.

Paraphrasing is increasingly important to do as the dialog gets further and further from your own natural way of speaking. If you're doing Shakespeare, or any highly stylized dialog, it's an absolutely crucial part of your process. And you won't want to do it. I'm warning you now that when the time comes to really dig in and practice your paraphrasing, when Working Toward Performance, it can be an agonizing struggle to come up with words to express complex thoughts word by word. You may want to call in the services of someone to act like a trainer who'll stay on you and force you to push through the burn.

Story: I remember sitting in a freezing warehouse in Melbourne, Australia working with Aaliyah Houghton as she prepared to play the title role in *Queen of the Damned*. At one point, while I was nitpicking and badgering her to tell me in her own words the meaning for every word of her Egyptian royalty dialog, that funny, fantastic girl collapsed to the floor in mock exhaustion, begging me to stop. Nine months later the small plane she was in crashed on takeoff in the Bahamas in August of 2001, killing her at the age of 22, and it put a hole in my heart.

▶▶ *Note:* Beware words! You almost certainly bring to your work a conditioning since earliest childhood that stresses conversational skills and the correctness of how you argue your case. We train our children to be little lawyers: Plaintiff: "He changed the channel!" Defendant: "I was watching my show first." Typically the worst contaminant to the vitality of a performance is an excessive emphasis on the words and a preconception of how they should be spoken. The truth is, as long as you're committing to the truth of your Action, you can pretty much be oblivious to whatever it is you're saying and it will come off just fine. It doesn't matter what you say. Even now your analytic mind is probably rejecting that last sentence. But as Emo Phillips said: "I used to think the human brain was the most magnificent organ in the body, then I realized who it was that was telling me this."

SUMMARY: BREAKING DOWN THE MATERIAL

Use of the Emotional Bridge

Can you play the Character straight from yourself? If the character is similar to your normal way of being, and the piece is in a naturalistic style, you can largely use your own natural responses and behaviors.

"If ____ is how I feel and if ____ happens: how would I feel about that and what would I do?" You determine your Actions by relating to the fictional Circumstances and imagining what your response would be and your resulting course of action.

Always use the Emotional Bridge first. No matter how far the character or style of the role may be from your natural behavior, first seek to base your performance on your personal truth by relating directly to the role.

The Questions

[The Piece as a Whole]

1. How Does This Strike Me? The Initial Response.

2. What happens? The Plot.

44

3. What is the style of the piece? The Genre.

4. Where does it take place? The Setting.

5. How do the characters interact? The Character Dynamics.

6. What is the piece saying? The Theme.

[As the Specific Character.]

7. Who am I in this story? The Part.

8. What would I be called? (Label as brief and vivid as possible, possibly a Stock Character or just an image) The Character Handle.

9. What's made me this way? The character's History.

10. What do I wish for most in life?/How do I want to be praised? The character's Life Drive.

11. What would quiet my urges? The character's Cravings and Repulsions.

12. How do things affect me? The character's Responses.

13. How do I go about getting what I want? The character's Actions and Behaviors.

14. How might I speak, move and perceive? Character Additions.

15. What do I want from whom? The character's Relationships.

16. What thing or things determines how I feel about this person? Relationship Histories and Current Objectives.

17. How do I relate to the props, costume and my body parts? Associations with objects.

[As Scenes.]

18. What's happened/happens? The Circumstance(s).

19. How do I feel about it? The Emotional Preparation.

20. What do I want because of it? The Objective.

21. **Who do I want it from?** Relationships.

22. **What obstacles do I face?** Mini-Objectives.

23. **How will I go about getting what I want?** The Actions.

24. **What special aspects of Speech, Physical Life or Faculties is required?** Specific Character Additions.

25. **How do I relate to each prop, costume or part of my body that I must deal with?** Object Associations.

26. **What is the required blocking or behaviors?** Stage Directions.

Change to Look Like the Character

Adjustments. Relate to events and people with responses not normally your own. Often referred to as the "as if," which is saying: The character feels about this thing the way I would feel about _____.

Additions. Adopt a Character Addition that alters your normal speech, movement, and the apparent functioning of your fives senses and/or faculties.

Actions. Strive for objectives that you yourself might not normally pursue, and in ways that you would not typically use, either ever or in this context.

chapter 2

Working Toward Performance

All right, you've put in the work and determined the vital information about your character and how they should be played, and guess what? By itself, this means nothing. You now have to put all that information you've gathered into practice so it will show up in the performance. You don't want to be one of those actors who can talk and talk so beautifully about their part, but when they go to do it —stinksville! Fast Eddy didn't say greatness came from a guy knowing what he was doing, by itself. No, you have to make it come off. So here's how you increase your likelihood of that happening.

Rehearsal is mostly going to be work you do on your own. Get used to that idea, right now. The reality is, it's often more than 95% on your own. Maybe you'll be lucky enough to get substantive rehearsal time with the cast and an attentive director, but even then, you'll need to grind out the major preparation for your part on your lonesome doing what musicians call "woodshedding."

Whether the work you do is done alone or in tandem with other artistic associates, it takes time to shape a performance. Only by doing a lot work can you make it look like it wasn't a lot of work. You're trying to achieve "disguised virtuosity." Like an athlete who's developed muscle memory, you want psychical memory. You want whatever you planned to be so habituated that, in performance, your attention can be where it should be, namely, playing the moments (*see* Doing the Performance). Be conscious where you should be conscious, so you can be unconscious where you should be unconscious.

Throughout this process you have to stay open to reexamining questions you've already answered, be open to new input, and be completely free to modify or abandon any preconceived ideas. Especially suspect will be your favorite little ideas, the ones you think are so very clever. You must be ready to — no, you must be eager to, as G. K. Chesterton put it, "Murder your darlings." It is through this process of active experimentation that you begin to find out how the information will play, and whether it plays at all. The ultimate determination will always be: Does it work?

PRESET RESPONSES

With the character's responses established by breaking down the material "As the Specific Character" and "As the Specific Scenes," a good beginning for "Working Toward Performance" would be for you to preset your emotional connection to the fictional meanings in the script.

Know what you know. You need to bring to life from your imagination the specific people, places and things referred to in the text. Whether it's "Mr. Jones" or "Mr. Jones' couch," if the character knows of him or it, you need to have a way of feeling about them.

This is, of course, critical for the major Given Circumstances before the scene and the major emotional bombs that go off during the scene; but beyond this, you'll need a way of relating to all the things your character is familiar with, whether it's something actually present or if it's merely mentioned. Especially important may be your character's personal items that can even take on a symbolic meaning and, by extension, reflect on larger meanings in the story.

Whether or not a specific personal history with a given person or object is explicitly mentioned in the text, you need to have an emotional connection with them. The audience doesn't have to know what it is; they only need to know that you know. This isn't to say every event or reference calls for a huge reaction. You don't want to distort the presentation and distract by making a monumental event out of every single thing, but the meaning of each particular thing does need to be distinct. So, if the scene requires you to get a file off "Mr. Jones' couch," I'm not saying you have to make that couch the place where you lost your virginity. If you did lose your virginity there, well, okay, then as you approach that sacred piece of furniture it will need to resonate appropriate to the experience, and if you lost it to "Mr. Jones," his name should resonate, whether in reference to his couch or anything else of his. But it might only be a place where you once spilled a cup of coffee and had to hurry to clean it up before he got back. You need to have a specific way of feeling about it.

Preset an organic response. For you to know something as the character knows it, it's probably not going to be enough to just run the thought through your head. Stella Adler said: "Until a fact is put through the imagination, it's a lie." Ideas are either weak or outright bad in performance. In order for it to be the full, organic response you need it to be means you'll probably have to preset it emotionally, set it into your body, and this can only be done through work with your imagination.

These preset responses should be made Pavlovian. That is to say, just as Pavlov conditioned a dog by ringing a bell and then giving it food so that the sound of the bell alone caused the dog to have a physiological response, you want to preset the stimuli, your bell, at the proper moments of a performance so they elicit the desired emotional associations in yourself.

It's very possible that if you don't have a true, emotional connection to the material, then, during the performance, the showman in you will recognize there's a gap where your response should be, and you'll be inclined to "act your response," in order to fill it in. This pretending to be affected is always a poor substitute for the real thing, when it isn't outright sickening.

Make your Relationships alive. It's difficult to overstate how important it is for your eventual performance that you create rich Relationships. Having an alive Relationship means that when that person enters the room it's an event. Every moment when you are in that character's presence should cause a specific feeling related to that Relationship.

As is always a useful analogy, consider how animals behave. The cat is happy when her master enters the apartment and is drawn to them, wants to sit on their lap. When the hated dog enters the room, the cat can never be truly comfortable; whether she affects an air of uncaring or not, the dog's movements are a deeply felt disturbance. It is at this primitive level that you want to connect to your Relationships in the piece.

Of course, after the character has entered the room, subsequent events will change the Relationship. Relationships are in constant flux as new moments play upon them. A scratch of her ear warms the existing Relationship, yet Kitty will find Mommy less lovable as she's being lowered into her bath.

Emotionally prepare. So now, my fine young Thespian, we come to the point where we teach you perhaps one of your most important tools as an actor: "emotional preparation." I've seen actors who, after being introduced to this technique, changed unrecognizably in the kind of work they were capable of doing. I've seen it so many times that the statement you sometimes hear — "You can't teach acting" — can only be described as idiotic.

▶▶ *Note:* **I know the "You can't teach acting" statement is predicated on the idea that the amount of talent you have as an actor is set, and that acting is a natural thing to do, but I think we can all agree that childbirth is a rather natural thing to do and women take classes in how to get better at doing that, don't they? How can you know what innate talent there is in a seed if it's never come in contact with water? The emotional preparation technique I'm about to describe here might be just the water you need.**

You can use this technique exactly as I describe it, or you can modify it to suit yourself. I've seen this particular technique work wonders, but maybe it won't suit you exactly, or it won't suit you fully for every part, and neither I nor anybody cares what you do in order to produce the appropriate, good quality emotion during a performance. Use whatever you want, affective memory (where you recreate the sensorial aspects of an actual event from you life) or music that ignites you emotionally, a photograph of your dead dog Rusty — anything that gets you there. Hell, go for it. It's only that I know just about all of these ways intimately, and I don't think any of them are likely to be as effective as what I'm about to suggest. And you can't lose it and it doesn't run low on batteries. Also, I personally might suggest you use that affective memory stuff sparingly, if at all, because, in my long experience with it, the kind of the emotion it brings up tends to have a tortured, self-involved quality.

And if you say to me, "Thank you very much, but if you don't mind I'll just work from relating to the circumstances in the scene," that's fine, too. During the performance I only want you to do that anyway. And if the events of the scene are completely relatable to you, and your responses and the character's would be exactly the same, I'm not insisting you preset any emotional responses to them at all. If, upon hearing "I'm pregnant" from the other character in the scene, you get the right reaction by living through the moment, no homework may be necessary at all beyond knowing your lines. But you're still going to have to deal with creating a relationship with Mr. Jones (and his, ahem, couch), so you'll have to take the time beforehand to relate to them somehow.

And maybe the event or the relationship in the scene is something difficult for you to relate to, or maybe you've done the play so many times you're starting to go dry, or maybe you just want to make sure you've done a little extra work and put a deep charge in the chamber; even if it's just so you're confident and therefore all the more likely to get the emotion because you're not worried about it. Then these are the times you can use this approach to fire up your mojo.

Here's what you do:

Pick a fantasy. Think about it, then choose a fictional scenario, a day-dream you could have that when played out might generate an emotion similar to the way you want to feel about this person or event in the scene. You can select a fantasy situation that is the same as what's described as having happened to your character in the story, but you're not limited to that. It might be that the daydream you employ is very different from anything written; it could be either an unmentioned episode in the character's life, or you can completely branch out and make it a fantasy that is totally personal to you, with nothing remotely to do with the character or the piece other than it elicits an emotional response in you that, seen from the outside, will appear identical to the one you envision appropriate for your character in that moment. If you do pick a fantasy that's different from anything your character would relate to, you'll then graft those feelings onto the part, as I'll describe in a moment.

If you are going to use a daydream about something different than what has happened in the life of your character, you will evaluate how your character would react to a particular event or person in the scene, and then ask: What fantasy event would bring about that same response in me? Using a circumstance completely different than what is mentioned in the text to relate to as a parallel circumstance is referred as an "as if" or a "particularization."

A materialistic egomaniac might respond to a dent in their car the way you would if someone injured your child; a hardened soldier checking a dead man's identity tags might feel about it the way you would if you had to fish keys out of a toilet; an innocent farm boy approaching a store clerk in the city might do it with the same feelings you would have if you approached a senator.

You can choose a daydream that will bring about a pure feeling: A fantasy of someone who rescues you from drowning will probably create a feeling about them as a pure idol. But maybe the fantasy you'll settle on is meant to create a blend of feelings: Someone rescues you from an attacker (making them an idol), but they're excessively violent in the process (a monster), and then they collapse in hysterical tears (a needy child). A fantasy of your ninety-year-old grandmother dying of natural causes could bring pure, deep sadness, whereas a fantasy of your sister being raped and murdered generates tremendous rage along with your grief.

In emotionally preparing for a part you'll most likely want to go through many scenarios to find what works best, and then overlay them to bolster your connections. There may be something you thought would bring you to life, but when you do a daydream about it, ah, not so much. You thought imagining something happening to your sister would emotionally destroy you, but it isn't nearly as powerful as fantasizing a little puppy being crushed.

▸▸ *Note:* **There was a play that attracted great attention because it began with a remarkable performance by an actor portraying a man about to commit suicide. He was so able to create the reality of this event, holding the gun to his head, pulling it away, putting it back it again; that it was absolutely excruciating to watch. Observers said it was truly as if you were about to witness the death of this person. When asked later how he was able to get to that incredible place in his imagination, the actor said that it was from the idea of stepping into**

a cold shower. He absolutely abhorred the idea of icy water rushing down his back.

Your job is to explore yourself and find what it is in this world of daydreams that hits your nerves: what repulses you, what do you crave, how does your own Life Drive respond to circumstances. Detective, investigate thyself.

Here's where those ethical pillars that I mentioned earlier for how your character may relate to the world, may relate to you. You need to enter in and get a feel for the real meaning of circumstances.

Suppose a lover cheats on you. What exactly upsets you about that?
Is it because it's a betrayal of the team? (disloyalty)
Is it that the body parts you touch were touching someone else's body parts? (impurity)
Is it your humiliation that they didn't honor the relationship? (violating authority)
Is it because it's an insult to the sacrifices you've made? (unfairness)
Is it the negative repercussions it could have on yourself and others? (harmful)

Circumstances play upon your Life Drive and bring about crushing disappointment or soaring exaltation in your psyche. The closer you get to the bone, the more vital will be your response and your ability to bring this fullness to an interpretation of your character.

What makes getting married so wonderful?
Is it the bonding with family? (acceptance)
Is it the new, uncharted waters you're entering? (adventure)
Is it the feeling of ownership? (conquest)
Is it the permission to give yourself fully? (expression)
Is it the guarantee of property? (security)

The subject matter to use in accessing the most highly charged fantasies is usually drawn from the profound relationships in your actual life, but daydreams should be freely drawn from anything in your imagination, without regard for how fanciful they may be. While the realities closest to your life, such as car accidents, grandparents having health problems or abandonment by romantic partners, will tend to generate the strongest and most dependable responses, all manner of fictions, such as fantasies about nonexistent relatives, make-believe professions, even putting yourself in a historical setting, can be very stimulating.

The entire driving force behind your work as an artist may be to explore the two or three most powerful images that first played upon your heart, but you were so little at the time that you have no memory of what they are. You have to be free to pursue these images in all their truth, whatever their origins.

The fantasy should be chosen without any mystical fear that creating a fantasy about something will make it happen, or put out into the world "negative energy." You're not doing voodoo and you're not trying to put a whammy on anybody. The whole process of creating Art ought to be under the umbrella of healthy creativity: an appeal to the Light. However grim or depraved the chosen fantasy is that you use to achieve an emotional value in a scene, your intention is for a larger loving purpose: to delight and enlighten. Cutting flesh with a knife is ugly, but in the service of surgery it becomes wonderful.

Whatever fantasy you chose, I recommended you keep it private. It'll help to retain its power, and, anyway, nobody really wants to hear that stuff. Believe me.

Select for the height and vividness of the meaning. There's a normal inclination to unconsciously minimize the severity of the events you relate to in order to better stay in control. But the goal of Art is to present life at its most vibrant, so it's usually best to select a fantasy Circumstance that exceeds in magnitude the Circumstance in the text.

▶▶ *Note:* **If you fear being seen as overacting because you've made a response too big — don't. What we think of as overacting is either when someone pretends to be having feelings that they clearly don't authentically have, or it looks self-generated and, even if they are truly emotional, it seems whipped up by themselves and not directed towards a person or object we can identify. Let's say you do make something disproportionately eventful, for example, you act as if it's a catastrophe that someone put a dent in your car. As long as you're really relating to it and the emotion appears to be coming from, and directed at, the dent itself or the person who ran into your car, it'll be interpreted as your playing a neurotic character, not that you, the** performer, are overacting. And remember, we tend to like watching neurotic characters. It might be wrong, yes, and you shouldn't do it because it distorts the meaning of the piece, perhaps even being unintentionally comedic, but it won't be called overacting.

Whatever the response, it should be specific and, even though the character may have an adjusted reaction that's less than your reality, that lesser meaning should nevertheless be fully brought to life. Fishing keys out of a toilet is a less meaningful event than taking them off a dead body, but, depending on the current state of the toilet, it is vivid. If you like cats and you walk into a room and find one sitting there, even if it's your least favorite breed of cat, it's still fun to meet them. Or at the other end of the spectrum, even the least offensive type of insect that crawls into your mouth will still get your attention.

▶▶ *Note:* Everything means something. You can see mediocre actors make this mistake when they play a bad guy who maintains the same sneering relish or lack of feeling for killing, regardless of the circumstances. In the film *A History of Violence*, a bad guy kills a little girl at the beginning of the picture, and it's supposed to be scary because he has no feeling about it. For me, I found it less frightening, or affecting in any way, to be asked to inhabit a world devoid of human truth. Okay, he's a psychopath, without any remorse for the killing itself, fine, but since he's not represented as mentally retarded, how could he have no feeling for the fact that killing a little girl is certainly going to bring incredibly intense heat down on himself and grave prosecution should he be caught? When Joe Pesci's character in *Goodfellas* shoots a boy for giving him backtalk during a card game, Joe Pesci and Robert De Niro are both genuinely upset. Not as upset as you should be about an arbitrary murder, but maybe as much as if he'd broken his mother's anniversary plate. When I worked with Keanu Reeves on Sam Raimi's *The Gift*, I suggested that he not play his character as some generic redneck who abuses his wife without feeling. I recommended he play it with an emotional value as if her character was like a schizophrenic sister he'd taken care of his whole life, and who had cost him the woman of his dreams; that this sister was violent and had to be treated severely to be kept in line, and so ill, day to day, she wouldn't remember anything he did, anyway. While I'm on the subject, there's a scene where he warns a boy to tell his mother, who's been harboring his wife, that she should stay out of his business. I suggested that he not act snarly with the boy, again to avoid the shallow redneck cliché, but rather that he like the boy, that his character might be a man's man, coach Little League and that kind of thing, and that he could be thinking he's being helpful to the boy and have the sensibility that "we guys have to stick together." For me this kind of intimacy with the boy, and the reality of the threat, not just being a mouthy jerk, makes it much creepier.

Once the desired fantasy is chosen you're ready to use it to work toward your performance.

Have a daydream. In a relaxed, private and secure environment, with eyes closed, initiate in your mind's eye the chosen daydream at its logical beginning. There's no need for extended preludes; set the stage just prior to the important event. If the fantasy is going to be about your being diagnosed with cancer, you don't need to fantasize finding a parking space and riding up in the elevator (although, I suppose you could if you wanted to); you can start as you're sitting in the doctor's office with your mother, waiting for the test results.

Experience the details in the first person, not watching dispassionately from the outside. Live through the fantasy with your five senses, open to each sight, sound, smell/taste and touch. We tend to emphasize vision, but the fantasy itself will probably dictate the important sensory elements: *the sound of your mother's sob, the antiseptic smell of a medical environment, how your mom reaches for and squeezes your hand.*

The fantasy should be allowed to take its course. It will naturally move towards a climax. Once underway, the daydream shouldn't be tampered with, and, as is always true, whether it's preparing or actually acting, disregard the conduct of your emotion. Afterwards you can evaluate how deep you think you got, if you must. Don't let anxiety get you to second guess yourself and change channels, as it were, interrupting the fantasy. The mind may be bombarded by extraneous thoughts and judgments, but these thoughts should be passively ignored and the process willfully allowed to continue. Emotional Preparation requires trust and relaxation, and you must be free to become lost in the specificity of the daydream. Like a raft pushed into the beginning of the rapids, it will naturally find its way to the central torrent.

Given that daydreaming is a natural thing to do, it might be helpful to reflect on how you've done this before in your life. Specifically, let's look at sexual fantasies. We're adults here. Nothing was forced, there was no jumping ahead. If you had a fantasy of being with someone attractive, you may have thought beforehand that you'd be drawn to, say, their rear end, but if you started gravitating toward their legs or stomach in the fantasy, you didn't feel compelled to stop yourself and go, "No, damn it, this is suppose to be about their ass!" You didn't insist, you were simply present with the details and let it go whatever way it wanted to go. You trusted that the fantasy would know best how to move you toward climax.

Associate the personal fantasy with the textual Circumstance. If you're not using a fantasy directly relatable to the fictional reality that the character has lived, and you're using instead a personal fantasy so you can channel the feelings from that into the material in the scene, you'll need to go through a two-stage process.

In this way, when the personal fantasy reaches its emotional crescendo, the next step is to associate these feelings with the event of the scene. You remain in contact with the peak experience of the daydream, then say to yourself: *Not only did this* [the personal fantasy] *happen, but this* [the event of the scene] *as well.* Relating to both Circumstances simultaneously: *not only has this doctor just told me that I have cancer, but I've just been told that I'm being fired as well*, or, *not only am I holding my child for the first time, but I've just been made salesman of the week, too!* The triggers for these preset emotional responses should be events in the scenes, whether they are caused by spoken words or nonverbal events.

A certain dissipation of feeling might occur as you relate to both your fantasy circumstance and your actual scene Circumstance together, but continue to relate to them both. Any literal thoughts about the process should not be allowed to confuse and interfere with the emotional truth of this work.

Let the fantasy go. The next step is for you to let go of the initial fantasy and to just continue relating to the Circumstance of the scene: *I'm being fired.* Not trying to actively dismiss the daydream, it isn't being amputated, you just leave it alone as you transition to an exclusive relatedness with the event of the scene.

Repeat. This process may be repeated as often as is desired with the same or different daydreams. If it's the same fantasy scenario, it will probably play itself out with slight variations and with different aspects of the daydream coming to the fore. What may have been the crescendo once may not be the next time, and you have to be open and flexible to go with these new variables.

There are some situations where the actor is asked to represent a profound emotional condition, as with a character living with a terrible loss or in a horrible situation: someone living with post traumatic stress disorder (PTSD). To create an extreme condition of this kind you'll almost certainly need to do repeated, severe emotional preparations to break yourself down. It can be very difficult, painful work. But you are an actor and it comes with the territory. A nurse walks into a room where someone is screaming in pain, knowing they will claw at her as she secures them to the bed; a pastor holds the anger of a mother whose child has died, for whom the idea of a loving God is now an obscenity. You must bear what you have to bear if you intend to call yourself an actor. Horace said to the artist over two thousand years ago: "If you would have me feel, you must feel."

I can only offer that, if you are willing to walk through the fire, you just may find on the other side a kind of joy. You'll perhaps get to that place where you can go into the darkest corners of the human experience with abandon because you know that you can return, braced by the fact that you take what you do and yourself seriously. And it is fantasy, after all. You do have a return ticket from any ghastly fantasy world you choose to create (another reason to maybe avoid working from actual events in your life). Winston Churchill said: "There's nothing more exhilarating than being shot at and missed."

Daydream only for homework. No matter how much preparatory work you do, or don't do, you have to understand that at some point, you're going to leave it all behind you. You're going to have to trust it, and go about your business on stage without ever once referring back to that personal fantasy. No matter how fanciful the material may be, once it's time to perform and you're living through the scene, there is only the reality of the scene and your personal daydream has no place in your conscious mind. Not the: "I'm going to kiss the most beautiful person in the world." you used to prepare for the moment, only: "I'm all vampire, and I want to bite that beautiful neck!"

Appreciate how a bomb goes off. Actors tend to want to go for results and assimilate events too quickly, thereby limiting the magnitude of an event. When you first learn of a major event, there's going to be a moment of stillness equal to how strange that event is. And I don't mean confusion or amazement. No, no, darling. Those are almost always acting faults because it means you're trying to process it above the eyebrows, when what you need to do is take it into your gut. Your state during these moments might be described as awe.

It's like when you cut yourself with a really sharp knife, and you go into that space where you know something bad has happened, and you know you're going to pay for it, but the storm hasn't hit yet. Another analogy I use is that a big event can be like dropping a bowling ball into a child's wading pool. The event hits, and the water, your emotional life, rushes away leaving an empty spot for a moment, with just the ball sitting there, then the water/feeling comes rushing back and fills the space with a whoosh. On a massive scale, as when you've just been told your child's been killed, or, egad, they cast the part with somebody else — it can be like a tsunami. The water withdraws at first, leaving an empty beach, and only later does the torrent roll in. During these eerie, still moments before the flood you can say your lines, you move around; we all get it, you're just something of a zombie.

My wife was once betrayed by someone and I said to her, "You're taking this pretty well." To which she replied, "Oh, no. I'm not taking it well at all. You just haven't seen my reaction yet."

This goes for good bombs and bad bombs both, and whether the rush of feeling is going to be grief, rage, terror or joy.

SET THE ACTIONS

Ah, those magnificent Actions. Your solid banister that leads you faithfully and powerfully through any part, in any scene. You've established them, either through extensive analysis or simple intuition or, hopefully, some combination of both, and you know what your character wants and how they're going to try to get it at any given moment. Now you can habituate those Actions. Once firmly set they will serve you either automatically or as a place to put your crumby, little mind.

Connect and do. To practice an Action you first want to get emotionally related (no Action is done in a vacuum). Then you connect to your Objective in that moment; then you employ the methodology you've decided your character would use to get it. The Action is happening before you even begin to speak, because remember: Actions are not the things you say. An Action is not dependent on saying words. Animals are always doing Actions and they don't do them with talk. The words we utter are solely for the purpose of furthering whatever the Action is we've embarked upon. It starts before we speak, and continues after we are done speaking. It should issue from every fiber of your body.

Speak using your own words. Now that you're emotionalized and doing the Action behaviorally, if you have dialog, the sense of what you say should be spoken in a total, free paraphrase. You have to own it. You broke it down already (If you need your cheat sheet to keep you on track, that's okay), you know the sense of what your character is saying, so, doing the Action, go through every meaning in your dialog and, once again, create it with your own words. You want to make yourself come into personal contact with the sense of what you're saying, in this context, and with this Action.

Use a Gist Phrase. What can be helpful for keeping you on track with an Action is to find an expression that represents the active meaning of what's being done, the gist of what is being put forth. This active meaning of what's being expressed can be spoken periodically while doing the Action, and during the paraphrase, and it will help reaffirm the Action. If it is an imploring Action, you could use the Gist Phrase, "Please help me." In practice you deliver it along with the paraphrase or the actual textual line: "[Please help me.] She's my daughter. She's all I have in this world." If the intent is to threaten, it might go "[I'm warning you.] She's my daughter. She's all I have in this world." And, of course, the line reading becomes very different.

The Gist Phrase is also useful because it will distill the Action down to its essential thrust. What may look on the page to be a long story with a lot of information and a list of complaints, can probably be distilled to a blunt statement of fact such as "This has to stop!" It will help you not to get lost in the ideas you're putting forth, and instead ground you to what is actually going on. Actions are simple and universal and their expression can be captured in short, to the point statements: "Get away from me." "Be fair." "Don't you like me?" "I'm here for you." "This is wrong." "I'm so sorry." "It's always been you."

Although you may utilize a paraphrase that's made up of contemporary slang and reads far different from what might be the very poetic or colloquial style of the actual dialog, I suggest you use a Gist Phrase consistent with how the character would speak in this piece. Yes, it should be personalized to you and your connection to those particular words, but, in order for it to endure throughout your process, the language you use for your Gist Phrase should not violate your immersion into this particular, imaginary world. The best Gist Phrase would be one you could use during rehearsal that wouldn't jolt the other actors out of their reality. And, heck, maybe you will use it later, during rehearsal. If you're rehearsing something by Shakespeare, it's probably going to be a bit jarring if you blurt out at one of your cast mates, "Chill out, dude!" Not very Elizabethan. And it's not really great for your sense of reality, either. But nobody should mind too much if you were to ad lib, "Easy, friend!" If that's what your character is saying openly with their behavior, anyway.

You've got to get your teeth into your Actions. Actions are vital. Actions are huge. Many actors don't understand this and their work suffers. Often when my wife and I see a performance from somebody who's previously been good, but now, in a different part, isn't at all, we say to each other, sadly, "They don't do Actions."

Even though your character is very upset and angry to meet an ex-spouse's new lover, in the scene you may be trying to come off as breezy, like everything is fine and normal. So you aren't going to say "screw you" with your behavior, that's not the message your character is trying to put forth; you're hiding that and trying to communicate a Gist Phrase more like "Everything's good with me." This isn't to say an Action has to always involve a suppressed emotional life. Your character, given who they are and the context, could just as easily be totally open about their feelings and be doing the Gist Phrase, "I don't like you."

Use a Psychological Gesture. You can enhance your deep connection to an Action by creating and practicing a gesture you associate with that Action. You can even greatly exaggerate the gesture when you rehearse it, using your entire body with an intensified physicality much larger than anything a human being would normally do, and well beyond what the style or character would allow for in the performance.

Of course, such an exaggerated Psychological Gesture would not be rehearsed with other actors unless it was in special situations where they were voluntarily participating in the exercise. Let's not frighten anybody. And a purist of Psychological Gestures would suggest that the physical gesture itself ultimately be removed altogether, without any physical trace remaining, and that you should only be left with its influence in your core.

Blend the paraphrase into the text. After doing a full paraphrase of all of your dialog while doing the Action, do it again, this time mixing in words from the actual dialog. Go ahead and use any words you normally use, but you might still paraphrase those that are foreign to you. Also, you might continue to paraphrase a sentence that uses words you'd use, but not in this way. For instance, the sentence "I would that I had flown to her" uses all common words, but it might be best for you to continue paraphrasing this sentence, "I wish I'd rushed to her side."

As the paraphrase is repeated, more and more of the playwright's words can be mixed in until, with each term and phrasing understood and integrated, a final version is done using only the lines from the script. Now you'll own the words completely and have a feel for how they're used to assist the Action. Nifty, huh?

It's only by going through this process that you have any right to consciously connect to the words you're saying. Otherwise, those words won't be incorporated with the Action they're meant to be serving, and will intrude with their contaminating ideas about how those words should be spoken, and make for line readings that are — how should I put this — well, crap.

Practice the big Action changes. At times you'll make a major change of Action, as when your character begins pursuing an entirely new Objective or they switch to a completely new method for getting the same Objective. When this happens, it can be tricky because, for the most part, it's by following your Action that an audience follows what's taking place. If you jump to a new Action inorganically, or without an obvious event that can be seen to have made you change, you'll leave everyone in a muddle. It's therefore advisable to lead an audience deliberately through your transitions from one major Action to another for the sake of clarity. If you do this well, these transitions will show your mastery and provide gratification for those basking in it.

And remember, it's crucial to feel the reason for the change before you make the change, and that you not just go to a new Objective automatically. The emotion is the impelling force that powers the change.

Sometimes the impulse that brings about the change of Action builds over time; in other situations, it is a new event that causes a sudden change. Say a man wants to get his wife back, and he acts romantic with her, but this fails to persuade her to return to him (gradual), so he changes his Action to pleading with her. Through the successive moments from the beginning of the scene she's been acting evasive (gradual), so now he becomes suspicious that something else is going on, and the curiosity eventually brings him to the moment where changes his Action to that of asking her what she's hiding. As she avoids the question, he continues with the Action of directly probing her until finally she tells him that she's been having an affair, and this new event (sudden) changes his Action so that he now wants to leave with his dignity. She continues telling him how she never truly loved him and that this new man has brought her new happiness into her life until the successive moments of this humiliation (gradual) cause him to change his Action to wanting to punish her and he strikes her. She recoils (sudden), and he changes his Action to trying to get her to accept his apology; she refuses and demands that he leave. Humiliated by the accumulation of events (gradual), capped off by her demand for him to leave (sudden), he once again returns to the Action of leaving with dignity. And... scene.

Let's first look at how to negotiate a change of Action when it's a new event that causes the change. This is when something out-of-the-blue happens to blow you off track, and supersedes your prior Objective, such as a knock at the door as you're about to eat, or if you're told your child has been taken to the emergency room as you're about to enter a conference. An event may occur that proves the Objective you were pursuing is going to be definitely unattainable, as when the plane you were trying to catch takes off without you, or the last match you had to light a cigarette blows out.

Using your awareness, you should practice going through the change of Actions step by step.

Changing Actions when the change comes from a single new event:
1. Do your original Action.

2. Imagine the new event happening.

3. Feel the impact of the new event, including that stillness before the flood: that "oh, no" moment before the pain from the newly sliced finger rolls in.

4. Instantaneously the power goes out of your original Action, as the reality of the new event envelops you. You drift, then suspend, then feel the rush of the emotion from the new event coming in, possibly causing you to vent (more on this in a moment), and then you reorient toward the new Objective. We will call this the Action Pivot Point. It's like a jet flying straight up that has just had its engine cut off: it continues a bit, loses speed, is suspended for a moment, then reorients as it falls back toward earth, its new direction.

5. You now plunge into the new Action, gaining momentum and driven by the force of the new event.

During the Action Pivot Point the audience is able to sense that you are going through this reorientation process and they're able to follow along on the trip from one Action to another. The duration of this moment of suspension is based on the event's strangeness and magnitude, but, given that it's essential to exist, even if for a fraction of a second, it's a good idea to practice it slowly so you can feel and finesse the steps your character goes through before they launch into their new Action.

With the rush of emotion coming from an event, you may have a venting, a vocalization, of this emotion. This won't happen if your character is repressed or if the new Objective is life and death; but if you do vent, you must feel free to say actual, intelligible text as part of this expression, and not wait until you recover so you can deliver your lines in a more composed, and boring, way.

▶▶ **Note: Be clear though, the momentary venting of emotion should not, by itself, be confused with fully taking on the Action of getting someone to register the type and magnitude of your feelings. If your venting does move into that Action, you, and we the audience, ought to be very clear who it is you want to get your feelings. If you just start doing an extended Action of trying to get God or the Universe or your own alter ego to register your feelings, we'll view your character as a crank.**

Doing an Action change that comes out of an incremental build up is slightly different. This would be the case if you're trying to open a plastic bag and it resists and resists until you change your tactic to violently tearing it open with your teeth. It could be the impulse to change comes from something that occurs episodically, as when you're trying to explain something to someone and they occasionally look at their watch until, on their third look, your curiosity overtakes your desire to explain and you ask what's so important about the time. Or the distraction could be continuous; say you're on a business call and your girlfriend starts doing a striptease. You maintain your business composure with the caller until you can't take it any longer and then, still businesslike, you tell them you'll have to call them back, after which you dive into your new Action of going after her.

Changing Actions that change as a result of an incremental build up:
1. You start by doing the original Action.

2. Feel the rising impulse coming from the distraction or from the growing agitation from your failure to achieve the Objective.

3. Contain this impulse as you continue to pursue the original Objective in the same way you have been. This containment creates a tension in you (and the audience feels it). It's like holding a board to channel water during an ever-increasing flood. Either there is an event that acts as the last straw or you feel your breaking point approach and hit, and the tipping point tips.

4. You give over to the rush of feeling, releasing you (and the audience). You possibly vent. There will be no moment of stillness before the rush of feeling from this event because, with a gradual building up scenario, it's been pressing on you for a while and you've been internally preparing for this eventuality.

5. Plunge immediately into the new Action.

▶▶ *Note:* **You need to watch for this build-up change and not just jump at changing on the exact line in the text where it seems obvious. You want to create the weather conditions getting into your bones well before you say the line, "It's so cold." In Sam Shepard's *True West* he has one brother say to another in the middle of a conversation, "Do you always work by candlelight?" If you're playing that part, the flickering candle should have been bothering you ever since you came into the room. You can get a scene off to a nice, rousing start by beginning it with the sense that your character has already been affected by a building up of moments that the audience didn't see prior to this moment.**

Do a Mirror Action. This technique is great for really making an Action your own. A Mirror Action is a personalized version of an Action wherein you imagine a Circumstance and a Relationship that would create in you the same feelings as the character in the scene. Then you practice this fictional Action straight from yourself. You use a tactic similar to what the character uses, possessed of the same emotional condition and with a parallel relationship. Being personal to you, however, a Mirror Action will almost always be for a vastly different Objective.

For example: to play a scene where you are an overly possessive brother threatening his future brother-in-law that he better treat his sister well, you could practice a fantasy scenario in which you coldly tell your neighbor that if he hits his child again, you'll report him to the police. If you're going to play a saint who offers a stranger help, you might practice earnestly asking someone who saved your life if they'll allow you to pay for their hospital bills. Playing an android asking someone directions so you can hunt down and kill your target, you might do a fantasy scenario wherein you are in a foreign country asking a policeman for directions to your brother's wedding.

You can then wed this Mirror Action to the actual Action of the scene by launching from your personalized Mirror Action directly into the one in the scene, perhaps using a Gist Phrase as a bridge.

Tell somebody about it. There's a nice, straightforward technique, a kind of variation on the paraphrase, that you can use that is really good for getting you in contact with the meanings in a scene. What you do is you imagine that the scene is now over, and that, as your character, you're telling someone who's receptive everything that took place during the scene, including everything that was said. You tell the story of what happened in the scene, after the fact, point by point, in specific detail. In order to talk through an entire scene this way, and spell out all your dialog, you will need to have a full understanding of what your dialog means, whether because you've done an exacting paraphrase or because the dialog is such that you naturally understand it.

You can have somebody do this with you if you want, but it's easy enough to do on your own, because all you're really going to do is imagine someone periodically asking you, "And then what did you say?" or "Then what did you do?"

I love this process for how it fleshes out the values of a piece, giving you an organic understanding of what's being said and how it should be presented. In my experience it always seems to reveal where you're giving something undue stress and where the real thrust belongs. Often when I do this simple exercise with an actor, somewhere along the way they'll say, "Why was I hitting that point so hard? That's not a big point. I'm an idiot!"

The beginning of William Shakespeare's famous soliloquy from *Hamlet* might go, "I was all alone and I asked myself whether I should live or I should die. That this was the only real issue. I asked whether it was better to submit to the punishment of a monstrous fate, or to use a weapon against this ocean of problems and, by fighting back, make them stop."

▶▶ *Note:* I picked this speech to use as an example, given that these are the most famous lines in drama, and I discovered that, even though I've known these words since I was a little boy, I never really understood, until putting it through this technique, that Hamlet's weighing the option "to take *arms* against a sea of troubles, and by opposing end them" would almost certainly have to be a reference to a specific weapon he could use to stop his troubles, namely the knife the play mentions he carries. This would very much influence this moment given the means of his suicide is there physically close at hand. Would he go for a stab into the heart or into the throat?

SET THE CHARACTER ADDITIONS

Once all the special physical and vocal behavior has been determined for each scene, the way your character speaks and moves and their faculties, including the functioning of the five senses, you'll have to drill those things that are different from your natural way of being until they become second nature.

Practice your Character Additions separate from the material. You should rehearse the Character Additions by themselves and often. You want to do them separate from the material to make sure you're executing them precisely without relying on the context to mask any lack of true ownership.

Do them while doing daily tasks, take them out into the neighborhood and embarrass and annoy your family and friends because you won't stop with the crazy accent or that funny way of walking.

Another way to practice Character Additions is to do visualizations. In a quiet, relaxed place, maybe before going to sleep, visualize in your mind's eye performing your Character Addition perfectly. Visualizations have a proven usefulness. They test people and find that, in certain physical tasks, people will show almost as much improvement from doing visualizations alone as they do when they spent that time actually practicing the thing.

Choose when and how to apply your Character Additions to the material. It's generally recommended that you rehearse a scene for as long as possible without incorporating the Character Additions, while the Character Addition is being perfected separately. This is to make sure that you're fully personalizing the part and avoiding externalizations that are prone to happen with Character Additions.

The general rule of thumb is the greater the behaviors differ from your own, the sooner they should be applied to the material. If it's a profound Character Addition: *brain damage, insanity, gunshot wound*, it will have such a huge influence on every moment that there's little value in working on your role separate from this fact, and doing so would be, truthfully, kind of silly. On the other hand, accented speech usually has little impact on the life of your character, but it does risk making you "act the accent," thinning your emotional life through cliché. Do a cockney accent and suddenly you're a jaunty character in the cast of a second-rate production of *My Fair Lady*. Put on a New York accent and automatically you become a blasé New York thug or a "hitter chick" smacking her gum.

Story: **Peter MacNicol was in preproduction for a feature he was directing, and he asked me what I thought about casting a particular actress in the part of a poor girl in the south. I got a picture of her doing the thick Appalachian accent and I spontaneously said, "I'm worried she'd have too much fun with it."**

Having said all this about delaying Character Additions, however, there are very real exceptions to this, because there can be certain, even small behaviors, that appeal to your deeper connection to the character. If a small thing, say, a way of sitting, or a slight beer buzz, or an accent, seems to open a larger door into the character, what I call Intuitive Embodiment, there's no point in not using all the time possible to explore it. Perhaps a proper English accent will bring with it for you a heavy sense of propriety, and a pained feeling of being cut off from the world because of it. Whatever brings you closer to the core of the character should be pursued.

The truth is, there's such a tremendous variety of Character Additions and styles to apply them to, plus the variations of your own temperament and how each part will require a readjustment of your approach, it's impossible to give pat advice on the subject. What I will say is that it's probably best if you have your Character Addition extremely well in hand before you apply it to the text, and, if possible, blend it in by first practicing it with the Actions and a paraphrase before doing it with all text. But the decision of when to add your Character Addition is a personal one and, really, I only offer the caution not to let the tail wag the dog.

Note: This issue of when to apply Character Additions goes directly to the topic in acting concerning whether someone works from the outside in, or from the inside out. Let it be known, I am a card-carrying member of the inside out school. I believe every role, no matter how stylized, should, first and foremost, be deeply personal. I heard Glenn Close say she was going to be glad to get away from the villainous character she was playing in *101 Dalmatians*. This would only be the case with an actress who approaches work on even such a broad role with the same personal connection they bring to their naturalistic drama.

SET WORK WITH THE PHYSICAL WORLD

Rehearse how you operate in the Physical World. You want to rehearse how you're going to deal with all of the potential elements of the physical world in the scene, the props, costume and body parts, both yours and others, that you touch. Of course, this work intimately dovetails with all the other work so far discussed in Working Toward Performance. Your temperament and Character Additions will affect your habits and mannerisms and how you then deal with the Physical World. It might be a direct relationship with these things, such as the one a policeman has with his handcuffs, or a handicapped person with their cane, or it could be a more general prop issue as in the choice of how your version of a policeman waters his plants, or your handicapped person puts his money in his wallet.

The way you deal with the physical world can say so much about who you are and can create such a beautiful sense of truth that you really should take every opportunity to practice what needs to be practiced. This way you can make a place seem lived in, a job seem second nature, and personal quirks personal.

We saw a towering performance given by Ian McClellan in *Dance of Death* by August Strindberg (less than a minute into the play, my wife and I turned to each other with raised eyebrows in an expression of "Wow"). At one point, he handed a wine bottle to David Straithern, a nice actor in his own right, but you could feel the life go out of that bottle in the most remarkable way as it lost all its Ian McClellan magic and became just a prop.

70

Learn from experts. If you have a prop or a costume that is unfamiliar to you, you have to go to someone who does know how to handle it and learn how it's done. Whether it's a saber or a parasol, there's a right way to use it.

I understand when he was getting ready to do *The Last of the Mohicans*, Daniel Day Lewis became one of only a handful of people alive who could run and load a flintlock rifle at the same time.

Use the same process for rehearsing the technical as Character Additions. Work on the physical in the same way you did the Character Additions, and, as I said, there may be a lot of overlap. Practice separately what you can until you have a good handle on it, then work it into the text with precision.

Let the Physical World tell you how it ought to be handled. Give yourself freedom to play when it comes to how you do things physically. Be inventive. Try new things, finesse things differently. Let your relationship with everything that's useful and everything that's decorative have a chance.

The Physical World is mostly crap. Watching Brando I learned (among other things) that, in most situations, it's probably good for an actor to treat just about everything they handle like it's interesting trash. There are huge exceptions to this with objects that have taken on a sentimental significance, of course, but the vast majority of what makes up the Physical World shouldn't be treated as very precious at all compared to human beings. Like so many aspects of what you do as an artist, this communicates the truth to an audience of something we already know. What's important is the souls around us, not the objects. You can be precise with what you deal with, enjoy things even — in fact, most of the time you should treat your work with props like intimate ritual — but that doesn't mean you won't let it all fall to the floor in a second at a hint that someone's feelings might be hurt.

Don't get too clever with props. While props do have this wonderful ability to convey both a lovely reality to the life of your character, and nice thematic and metaphorical meanings in the piece, these effects are almost always better if they are subtle, even unconscious, in the mind of the audience. There are some actors who become enamored with this power of props and how they can be used to send messages, and they end up focusing on them to the detriment of the true thrust of a scene.

For example, this is not a conversation you want to have:
Actor: Did you like that thing I did with the glass?
Friend: I saw you doing something there. What was that?
Actor: Didn't you get it? It was like the glass was my heart and during the scene it fills up.
Friend: Oh. I just didn't know why you would keep pouring wine into a glass when you hadn't drunk any of it.

SET THE TECHNICAL

The work on the technical aspects of a production — the blocking, stunts, and so forth — are going to be determined much less by you in isolation and more from a joint rehearsal process and the demands of the specific production and its director. Once staging decisions are made, you'll still want to work on these technical matters privately as much as you can.

Use the same process for rehearsing the technical as Character Additions. As with the dealing with the Physical World, you should get yourself well rehearsed with the staging requirements in the same way you do the Character Additions: hanging up your coat or loading your flintlock rifle while you're running, and they often overlap, such as when falling down drunk or getting shot. Those things that are technical should be worked on separate from the material, and then done with the exact text.

Practice the complicated until it becomes ordinary.

Don't chafe at the bit. There can sometimes be the feeling among actors that the technical demands of a production, even the technicians themselves, are at war with the creative process. This feeling is perhaps understandable, given that technical matters exist in a totally different world from what is imaginative and they certainly impose restrictions, but it's wrongheaded to view them as adversarial. The Imagination is huge and brave and sturdy and it will only withdraw when insulted directly, something the impersonal, technical requirements are unlikely to do on their own. That insult is much more likely to occur when your own insecurity and ego cause you to obsess over a distracting working condition or an insensitive stage hand.

Taken in the right way, technical restrictions can act as a means to focus all of the energy, that light of creativity, into a tight, white-hot laser.

MEMORIZE THE LINES

Get the lines down cold. You must learn your lines exactly and know them by rote. Period. Often an actor is told by a relative, "I don't know how you can memorize all those lines." And the actor will smile at the quaintness of this remark, because there's so much more to the process of acting a role. Yet these laypersons in their innocence have in fact hit upon one of the most fundamental tasks you have as an actor. If you're going to do it right, you have to take the time to know your lines cold. Some people have more difficulty than others at memorization, but anyone can do it if they put in the time. If it takes you longer to memorize something than it does somebody else, well, that's kind of your tough luck.

You can be learning your lines at the same time as you practice all the other things you have to practice, including your paraphrasing, because they really have nothing to do with each other. Most of what you do while acting is natural, channeled through an imaginative talent, but using someone else's wording to say what you want to say is artificial, and because those words are artificial to you, you have to know them really, really well.

You can think you know your lines because you run them so easily in the peace and comfort of your living room, but then, when you get in the hectic, intense bedlam of the acting situation, they go right out of your head. When you forget your lines, you then reach for them out of your memory, much as if you left the set to go get the script backstage, and this makes it impossible for you to be totally present in the scene. Searching for a line breaks your concentration, losing some of the vitality of that moment, and it will also bring into your mind that you're an actor on stage who's made a mistake, with the possible consequence of causing you to get mad at yourself for being incompetent. The resultant stinging impulse of self-reprimand is probably not something the character is feeling in this moment, so that, too, maybe especially that depending on how punishing you are on yourself, removes you from the scene.

You'll know you know your lines the way you need to when you can rattle them off monotone, like a robot, as fast as you can speak. Once you have the exact text perfectly and firmly committed to memory, you're free to be fully present and relating to the person you're speaking to in that moment. Be conscious where you should be conscious, memorizing your lines as homework, so you can be unconscious where you should be unconscious, spitting out the exact text without hesitation.

Apart from knowing them well, the really big thing is:

Don't memorize line readings. The lines should be memorized without the inflections that come with having associated meanings with the words. You must learn your lines like you would if they were a list of numbers. If you don't do this diligently, then your preconceived ideas about how those words should be said will get habituated, and you won't be free to say them fresh and how they really ought to be delivered when that moment comes. Memorizing line readings happens very fast, and once you get stuck with a set line reading it is extremely hard to shake.

And — you aren't going to want to do what I'm telling you right now. Because memorizing lines without any inflection is the most difficult way to do it, you're going to want to make those associations with the words so they stick in your head better. Virtually everybody memorizes their lines with some contamination from these preconceived notions, it's just the degree to which you're able to fight off this crud.

One of your worse obstacles to acting well is going to be the way you unconsciously connect conventional associations with the words. You're going to tend to attach the sensibility to a word or phrase that is the conventional meaning of that word or phrase. The result will always be a line reading that is in some way stilted. You know, of course, that the line "This is so boring" can be said with the subtextual meaning "I'm going to scream!" But if you've memorized the word "boring" with a connotation of boredom, it's going to pervert the true moment, so that when you go to render the line you'll start automatically rolling your eyes with boredom.

▶▶ *Note:* Taking words too literally is a constant danger. John Patrick Shanley is a great writer who puts a crazy amount of trust in actors. In his play *The Big Funk*, a jaded woman is given a bath by a man, and it's this kind of beautiful baptism for her, but during the event she says, "I hate baths." When an actress I was working with said this line I was so startled that I stopped her and had to check the book to see if that was, in fact, the correct line. It was, and my jaw dropped with awe for Shanley's nerve. This talented actress had delivered the line, "I hate baths," the way you would naturally assume a line like that should be said, but it had cut the legs right out from under the scene. She'd started connecting to an old, petty dislike, making a complaint, and it had steered her out of the experience she was having of entering into a wonderful, albeit frightening, world. I coached her to stay with the truth, and not be swayed by the convention, and so to deliver the line more as if she was girlishly looking for reassurance — more as if "This isn't normal for me, in the past I always hated baths." But can't you see how less artistic it would have been had Shanley had her say all that instead? Another example of how being literal can hurt you, although not as devastating to the scene if you don't get it right, would be in David Rabe's play *Hurley Burly*, where the character of Bonnie is blaming Eddie for setting her up with a guy who threw her out of a moving car (with the Objective of getting him to reassure her that he will use more caution in the future). During her rant he tells to "get to the point." She responds, "No." If the actress does that "no" literally, it becomes, at best, foolishly obstinate. A better take on the line is for her to use that "no" as a rejection of him trying to dictate terms to her of any kind.

To put richness in line readings is not to have a pat way of saying the words, it is to have something to say. It is to understand what it is you're saying, so you can connect emotionally to the values in those things, and so you can better put forth the simple message of the Action (your Gist Phrase).

I hope you know you shouldn't be practicing how you're going to say your lines over and over again. So amateur. How you say them should be left to whatever happens in the moment as you live truthfully through

75

the imaginary experience. Okay, alright, there may be the rare exception when you're going for a comedic reading or something, and there's a particular tempo and snap you're listening for, but even then you'd better be damn sure you know why the sense of it makes it get punched that way. That sense should be the real purpose of your concentration, not a set line reading, or it's unlikely, in the end, to work.

You experience in the extreme what it sounds like when lines are spoken with only their conventional idea supporting them when you hear one of those commercials that guys do on the radio or local TV for their own store. They have that tone, that disembodied, hollow tone. It's funny, yes, because they're egotistical fools to be doing these unprofessional presentations themselves, but it's really rather chilling to the ear. This is what people in hell must sound like.

Some actors are better at faking line readings than others, but even the best can't fool all of the people all of the time.

Use tricks to shake up your memorized line readings. Because you're an animal, and animals are given to locking into habits, you will have to constantly deal with this curse of getting stuck on pat line readings. You want to be able to run your lines fast, and with a robotic absence of all meaning to them, but you can also shake habitual line readings by intentionally messing up how they might be said by arbitrarily playing around with the emphasis.

Read through them and, every time, absurdly punch a different word or words, in the sentence. Sing them and jack them around randomly like a crazy person. Say or sing them like someone who doesn't speak this language.

Here's my message for you that will sound heretical to many: Disrespect the words!

ALLOW THE PERFORMANCE TO DEVELOP

When all the components of Working Toward Performance are operating together, it's possible to let go of the controls a bit, to let things integrate organically and trust it will all shake out all right. I'm not telling you to be sloppy in your discipline, or to stop building onto the portrayal, it's only that, at a certain point, you may want to relax your exacting focus on specific pieces of the performance and let it breathe some, allowing your Intuitive Embodiment to do its work.

Welcome new things happening. As a part develops, new things can start to happen that weren't planned. Character Additions may modify into behavior you don't recognize as deliberately being executed. You might, for example, gesture more with your hands when using an Italian accent; well, maybe that's how you'd actually behave if you were raised in Italy. If you're performing a role with a physical defect, a shyness might come over you, or, for that matter, you might get more pugnacious as a compensation. New things are to be welcomed, and shouldn't be rejected as inconsistent with the original design just because they weren't deliberately premeditated. It's possible your conception wasn't fully balanced, and that the deeper mind is appropriately tuning things.

▶▶ *Note:* I gave myself a small part in the movie I just made (a perk of being the director), and, while I'd planned certain Character Additions such as an Oklahoma accent and a feeling that my eyes were made of wax (an effort to convey the woundedness of a man whose son has been murdered); better than halfway into doing the performance I noticed I was keeping my chest very full, especially right under the armpits. I was alarmed at first that I'd taken on this uncharacteristic tension, but then it occurred to me that maybe the character would carry himself this way, that it really wasn't actor tension and was actually how this upright man might be holding himself in this situation.

It's also possible that entirely new insights will be offered up out of this Intuitive Embodiment of the character, and you should openly entertain the validity of these new behaviors and emotional reactions and desires, regardless of how they upset the applecart of your original design. You may find that a piece of jewelry or a hair style or a costume you once thought of as perfect, seems less and less so as the part develops. Get rid of it and find a better fit.

Let the character speak. There's not a lot of point in talking too much about this deeper mind stuff (and it even kind of gives me the heebie-geebies doing it). Suffice it to say that your ideal situation as performer is to put what you can in place, then get the hell out of the way and have it channel through you.

TRY SPECIAL METHODS

The specific approach described in this manual is designed to be a single, comprehensive system that will work for everyone, but of course it's not meant to be the last word. There are many wonderful ways of stimulating your imagination, and, bearing in mind that an approach that works for a particular role might not work as well for a different one, and that something inspirational for one performer might leave another cold, you ought to be constantly seeking to discover and create new techniques for yourself and for each situation.

Caution needs to be taken working with Special Methods, however, because some of these approaches risk becoming fanciful pastimes in themselves, and that isn't funny if they take away time you should be spending doing something that will actually develop and improve your performance.

Some Special Methods for the actor to practice alone:

▶ **Study the real world.** In conjunction with all the necessary research for a part, if at all possible you should spend time in the same type of environment as your character, and, if possible, actually do the same job the character does. This practice will feed your performance in many subtle ways, as well as instill confidence that you have a deeper understanding about this lifestyle. Benicio del Toro told me that, if he plays a dentist, he wants to know more about dentistry than anybody else on the set. My wife went into a holding area with over a hundred psychiatric criminals, just herself and the female chaplain she was researching to play. She said it was the craziest thing she's ever done, yet, she brought that authority to her part and crushed it.

▸ **Get a personal object.** You can find a personal object for your character, such as a watch, a necklace, or a lucky coin. You can then perhaps create a fantasy around this object: *your mother gave it to you on her deathbed; your first love gave it to you after the first kiss; it was taken from a bully the first time you stood up for yourself.* You can then keep this with you while you're acting, maybe even while you're off stage as well, to help keep the part simmering inside on some level. This object can either be seen by the audience or not, used during a moment of the performance or not.

▸ **Find the right song.** You might try to find a piece of music that stimulates a response consistent with the life of the character.

▸ **Find something like your character or what your character relates to.** You can find an object that either typifies your character in the abstract, or something that resonates with the same meaning as something in the piece would resonate with your character. It could be anything: an old shoe, a rock, a figurine, a perfume; perhaps it's a photograph of something evocative. This object can then be used as an intuitive reference for the desired feeling.

▸ **Write in a journal.** You can write an entry in a journal for a day in the life of your character.

▸▸ *Note:* **This would be one of those time consumers I might caution against going overboard with. Note that I mentioned one day, and not a year in the life. Writing is writing, and it's more a mental activity that won't probably penetrate to the visceral level where you want to connect the way a sensual daydream will.**

▸ **Draw a picture.** You can draw a picture of your character or other characters, or anything your character relates to, perhaps in the abstract, but certainly without judging your drawing skills.

▸ **Do something in character out-of-character.** You can go somewhere in character that is unusual for your character to be, or practice doing something as your character that is unusual for them to be doing: as a psychiatrist, go into a church; as a bitter

79

miser, feed a dog; as a brutish thug, go to a museum; as a priggish secretary, go to a nightclub. This can give you a better sense of your character as you feel the contrast, the chafing points in this out-of-character environment or behavior. Maybe you'll be surprised to learn it isn't so out of character.

▶ **Meditate on your dialog.** You can read your lines out loud in a ruminative, meditative type of state, allowing yourself to be freely played upon by whatever associations arise.

▶ **Get a sense of history.** You can practice your part with a sense of historical continuity. Try to feel how people in history in this same situation performed this behavior in exactly the same way.

▶ **Analyze your dreams.** You can write a letter to your unconscious mind asking for aid in investigating a particular aspect of a role. You do this before you go to bed, and then you set an alarm for three or four hours later; upon waking to the alarm, write down whatever dreams you were having; then go back to sleep and, upon waking in the morning, write down those dreams you remember. These dreams are then contemplated and an interpretation sought. The letter might start out something like: "Dear Deeper Mind, Please reveal to me the nature of my character's relationship to his father." Yeah, I know this sounds whacky, but what the hell? It's at least putting you into the right part of the brain.

Some Special Methods possible for rehearsal/performance

Some of these Special Methods can be helpful for you if you're fortunate enough to find yourself in a long run of a play where using new things can aid in keeping your performance fresh in spite of constant repetition.

▶ **Imitate how someone else would do it.** You can play the part imitating how an actor you know of, perfectly cast or not, would play the part. Gary Oldman said he always does an impersonation when he plays a part, just that he's so bad at imitation, nobody ever picks up on it.

▶ **Live with a vision.** You can operate as if your character has certain knowledge of how they will be living in five years, or twenty years, or how they will die. Perhaps you've acquired this knowledge through a dream or visions you've had your whole life, or maybe an angel showed you. It could be in fantastic luxury or terrible poverty, alone or surrounded by loving family, doing something heroic or something stupid.

▶ **Know of past lives.** You can operate as if your character has an awareness of being reincarnated as this person that they are now, or that they are an entity from another planet exiled into this character's life form.

▶ **Emphasize various values.** You can concentrate on a particular aspect within the rehearsal or the performance, such as: an awareness of the physical environment, spontaneity, privacy (a strong fourth wall), variety, intention, pacing, or even a specific part of your body, perhaps one of the seven chakras.

▶ **Treat the piece with a new sensibility.** If it's a comedy, you can pretend it's a drama, if a drama, act as if it's a comedy. What if it were a musical? You can treat the piece as if it's in the style of a different author.

▶ **Experiment with the atmosphere.** You can seek to feel the atmosphere the piece is taking place in. As if scented, or fogged, or electrically charged, or as if the ceiling is low, or the floor could give way, or that the place is haunted by spirits, or fated to hold you. You can sense that the atmosphere itself is pulling the performance from you.

USE RITUAL

Devise your own triggers. I watched as weightlifters at the Olympics who were about to compete started lightly tapping themselves on the forehead, and the announcer pointed out that this was a technique they were using on the recommendation of a particular sports psychologist. They'd been taught to give themselves a trigger, a post-hypnotic suggestion, so that when the time came, they would no longer think of themselves as husbands or fathers or responsible citizens. By tapping themselves on the forehead they were signaling to their inner minds that they were now pure, weightlifting machines.

Maybe you can develop some kind of signal like this for yourself. You can engage in some kind private ceremony for every time you act, or maybe you'll use a particular type of ritual for a particular part. Perhaps, when you put on the jewelry of your character, you'll give yourself the sense that you are now entering into that character's skin.

You might count backward from ten as you imagine yourself walking down ten steps, or say a prayer to St. Genesius, the patron saint of actors, or — slap yourself in the head. But don't underestimate the power of ritual to stir and arouse the forces of your deep mind.

Turn on and off for especially heavy parts. Ritual can be particularly helpful if you have to live within the gut-wrenching reality that some parts call for. These might be characters afflicted by external trauma, such as living in a concentration camp or having a kidnapped child, or maybe their pain comes from an internal condition, such as a mental illness or overwhelming guilt. It's never going to be easy, but if you have a monstrously taxing role emotionally, I suggest you separate yourself from it the best you can when you're not in character. I don't say this to keep you from being miserable or from alienating the people in your life. What do I care if you or anybody else is miserable, as long as your acting is good! I recommend you ritualize entering into the part, and then stepping out when it's over, so your psyche is more inclined to let you fully immerse yourself in whatever that god-awful reality is, without resistance, because it knows there'll be boundaries and limits on how long the self-inflicted torture has to be endured, and that the consequences on your actual life are minimal.

TAKE DIRECTION

As we start talking about the issue of direction, we now bring into the picture another person and therefore, I'm afraid, it starts to involve social skills. This is not my area of expertise. I strongly suggest, however, that you herewith consider yourself a student of this science, and develop for yourself a deeper understanding of protocols, salesmanship, and the Byzantine politics of show business.

The director is supreme. Presenting something for the theater, film, or television will always be an extremely collaborative effort, but it seems these presentations are best served when they issue in their final form from a single, artistic vision. Historically that vision belongs to the director. While it's true the greatest artistic contribution may come from the author, and the most influential power on a production might be with the producer or the star, and — in film and television — the editor profoundly influences the final product, yet it is from the director that the actors traditionally take their marching orders.

Don't expect any direction. Imagine if your electrician came to you and asked your opinion about how he should wire your house. He's very earnest and open and all, but he's not sure if he should create a large central conduit or whether each line should have its own separate *framazink*. What would be your response? Probably something like: "I don't care! Just make it work and don't burn the place to the ground!" There's every likelihood your director knows about as much about acting as you do electricity. He may have come to directing through writing, producing or editing, and, regardless of how many shows he's done, may have very little understanding of what you do. This can make your director feel intimidated and out of their depth when talking to you about your performance. Some may even fear and resent that you are capable of revealing them as less than godly in their expertise. An actress I know once asked a director if he would like a moment played one of two ways, to which he snapped, "Is this a test?"

A director has a lot of decisions to make and they have to deal with a lot of different aspects of a production, so their time is precious. Insecure actors sometimes fear that when a director isn't saying a lot to them it's because they've given up on them as a lost cause. It's much more likely they're quite happy with your work, and so they're able to spend time addressing other concerns.

A director may be hesitant to compliment you because they fear you could then say to them, "Of course, I did it well. What did you think I was going to do?" Or they might be hesitant to talk about the specific things they like that you're doing because they're worried, and rightly so, that mentioning it will make you self-conscious about it. You were great doing that thing with the lamp or the cup until somebody told you how great that thing is you do with the lamp or cup and now all you can do is screw it up.

Be self-sufficient and don't require or expect any direction. Making choices, practicing those choices, and doing the thing itself — acting — can be done with very little conversation about it with anybody. If the director wants to join in, whether to fine-tune or to contribute more significantly, welcome this as an opportunity, but be prepared to go it alone.

Be receptive and flexible. Because of the nature of the process, you can't really tell how something you're intimately involved in might be projecting. You also may not have an appreciation for the balance of the entire production as a whole. This then requires you to bestow a certain amount of trust on the perspective of outside observers, particularly the director, whose overall vision is used to shape the writer's intent.

You have to be ready to change your performance based on what you're told. It might be just a slight modification, or it might be something quite large in scope that requires an entirely new assessment. You can't be too precious about anything, and you shouldn't fear losing control of your part.

Somewhere the idea got around that a director giving an actor line readings is a terrible thing. It's not. I'm sure this taint came as a result of directors giving line readings without their having any sense of why the line should be said that way, and so, unable to convey why one way of saying the line was better than another, actors who have been left trying to imitate the line reading felt used as puppets.

You just have to take it upon yourself to do the extra work to figure out what he's going for, so you can make it work (and, yes, I know that can be upsetting when you're being pressured to do it on the spot). Whether you're performing to exacting direction or not, the part will always belong completely to you — you're the one inhabiting it. The actor is the instrument and its player, the writer is the composer, the director, the conductor.

Translate results into process. During the heat of rehearsal, pinched for time, even a decent actor's director is capable of requesting that you "Get angrier here." If you just jump at this direction and try to "get angrier," you'll end up acting an inorganic result. You need to go through your process and find a motivation to get angrier. It might be more heat in the Relationship, it might be a greater feeling of threat to the Objective or a greater feeling for the Objective itself, but it's up to you to find the underlying reason to "get angrier."

Fulfilling a director's request can no doubt be difficult to do at a moment's notice, and in certain instances you may need personal time to flesh out or finesse the desired result. It's possible if rushed during a rehearsal, and not actually filming, for you to bite the bullet, apologizing to your muse all the way, and put forth an indicated representation for the director, knowing you'll develop it later and fill it in when you have the time. Like sketching an outline in pencil and then going back and putting in the color later.

Be open to trying a different process. Just because you're available to experiment with different kinds of direction or alternative techniques doesn't mean you're abandoning your own beliefs or surrendering your artistic purity. Rarely, if something has no worth, will it stick. If you use the system presented here you can render a total, valued performance all on your own, but that's not to say that there won't be something to be gained from other types of exercises a director may want to introduce you to.

Ad-libbing scenes that don't appear in the production, doing the scene using gibberish or singing it, switching parts, playing it as children or animals, all manner of theater sports and rehearsal techniques can be tried, and, being the enthusiastic and confident actor that you are, you should always be ready to explore your work and, if nothing else, develop a team spirit. When you have your own, solid technique, there shouldn't be a fear that any type of rehearsal will shake you, no matter how foreign, or, okay, what a nutball waste of time it sometimes is.

But don't give up your sense of truth. Sometimes, unfortunately, when pushed to the extreme of a really bad direction, you need to hold onto what you know is true and right. If it's not just from a reluctance to do more or uncomfortable work, if you're sure you understand what the suggested interpretation is and that you aren't just defensively misinterpreting the direction, or fearing that if you take the direction it's an admission that you were stupid to have been doing it any other way in the first place — if it comes down to what you honestly feel in your heart of hearts is an artistically unacceptably direction, then you will probably have to fight the good fight. A soldier, by law, must not carry out an order that they know to be immoral, and the actor is, after all, the soldier on the front line of any given presentation.

There are many ways to fight this fight. The first and best resort is the tried and true weak smile with shrugs of helplessness at your inability to perform the god-awful directions that you have no intention of performing. Affect deafness to off-putting remarks. Just keep lying that you're trying: "You mean that's still not what you wanted?" Violent argument should only be your last resort. In between there somewhere you might have blank stares, or laughter that they must be kidding, progressing to the more grave, going public by opening it up to other actors in the cast, or going privately to a producer. Every situation is so unique in this area there can be no pat advice.

Thankfully, these situations are very rare and the issue is much more often a problem of communication and interpersonal relation. Should the worst of artistic conflicts arise, however, you must trust yourself and hold to that thing that made you an artist from the beginning, knowing that, without it, you're no good anyway.

Get your own extra set of eyes. It's difficult for you to accurately judge how elements of your performance are playing because you can't watch your own performance live, and, even if you are able to observe it recorded, you may not be able to give an objective assessment. Watching yourself act without having a nervous breakdown can be a feat by itself for many fine actors, never mind evaluating themselves objectively. So, it's probably a good idea for you to have artistic associates who can give you notes about what they see that you're doing if you have the chance.

SUMMARY

Prepare a Structure for Your Performance

I can say this a lot of different ways: make it unconscious, habituate it, get it in your bones, and so forth, but it really comes down to what the cab driver said to the guy who asked him if he knew how to get to Carnegie Hall. Practice. Practice. Practice.

Set Your Emotional Responses. Fantasize either the events in the character's life, or personal situations that emotionally parallel everything the character would feel, then associate these emotions with the meanings in the text. Assimilate the experience. Be with it and feel the feelings.

Place your Actions. Practice doing the things the character does using a Gist Phrase to keep you on line. Do the Action separate from the text with a Mirror Action (doing something personal to you that looks just like the exact Action you want seen). Do the Action with the text. Practice going through the big changes of Actions.

Make the words your own. Paraphrase the text by putting it into your own words as you do the Action. Then mix the paraphrase with the actual words from the text as you do the Action. Do all text with the Action. Tell somebody, as your character after the fact, everything you said during the scene. ("So, then I told them….")

Memorize the lines cold. Learn your lines as if they were numbers, without inflections, cold. Know them so well you can rattle them off robotically, as fast as you can speak.

Place the Character Additions. Practice the Speech and the Physical Life apart from the text. Integrate it with the text when most fit. Practice executing predetermined behaviors that erupt during the scene.

Place your work with objects. Finesse your behaviors with props, costume and body parts. Make it look lived in.

Place the Technical. Run the Show, working through the blocking and the choreography, and all technical requirements. Allow no distractions.

Simplify

Streamline it. Remove whatever conventions of form and detail can be done without and still maintain the spirit of the whole. Be ruthless. Martha Graham said of this process, "That simplicity which costs everything."

Make it look effortless. The ease with which you render your work is the mark of your professionalism, but it takes skill to conceal your skill.

Encourage Intuitive Embodiment

Welcome the Deeper Mind. Commit to the reality of doing and seduce your deepest belief.

Know where and when to work. Make huge investments where you think it will count and surrender the rest with Trust.

Let the character speak. Accept new manifestations resulting from an internal shift, and welcome unforeseen and nuanced ways of doing things.

chapter 3

Doing the Performance

Now we get to the important part, the only part that really counts. This is how you earn your money. You've got to make it come off. And, if you've done your work, it's easy. The idea has been that by now you've gotten yourself so prepared that the actual performing is going to be a lark.

The motto of the Roman legions who took over the world was: "Our drills are like bloodless battles so our battles are like drills with blood." If your drills have been intense enough, when you finally step on stage and go to battle, it's a romp with — not so much blood in your case, hopefully, but tears and gales of laughter.

Almost as important as anything you have to do when you're acting, is be okay that you don't have to do that much. You don't have to work it so much as simply find, and stay in, the right spot. Just like when you're riding a running horse there's a spot you want to be in. It's not a passive place, you're not a bag of oats in the saddle, you're participating full out, but you're letting the horse do the real work. Tennis players and linebackers are feeling for their spot when you see them rocking back and forth waiting for the ball to go into play. When you ski deep snow or are acrobatic on a bicycle or a skateboard you have to be there in that spot. It's wobbly and hard to trust, but, like a gyroscopic, spinning top, it has tremendous power to hold a point. If you haven't intensely prepared, you have no right to that spot; if you have, then it's yours.

Performance should be considered more or less the same as a rehearsal and there usually ought to be little or no distinction between the two. Every Performance is a working rehearsal, with the work constantly evolving and improving, and every rehearsal, with few exceptions, no less than your full effort. It's true that when rehearsing there may be a lessening of the fire, a softening of the attack in certain moments. Different aspects of the work may be emphasized in rehearsal, and you might do things you know will never be seen by a paying audience, but acting is acting. If you practice Ping-Pong, even if you do an easy volley, the tempo of the ball itself demands a certain minimum effort. For you as an actor that tempo of is the pulse of human vitality.

Having said this, there is, of course, something special about actually performing for an audience. There are powers involved. Adrenaline and mission and that unnamable thing that is art can come together for those precious moments in the spotlight. From the beginnings of culture, the performer has stepped forth and created a communication with other people, telling a story with his behavior and emotions. From the beginning it has been considered wondrous and valuable.

LIVE THROUGH THE EXPERIENCE

The first thing, the main thing, is to live through the experience. Acting is pretending. It's so basic, animals do it. When a kitten stalks and attacks her sister she doesn't deliver a killing bite because she knows it's pretend. A deep part of the human brain, called "the primitive mammal brain," is where we process play, and this endowment is separate from the intellect. When a five-year-old is asked to pretend she's a princess who's going to be rescued, her first response isn't to establish the gross national product for her hypothetical kingdom. She grabs a towel and makes it her royal cape. You should seek, beyond all else, to engage this enthusiastic aspect of your deep mind.

Begin before you begin. The acting begins before the curtain rises, before the entrance. Marlon Brando said, "Just because they say 'Action!' doesn't mean you have to do anything." You're going to need to resist the tendency to feel "on" the moment the spotlight hits you, flaring your nostrils, widening your eyes, demonstrating how alive you are and generally behaving like a trained seal, performing for your fish. Have some pride, for God's sake. The audience should find you taking care of business during a process that's already begun and is flowing.

Relate as if it's really taking place. You should seek to engage totally with the imaginative world. You should imagine: If this were really happening, what would I feel about it? That "if" is chosen advisedly as a non-coercive posture, meant to seduce you into joining in. Making demands on the imagination is pointless and, if anything, a bit insulting to your muse.

Accept that it's a performance. Sometimes after a good performance I'll compliment an actor and they'll say something like, "Yeah, but I didn't feel all the way into it." First of all, let me tell you something — if you ever were all the way into fictional reality, it would be what's called psychosis, and you'd be a danger to yourself and others. You might choose to, say, lean against the fourth wall that you were now hallucinating to be a mantle and fall into the orchestra pit.

▷▷ *Note:* Stanislavski said he felt the need to develop a craft for his acting after he gave what he thought was a really good performance, only to have some friends he trusted say it wasn't so good. I'm now going to tell you what the worst thing about acting is, apart from the difficulty of trying to make money for doing it. You can't tell how well you're acting while you're acting. Like a lot of things, acting has elements that are "counterintuitive." Just like it feels good to do heroin, but it's bad, and it feels bad to go to the dentist, but it's good, there are times when you're doing the wrong thing, but it feels right, and sometimes you're doing the right thing, but it feels wrong. I won't go into all the reasons why that's the case. Most of it has to do with social conditioning. But guess what? Being an actor was never supposed to be about whether you were having a good time. It's supposed to be about whether you're getting your job done in sending the messages to the audience that they need in order to enjoy the show. And they don't really need you to be all that emotionally connected to do that. Sure, it's nice because staying emotionally connected can help keep you on balance playing moments — dandy. But if you are in the process of trying to crunch the moment, no matter how assailed by extraneous thoughts you are the whole time, the audience will only see a character who is engaged. Besides, how do you know if you're connected emotionally, or not?

Because a tear rolls down your cheek? You shouldn't be judging the conduct of your emotion in the first place, and the part of your brain that does the good acting can't ever tell you how it's doing, anyway, because it doesn't speak language. Haven't you had the experience in life where, during an intense event, you thought to yourself, "I'm not that emotional about this." And then, shortly thereafter, you had a massive wave of emotion rise up out of nowhere and slam into you. So, yes, I guess you were emotionally connected and you didn't know it, Einstein.

The reason actors will feel after a performance that they weren't fully inhabiting the reality is because at some point they were distracted by the voice in their head. That voice is going to be there, that's okay, you just don't have to listen to it. Treat that voice in your head like it's a frightened passenger talking to you while you're driving. Some passengers can be trusted and some are scaredy-cats who don't know squat about driving and only really want to get you to pull over and stop the car. They'll scream at you, telling you you're driving too fast or on the wrong road or that you don't know how to drive, whatever works to get you to pay attention to them and slow down. My suggestion is, whenever that panicky, critical, shaming voice tries to talk to you, jam on the gas. Teach it some manners.

While one part of your brain is engaged imaginatively, generating emotions that are consistent with the imaginative experience, another aspect of your mind can operate unimaginatively and perform the necessary technical requirements, even making snap artistic choices on the spot. With experience, you learn to nurture and distinguish this voice in your head, the cool one you can trust. You'll need this separate self, and, by extension, an awareness that it's a performance, if you're going to execute many of the things you need to do as a major actor, whether doing Actions, executing Character Additions, or fulfilling Stage Directions. This very process of aware execution, this knowing what you're doing, working in tandem with your imaginative belief, is part of what elevates the art of acting to greatness.

Also, if you're in some way in contact with the reality of yourself acting, not only are you able to properly implement those things necessary for your performance, you can also connect in the back of your mind to the importance of your mission as an artist. Knowing that you are not just holding court by yourself, that you're actually working to serve others by moving their hearts and improving their perspective can give your work tremendous power.

Perceive what's now. In order to live through the experience, you have to perceive what's taking place at this moment in the imaginative world. You turn your senses to what the character would be receiving, and ignore everything else taking place beyond the fourth wall or out of frame. In the back of your mind, using that special sense — that magic, peripheral intuition — you take in the audience and ride the wave of their spectatorship.

The focus of your concentration should constantly be seeking more specificity about what is happening at this moment in the fiction; and by specific, I mean accurate, not articulate. An animal takes in things very accurately, with no language to articulate it.

Seek an opinion. While perceiving what's taking place around you, you simultaneously pursue your response to those things. It's not enough to just take note of them. You're not a dispassionate, visiting scientist observing what's unfolding and you're not a spectator watching from the bleachers — you're involved, you're in the arena.

You should always be on a quest for an ever more personal emotional response to what's specifically happening. And I'm not talking about a self-conscious monitoring of your responses unto themselves, taking your own emotional temperature and reflecting sentimentally on how you feel. Yick. That's the kind of thing that gives Method Acting a bad name: the brooding young actor trying to get in touch with himself, an isolated entity, adrift in the world, who your average, English stage professional wants to bash in the head. You're going for vivid responsiveness out of your immediate participation with the environment. A continuous: What does this mean to me? Embracing the impact of ongoing events with a driving curiosity.

Stanislavsky said, "The source of an actor's inner life, is the object upon which he puts his attention." Wow. That's really it. The attention, and the resultant opinion, must be about something outside yourself. Even when acting the part of someone working out a puzzle in your head, that puzzle is, in this sense, outside yourself, just as if it were a physical task on a table.

Seeking your response is everything, not labeling it. Ideally, the impulse issues from you in its purist possible condition, and the dialog is simply used to serve that impulse and its resultant Objective. When someone is about to have a waitress spill hot soup on them, they don't deliberately choose the words to best explain why this is a problematic course of action for the server to embark upon. That's where you want to speak from. When a baby takes hold of your finger, and you say something about it to the child, whatever you say is exactly right. That center, true-you place is where your voice should always come from.

Your responses should be to the things experienced, and not a disengaged overview. Not an announcement, but a fresh, spontaneous reaction to the event you're experiencing. Your exclamation may be the result of a build up of impulses that brings about an emotional flare, so that after the third mean remark you have an especially vivid, *"You're a bastard!"* or, with one more tap, you may finally snap, *"Stop that tapping!"* But it should come sharply and reflexively in reaction to the last thing experienced. It may only be a last straw, but that last straw is specific. There should be no pause and then your judicious commentary: *"Let me tell you something about yourself"* or *"I must address the tapping that has been going on."*

"What are they doing and how do I feel about it?" Perceiving the now and seeking one's own opinion about those things is what's called "being in the moment." Of course, you're always in the moment. Everything in the World exists in the moment, but what's meant when someone suggests for you to "be in the moment" is that they want you to have your full attention there.

Carl Jung said there are the four means by which we experience the World: our five senses, our emotional responses, our intellect and our intuition. Our sensual and emotional lives exist totally and constantly in the present, it's our intellect that's broken free and can cast back into the past and project into a possible future, scanning various pictures and word combinations. As for Intuition — well, we can't account for where the intuition is (we can't even define it). The trick is to use your will to direct your intellect to what's happening in the Imaginative World right now, study the experience of your senses and the way you're feeling about those things now and (keeping faith the intuition will tag along) bingo, you're fully present in the moment.

IMPROVISE

The term "improvisation" will be used here to mean that you're taking part in a new, unpredictable experience. The term "ad-libbing" will be used for that process of actors concocting their own dialog while they're acting. Ad-libbing can be part of an extremely useful exercise, and may even be viable for a final presentation if the style of the piece is conducive to this, but, regardless, you should always be improvising, even with the most exact word for word rendering of, say, Shakespeare. Whatever you act, it should unfold as if the dialog is only now being spoken for the first time. This can best be achieved if you operate with a sense of improvisation, not in lock step toward known conclusions.

While improvisation is immediately achieved upon total commitment to moment-to-moment reality and Living Through the Experience, I'll address it here through additional Craft techniques.

Believe anything could happen. There is a simple instruction you have as character in a fiction that is difficult to follow: Don't know what you don't know. Having read the script, you're going to know exactly what's going to be said, and after one rehearsal, you're probably going to have a pretty good idea of how it's going to be said. This inclines you to dreaded "cue-to-cue" acting. Cue-to-cue acting is when you say your line, then wait for the other actor to say theirs, then you say your next line, then wait, and so forth, like playing an orderly game of cards. If the actor opposite you has a large piece of text to say, you'll be tempted to take a nap during the bulk of it, and only when you hear your cue approaching will you rouse yourself, push off from the wall you've been leaning against, and launch your set remark into the room.

You need to transfuse your performance with a belief that, right now, anything could happen. What is written in the script as "yes," could this time be said "no." This applies both to what other characters do and what you do. You have to believe that the person opposite you could suddenly have a complete turnaround in their opinion, that you yourself are open to having a sudden flare of anger or elation. There could be a sudden knock at the door, a shout in the street, whatever. Anything is possible.

Be surprised. Surprise is the life's blood of acting. It propels you from moment to moment. Whatever takes the attention must be responded to at the height of the meaning and with the deepest feeling. Everything is significant and everything is special.

If you aren't surprised, it means you aren't affected. Every event you are in contact with will surprise you and generate curiosity. While this doesn't make a certain kind of logical sense, it is nonetheless true. I don't know why it is you keep being surprised by how cute your kid is, you just do. As long as a person isn't on automatic, even the least surprising type of event, some ordinary thing that happens exactly as you would have predicted, registers as slightly surprising.

For example, you come home from a long day and your sister has a wonderful meal ready for you. Even though she's been doing nice things ever since you can remember, and there's no reason to be surprised now by this particular gesture, still, your response should be something like, "What makes you such an angel?" By the same token, if your father is harsh to you your whole life and you come in and, true to form, he makes an unpleasant comment. Maybe it doesn't surprise you as much as if had it come from the angelic sister, but there's still surprise and it expresses itself with curiosity (as Heath Ledger's character asks of his father in *Monster's Ball*): "Do you hate me?"

At the core of being, at the very spark of life, there is wonder for how the World keeps laying itself out in front of us. In each moment, though it might not be explainable, something new is learned. A character can have an adjusted lower level of surprise to a particular type of event, but they are never devoid of surprise. They may be jaded or world weary, but this only makes for a dampening of expressing the surprise, after the fact; they're still surprised in the first place. Even the most deadpan of characters, unless they're brain damaged, are deadpan because of low affect, a lack of facial sparkle, not because of a lack of internal reaction.

Fight anticipation. The tendency to habituate is organic. Therefore anticipation is always pressing in and, like weeds in a garden or rust on iron, it must be constantly battled. The moment you fail to fight antici-pation, it is surely creeping back. Habit is an extremely powerful force and it's trying to make you fall into routine. If you're going to habituate something, habituate a work ethic that insures you're always fighting off this hypnotic trance.

What's surprising has power, and the animal nervous system espe-cially hates bad surprises. It was found that rats could tolerate numerous electrical shocks as long they came at regular and predicable intervals, but that only very few shocks delivered at irregular intervals caused rodent nervous breakdowns (yeah, I know, I'd like to give those rat-torturing creeps some shocks of their own, too). Surprise increases stress tremendously. Because acting already amplifies your stress levels, you will unconsciously anticipate surprising moments, the better to maintain your stability.

It might be best for you to try to fool yourself and anticipate the opposite of what you know is actually going to happen in a scene. Really try to believe that when you ask her to go with you she's going to shout "Yes!" and hug you. Instead of the curt "No" that you read in the script to be her response.

Love the unknown. Dare to be naïve. Be willing to be in what John Keats called a state possessed of "negative capability." *Be in uncertainty, mystery and doubt without reaching for facts and reasons.* There is in everyone a fear of the unknown that seeks stability and makes us clutch for the illusion of certainty.

Hold close to that lawless beast that is in all of us, that thing that doesn't care about rationalizing or proving its point or labeling every-thing. Don't understand what's going on around you, just interact with it. You have to make choices, and make them boldly, but these are places to jump off, not descriptions of where you expect to land. An artist knows that understanding is emotional and allows for what is unsolved, loving both the questions themselves and the Mystery.

Albert Camus said: "To understand is almost the opposite of existing."

Lao Tzu: "With expectation you experience limitation, without expectation you experience subtlety."

With my wife, Joanne Baron,
at a seminar I lead
with Anthony Hopkins.

▶ *Story:* I was conducting a seminar with Anthony Hopkins, and he started out by saying, "I don't really know what I'm doing. I just try to say the lines and not trip over the furniture." And I think, "Oh, great. These people have devoted hour upon hour to the study of this noble craft and that's what the master has to say to them." But then he goes on talking and pretty soon he says something like, "So, I've read my script perhaps as many as thirty times." And I think, "That's not just not tripping over the furniture." And it becomes clear that his opening remark was only meant to convey that he doesn't want to present himself as a know-it-all, and that he makes no claims for having a lock on how to get it done. That he will do his work and then surrender it in performance to whatever it's going to be. Similarly, after that great performance of Ian McClellan's that I mentioned earlier, my wife and I met him and my wife just broke it down, effusively detailing what made his performance so inspirational: clear, specific, lived in, authentic, yet elevated, etc. When she finished, he smiled sheepishly and said, "Well, I'm glad I've learned a little something after all these years."

Avoid cliché. Conventionalism is trying to substitute an idea for what is genuine. You do it so you'll be thought well of as a personality, clever and all, and so you can remain safely removed from awkward uncertainty. It also allows you to present a pretend person, not the real you, so that if that cardboard stand-in gets criticized, you avoid that sharper sting of having had it directed at who you really are.

Even a good, external performance needs to be free of convention, not just going through the motions, but something freshly created now.

FOCUS ON WHAT'S IMPORTANT

Where you put your attention is usually how the audience follows the show. In some sense this process defines the art of acting. A musician channels a series of notes through their instrument, a painter looks at a bowl of fruit and interprets it onto canvas using a particular type of paint — you engage with the imaginary and pass it through your humanity.

If you don't connect to something that the audience feels should affect the character you're playing, they sense something's faulty in the system, something is being lost, and, finding you untrustworthy, they will stop relating to you.

Focus on what is most important at this moment. If the character is like you, and you've used the Emotional Bridge to break down the material, then the free, unadjusted, "moment to moment" reality can be the focus of your attention.

If the character you're playing has a different sensibility than you, however, they may prioritize something different from what is natural for you to focus on. If this is the case, then you'll need to use the material you discovered in Breaking Down the Character and the Specific Moments to gauge where your character's attention might be drawn.

Of course, most points of focus will be Universal. Everyone in the room will turn to the sound of a glass breaking, then zero in on the embarrassment of the one who broke it, and what defines the character is their response to that event, whether it is, say, humor or disapproval. But it's possible that a given character type is particularly alert to certain things. A reformed alcoholic may focus on the drunkenness of the person who broke the glass; a restaurateur, the competence of the staff; a policeman, on whether a fight is likely to ensue; a "flirt," on the man nearby and her opportunity to play as if startled and so draw closer to him for protection, creating sexual undercurrents. All of your character's tastes and preconceived ideas will come into play. If you love shoes, then what someone wears on their feet gets your notice.

Attend to the single most distinctive feature for your character arising from all of the imaginary events. It might be a single detail. If a man enters the room carrying a gun, your focus will be on the gun. But it could be a collection of details that coalesce into one singular event, for instance, if the man carrying the gun is wearing a policeman's uniform and he's wounded.

The event in totality, known as the Gestalt, includes all past events that have added up to this point, and all that is now presently unfolding. These things come together to create a singularity: this is the context. The context will affect your relatedness to things and what your attention is drawn to as special. At a fancy event, normal street clothing stands out as sloppy; on a rifle range, a gun is not out of place.

Include everything. The attention should exclude nothing within the imaginary world. Everything has some significance, even if it doesn't alter your central focus. A friend of mine was held up at gunpoint by a guy wearing an elegant suit, and he said the suit made the experience very disorienting. Maybe it was because the robber sensed this that he felt the need to reaffirm where the focus should be by holding up the revolver to my friend's ear and shaking it so that the bullets rattled, while he said, "Hear that? It's loaded."

Isolating what's most important, you should nonetheless be taking in everything, and be ever ready to focus on the next event.

EXPRESS

Simultaneous with entering in and Living Through the Experience is participating. Being affected, you should seek to be effective. When these two things are done simultaneously it becomes one thing, one existence. The receiver gives and receives in a continuous flow so that there is no separation between the world providing the stimuli, and you the one in exchange with it.

To participate is to freely express, to open a channel to the environment, so that, just as nothing that is received is denied, all that you have to express is released. You seek an opinion about what's in front of you and, without pause, allow it to flow back to the World, without restraint. If you are extremely emotional, or not so much, it doesn't matter; you are as relaxed as you are emotional.

Of course, this is saying a mouthful when you consider that Stanislavski said it takes twenty years to learn how to relax as an actor.

▶▶ *Note:* Yes, I know there'll be cases where you're playing someone who adjusts the size of certain expressions, as when they're in the presence of a severe parent, or because your own reserved nature dampens expression. It's a mistake, however, to believe this means that your actual expressiveness has been diminished in any way. Regardless of the

Action you feel best to apply to a given situation, your impulses are still in free flow, and while your Action may take the form of reserved conduct, whether because of something external inhibiting you, as with showing obedience to a parent, or because of your own stance as a hard-ass, your expression of this Action is nonetheless fully released.

Believe you will be received. One of the major obstacles in acting is the failure of simple assertion. This comes from your lack of faith that you're going to be heard. But remember, even if the person you're trying to communicate with is resistant, perhaps even acting oblivious, you must have faith that you can get through to them.

Asserting yourself is problematic for several reasons. One of them is that, as a child, you were probably treated as less than a full person and you learned when you did assert yourself that the result was often not good. Someone at some point was passing out cookies and you got impatient that it was taking them too long to get to you and you yelled, "Give it!" To which they responded, "You're too old for that, so now you're not getting any." In this way you learned it would be more efficient if you acted helpless. Typically we teach our children to get what they want by being pitiful and annoying, rather than directly assertive.

Also, making a weak effort to assert yourself has the benefit that, should your attempt prove unsuccessful and fail, you can then retain at least the comfort of knowing it was only a partial effort, and therefore can't be considered a total failure of your competence.

Watch how fully and easily someone commits themselves when seeking an Objective they're sure that they'll achieve, like ordering a cup of coffee or picking up the phone.

Don't try to be clear with the Body. An obvious mark of unskilled acting is a performer trying to articulate what they say with excessive gesturing, putting on a pantomime show to make everything comprehensible. This comes from the mistaken belief that each thought needs to be made clear for the benefit of the audience.

While it's true that a great performance will have great clarity, this comes through presenting universal, human behavior, not by spelling out individual thoughts. Demonstrating the meanings of things physically in order to be understood actually has the opposite effect and makes things less clear. It distorts and distracts from the essential humanity that an audience is really following. I once saw an actor, and I use the term here loosely, who felt virtually every idea had to be tortured out, and so rendered a simple sentence thusly: "I (gesturing to themselves) thought that you (gesturing to them) were someone that I (gesturing to themselves again) could lean on (cocking their head to the side in mock leaning).

Now, depending on the character, it's perfectly acceptable to use demonstrative, physical movement if the dialog represents something that is physical, and your character is recounting a physical event, or if they're instructing someone to do a physical movement. You could clench your hand, as if holding a knife, and gesture as you say, "I stabbed her." Or you could cup your hands in a spontaneous demonstration as you said, "Carry it very gently."

It can actually be helpful for you to visualize the things you're describing, and this may result in demonstrative behavior, but it should be confined to important acts and always serve your message, not be the presenting of isolated pictures. Therefore these types of gestures should very rarely exceed a rough sketch type of demonstration and stay well away from white-faced, leotard-wearing pantomime.

DO THINGS TRUTHFULLY

Everything is doing something. We can't conceive of reality without a verb. Even a rock is *sitting* there. The very name we have for our species comes with a verb, a human *being*. You'll always be doing something, you should just make sure it's something that has to do with the character you're playing, and not as an actor playing it safe.

Behavior generates emotion. A cognitive psychologist asks, "Are you running because you're frightened, or are you frightened because you're running?" This truth is a wonderful thing for an actor. You do the behavior and the primitive part of your brain asks, "Why are we doing this?" It checks and when it finds the only answer to be the fantasy you created before you started acting, it then throws the appropriate emotion into your system consistent with having this situation happening to you. The more you commit to the behavior, the more the feedback system keeps dumping that emotion.

Commit to the task at hand. Having broken down the material and knowing what the Action is for this particular part of a scene, you can now really go after each thing you know you want to do. This involves concentration. You have to improvise and play each moment as it presents itself, with your nose constantly to the grindstone.

If a bear is chasing you, your Action is to efficiently put distance between you and the bear. You play the moments, dodging trees, jumping over stumps, climbing a rocky hillside, always aware in your nervous system the cost of failure, but attendant to the immediate details.

Keep going. Fear tends to favor a frozen state as the first defense in moments of uncertainty. Animals do this so as to stay camouflaged and not draw attention to their position. Children are taught that freezing and doing nothing will much less frequently get them into trouble. A child can blank out and avoid responsibility, whereas if they react to, say, daddy getting upset, it may not go so well (when daddy feels guilty he can get mean).

But we have a second, primitive response to danger. If the deer knows the wolves know where he is, he knows he has to keep moving. I heard a journalist tell a story of how he was in Afghanistan when the American forces bombed the wrong building, killing a lot of innocent civilians, and when the people of the village realized he was American they attacked him with murderous intent. He said that, as he looked at his blood smeared on the side of a bus he'd been slammed against, he had the distinct thought that this was how he was going to die. But then he remembered the advice of another journalist who'd seen action in Beirut. The guy had told him that if he ever found himself in a hellish situation, where it was really hitting the fan, "Doing anything is better than doing nothing." So he punched his closest attacker in the mouth. There was no way he was going to fight off these fifty people who were trying to kill him, but it made the crowd pause for a moment and they backed off, giving him a little ground, and, in that pause, an Islamic holy man came forward and wrapped him up, protecting him, and hustled him away so he lived to tell this tale. That's the kind of situation you're in while you're acting. You can't stop and think your way out of it. When you're acting you're in "the kill zone." The wolves have you on the menu. You have to keep going.

You must constantly stay in motion. Not physically in motion, of course — you can be fully in motion while portraying someone who is stock still, threatening or waiting — but even if it's waiting, it should be active waiting, with intention. Like a cat at a gopher hole. Within you there should be an ever present, internal metronome ticking away that insists you stay in the rhythm of life impulse, not calculating brain time.

Don't rush. While at the same time there is not to be a moment of delay, there should not be a moment cut short, and, while the ticking metronome should not tick off an extra click, it should always tick off the full number required to get the job done.

Watch a good food server in a busy restaurant and you see maximum efficiency at work. Any laxness would attract the disapproving eye of the manager, yet any greater speed would cause plates and glasses to break. John Wooden, in encouraging his basketball players to thread this path between haste and delay would say, "Take your time in a hurry."

BE AUDACIOUS

Commit everything you are. You must turn every cell of your body to your purpose, your absolute resolve, your best beyond your best, your wildest intent. If you don't, you won't awaken the true genius in you. It is only when you convince that deep primal thing that it must help you now, because there is no tomorrow, that it gives up its gifts and provides you with the magic.

We narrow ourselves to be more discreet, to only show those parts of ourselves we think will be well received, only that which will leave those around us comfortable and not offended. We hide the multifaceted beings we truly are. Screw that. Bring it all, and, if they can't take it, that's their problem.

Follow through. This is extremely important, and I catch actors making this error all the time. They say their confrontational line and, gosh, now it's their partner's turn to speak so they rock back and fade so the other person can deliver their pretty little line. Never mind they didn't get what they wanted. Never mind they were interrupted before they could really make their point. They, the actor, know what's coming so they kindly give ground and clunk — the tension goes out of the scene. They deny the audience an exciting experience so they can save themselves from being disrupted and jarred by having anybody cut them off.

A boxer's technique is to think in terms of targeting, not the opponent's face, but through the face to the back of the guy's head. A professional football player who really wants to put the hurt on somebody tries to tackle, not the spot where their man standing, but as if he's going for a hit on a man standing behind him.

Risk. Keep your youthful sense of adventure. The truth is you either dare or you dwindle. Creativity requires a constant infusion of fresh spirit and the desire for safety will always resist this challenge. Only if you're willing to risk going too far can you discover how far you can go. Dare to be wrong, but believe that today is your lucky day.

You can go forward into the unknown or you can go back toward security and stagnation. Every excellent thing is on a razor's edge and has to be fought for. Everything is dangerous, and your desire for safety and certainty will stand against every wonderful thing you do.

Don't bet anything on "no." Really go for your Objectives. Really believe that, regardless of how you've read it works out, this time you can get through. People will often hold something back in anticipation of failure. This is the understandable tendency to hedge your bets, to bet a little on "no" even while going for "yes." In this way, if "yes" doesn't happen, it won't be a total disappointment and you can salvage a kind of bitter victory in having accurately predicted that it wasn't going to work out.

If you want us on your side, your character has got to do exactly what they want to do at that moment on stage. I'm not saying your choices will be unambiguous, and it may only be by the slimmest of margins that you opt for the path you take — *stay with the girl or take the job of your dreams; tell your dad to shove it or bite your tongue because it would upset your mom* — but, whatever way you choose, you can't be namby-pamby about it — in for a penny, in for a pound, that sort of thing — you're going to have to commit 100% to that Objective.

Get ugly. We're, just about all of us, trained to be nice little boys and girls. This is good for the smooth operation of society and it served the comfort of those who raised us, but it isn't the artist way. You're supposed to be representing Life, and all living things are scrappy. A sparrow got trapped in my garage, so I threw a shirt over it. I reached into the shirt and got hold of it, and, really, what could be less threatening than a sparrow? But as I was walking out of the garage to set it free, it started chomping the hell out of my hand. This sparrow wasn't like, "Please, Sir, let me go. I'm just a little bird." It was more like, "I'll mess you up, you Bastard!" They're toothless, of course, so it was completely ineffectual, but bless its little fighter heart.

So, when you go out there, get your mean on and make no apologies for it. I'm not saying you should cop an attitude like a jerk: nothing snippy, sneery, or snotty. Please. And I'm not saying you shouldn't be loving and empathetic, be hugely loving and empathetic. But if you have to kick butt, kick butt.

Don't protect your castmates from the truth. You don't want to consciously or unconsciously hold yourself back from being wild and having an edge because it might be off-putting to the other actors in a scene with you. As long as you stay in character, don't get near them physically and don't throw anything at them, they have no complaint. If they can't deal with your intensity, they shouldn't be on the same stage as you. Let them go prance around somewhere where they can pretend to be the wind or nice little elves or whatever. Not in the arena where you work. Of course, you know the good ones, the ones you want to work with, love you for bringing the nasty.

BE VULNERABLE

When I'm talking about a particular actor with someone who really knows something about acting, we'll have a long discussion about the various aspects of the actor's talent, their craft and interesting choices, yet it seems we inevitably get around to the bottom line of what it is that makes them compelling and it's one word: vulnerability.

Be affected. Those who are vulnerable are played upon by, and in full exchange with, the World. Thick oven mitts prevent a person from being burned, but they make a poor representation of the human hand, and you can't button a shirt while you're wearing them.

Real vulnerability is frightening to display, but it is in fact very powerful because it allows you full use of yourself. That armor you wear comes with a trade off. The thing that blocks what is painful from coming in also blocks your effectiveness from being projected out. I'll tell my students the first day of class that we don't want them to be porcupines, waddling about loaded down with defensive quills, or turtles dragging themselves around in their thick shells. They should be like naked squirrels and lizards who succeed not because of how protected they are, but because of their responsiveness and dexterity.

And don't mistake vulnerability with just being vulnerable to attack. It also means vulnerable to wanting something very badly. That's scary, too. Even a big powerful lioness demonstrates vulnerability in how keen she is to get a grip on the gazelle. She wants so much to have meat for her cubs.

When students ask me why they've made a particular mistake I have a pat answer: "You didn't want to be disoriented." From your first day of school, or before, you were shamed out of showing that you were being affected too much. You learned quickly from the older kids that it was uncool to care about baby stuff, and the best defense was to act as if just about everything was baby stuff. You learned to be always on top of it or you'd get scorned. Much better to roll your eyes than to flush with feeling. Show feeling and it was like putting blood in the water with sharks nearby. Those sadistic little boys and girls would make their daily entertainment tearing you apart. But you're not on the schoolyard anymore and it's time to put away childish things and admit that you aren't already dead and that you're actually capable of being affected.

It strikes me as so paradoxical (and telling) about our society that we have made James Dean an icon of hipness. We have posters of him blasé and smoking a cigarette in a leather jacket, or with his feet up and a cowboy hat tipped down over his eyes — sleepy, so cool. Watch a James Dean movie. He is as uncool as they come. Begging his dad to love him, hanging desperate and needy on the slightest opinion of the girl. Our

108

effective tough guys aren't really so tough. Tommy Lee Jones or Gene Hackman may play those hardened realists, but we always sense the sensitivity just below the surface, and how they can be cut to the bone by a small insensitive remark from someone they love.

Expose yourself. Your goal should always be to be more naked, more universal. It's true that if you are open and vulnerable, then people are going to see you for who you really are, your authentic anger, your pain and joy, and they may not respond as you'd like. You must risk this. You must allow yourself to be known. The actor taking an emotional blow, even though they are cut to the center of their heart, can continue to live and engage, fed constantly by the vitality of their life force. Your credo must be, whatever the cost: "More Life!"

Besides, let's get real. That's what they're paying you for. The audience wants to sit in safety in the theater, living their lives of quiet desperation and watching you up there getting hammered.

Lose your vanity. There are some actors who succeed by nothing so much as their willingness to surrender their vanity. Phillip Seymour Hoffman impresses me in this way. Go ahead and get the best make-up and costume to flatter yourself if that's appropriate for the role, but once the acting gets going, let it go, man. Maybe it's time to be yourself, your real self, and stop playing to the crowd.

Don't be so put together. Don't worry if a strand of your hair is out of place. When it comes to freedom of the spirit, living white-hot life as it should be lived while you're acting — ugly is beautiful. Dress it down, raw. Like your heart put on a face and walked right out on stage.

Move people. Just as you should be seeking to move the characters opposite you and not speaking exclusively to that other character's mind, you should be very clear that your job is to affect the people of the audience on the deepest possible emotional level. Let their minds take care of themselves.

Play to their hearts from your heart. Rumi said: "Only from the heart can you touch the sky."

Lead them from what is known. If you want to reveal something to your audience, you have to begin with a shared language and transport them from there.

You probably never take an audience somewhere entirely new, but rather, through shared communication, you'll remind them of a larger Truth they already knew on some level. The greatest revelatory experience is not an "Oh!" (How amazing!), but an "Ah!" (Somehow I already knew that!).

EXECUTE

Execution is needed to perform the physical demands of a piece, such as the blocking, the work on Character Additions, and those things that have been choreographed to enhance the presentation. While one aspect of your psyche is completely plunging in and playing pretend, another part may be needed to remain cool and calculating in order to get some necessary work done.

Be tough minded. It is an act of conscious will to perform the necessary tasks while acting. It's a choice to stay focused and not allow distractions.

The tough minded do not have excuses always at the ready to rescue them with the status of victim. The tough minded do not look for opportunities to reaffirm and shelter themselves in the identity of incapable persons or perennial bunglers. They don't rely on cheap expressions like "I knew it wouldn't work out" or "I don't know what happened."

The tough minded live by the motto of the French Foreign Legion: "They were never defeated, only killed."

Do the next necessary thing. Everything should be done one step at a time. Every journey, no matter how agonizing or long, is just a succession of single steps. It won't help to look down the road to see how difficult what's up ahead might be. No matter how complicated the blocking scheme or how elaborate the behaviors required of your character, if it isn't physically impossible, it can be done.

Maintain poise. What's called "choking" is not fear, it is the fear of fear. When fear comes, you can get the sense that you'll be overwhelmed, and when this happens you might hastily look for a way out of the troubling situation. This can then cause a lack of concentration for the task at hand which causes a mistake that then affirms your initially felt dread. So you become trapped in the cycle.

To maintain poise is to accept the fear and know that you can still function regardless. While fear usually makes us move away from the thing that's causing the fear, with resolve, the energy generated by your fear can also be used to blast through the challenge. Here's another one for you, an Arabian proverb: "As danger approaches, sing to it."

Stress can either promote a lack of focus or it can drive one to have more focus. Adrenaline will shut off unnecessary stimuli to the extent that people who've been shot during gunfights were completely unaware they were wounded until after the need to defend themselves was over. Shouldn't you be able to ignore that guy in the front row who just looked at his watch?

Distraction comes from either scanning ahead, anticipating incoming threats, or from examining what's past for possible reasons that you might have done something wrong for which you will be punished. You can't allow yourself to slip into a state of shock, the child avoiding responsibility, playing possum, I suppose. You have to tell yourself that that particular option, the "I'm a nincompoop" option, is off the table.

The trick to maintaining poise is to keep faith, don't let your imagination run to all the ways it can go wrong or to the repercussions if it does. Be meticulous, using creative adaptations.

Be patient. You must adhere to your methodology. In the crunch, when things get hectic, it's easy to jump ahead and just go on to the next thing, so as to get the whole thing over with. Kind of like someone on a tightrope who feels drawn to the platform's safety, in your case, the end of the scene. You have to discipline yourself not to dash for it. The quick solution and the easy externalization offer a false shelter that must be guarded against.

TRUST

Almost every instruction on Doing the Performance eventually leads back to the exhortation to Trust. Trust the deeper mind to engage on an imaginative level with the suggestion: "If this was taking place...." Trust that what you express will be received. Trust that doing the truthful thing is enough. Trust that it will work out okay. Trust in your methodology to execute.

To possess trust is a great thing. I suggest you get some. Many highly effective performers excel in nothing so much as the amount of trust they have. Maybe it's earned because of a tremendous work ethic that provides security in the knowledge they are totally prepared, or maybe the actor brings it to their work because they just have that kind of bravado in life, but however you come by it, trust should be applied throughout a quality performance.

Ultimately, no matter how much preparation has been invested, you have to trust your homework to show up, and know that, even if it doesn't, you'll still function with competence if you keep playing pretend and concentrating on the moments.

▶ *Story:* **There was a director I knew who'd make his rounds to the anxious actors on opening night before the curtain, visiting each in their private places where they would be intensely getting ready, and to each he'd whisper a single remark: "It's too late."**

Whatever work has or hasn't been done, it's too late to worry once that curtain rises or they call "Action!" It's too late to look back, too late to want it any other way. It's time to take the leap. It's time to Trust.

Respect stillness. Just as great music values the silence around the notes, you need to allow that doing very little can be very effective. Never passive, you can nevertheless do all kinds of dynamic activities, such as coil, hold, submit, receive or recharge, without moving a muscle. It can be hard to trust that you're still being entertaining even when you're not constantly hustling for coins to be thrown in your hat, so get hold of yourself.

Have faith in the preset emotional homework. You need to stay in the moment, kid. Work off the other actors, do what needs to be done, and have faith in your preset work to come to life when it's called upon. You don't want to be looking ahead: *Four more lines until the big moment... three more lines until the big moment....* You have to allow the preset emotional work to come forth organically, without manipulation.

You must beware trying to oversell and indicate meanings on things you think are important. Please don't. Personal objects that you've imbued with special meaning may be especially prone to this, and can become so artificially emphasized that what could have been a lovely subliminal texture instead creates a confusing distraction. (Director: "It's not a scene about a beer bottle!")

Allow everything. Everything that occurs in the acting environment should be embraced as a beautiful inevitability. Each unforeseen event, every mishap — everything is an opportunity to be freer and find something new. Luck favors Art, and vice versa.

Forgive. To trust is to have a light touch, and this is greatly aided if there's no fear that a lash of self-punishment will come down on you if you make a mistake. Self-punishment will badger you to try to be more graphically emotional, but because you can't truly judge the conduct of your deep emotion, this judging only serves to distract and disconnect you from what might have been, if you'd left yourself alone, a wonderfully deep experience.

Fear that you'll make a mistake inclines you to reflexively bring out the shield of defensive excuses at a moment's threat — *I didn't have enough time, those guys were distracting me back stage* — instead of hanging in there and making it work. Some of the greatest work is great because it was achieved through overcoming a rough patch.

The cure for all this self-condemnation is forgiveness. You ought to have an umbrella of forgiveness over the entire proceedings. Not an excuse or an allowance for poor quality work, but, at least while you're actually acting, a loving understanding of your own humanity and the unpredictability of the artistic process that gives you a get-out-of-jail forgiveness card for every occasion.

The marvelous thing about acting is that you can make multiple mistakes, and yet hit a great moment and that will be what the audience leaves the theater with. If it's film, the mistakes can always be cut out. One good moment forgives scores of lesser ones.

I've seen it many, many times. In my class I ask people not to applaud (to keep the sense that it's all rehearsal), but sometimes the class is so affected by what they've seen they can't help themselves and they burst into an ovation when someone finishes with a bang. On occasion, I'll stand up and wave them down and point out, "Yeah, yeah, alright, they were wonderful — but do remember how flat it was through the first three quarters?"

I tell my actors going into an audition not to ever worry about flubbing a line or not being as full as they thought they should be in a moment, that they can be terrible, terrible, terrible and then have one moment that raises the hair on the watcher's arms, or stabs that thing through their heart, and, suddenly, you're first choice.

I swear, whole careers have been made on one moment. I always use sports analogies when I teach, but here they fail. The reality is, in sports you can get so far behind in the score that there's really no way you can get back into the game. But for an actor there's always a magic Hail Mary pass, and while the curtain's up, the game is never lost. One moment is all you need. One beautiful moment that will be missed if you're too busy fretting over what's come before.

ACCEPT THE PRESSURE

One of my friends was playing the lead in a film and he said the producer announced early on at a dinner that the entire success of the film depended on whether or not he was great in his part. After that, he said, the producer would occasionally pass him on the set and in an ominous tone say, "Pressure." Well, my friend finally suggested to this producer that this probably wasn't the best way for him to approach his work. Actually, I think he might have promised to stab the man in the neck if he said that word to him again. In any case, whether you have a schmuck like that reminding you of it or not, pressure is a reality you have to deal with.

Know that nerves won't hurt you. Some actors can have really awful stage nerves. That's too bad for them. It means you'll be uncomfortable while you're waiting to go on, but it doesn't have to have anything to do with your acting. Once on stage all that energy can go into concentrating on what you need to do.

114

I don't mean to be callous about it, and I do suggest breathing and vocal exercises if you have this condition — they can have a surprisingly relieving effect. But you're an actor and we're concerned now with your acting and your being good at it, so any discussion of the discomfort you may have associated with the doing of it isn't really my business.

Your only problem when it comes to actually acting with this regard is if the nerves put you in such a tizzy that you don't take care of business, and look for distractions through absentmindedly forgetting something, or backstage bickering or drama of one kind or another that you might use to act out those nerves offstage. That this offstage nonsense prevents you from having your head in the game and getting yourself appropriately prepared, now that's what's going to piss me off, Sunshine.

Know it's normal. It's normal to be nervous. And I don't mean just for actors, I mean for *Homo sapiens*. You're built for it. We've been getting ready for big events since we've been around. Whether it was a midwife coaching a new mother on what she might expect when the contractions started, or the uncle telling his nephew what will be expected of him when the wild pig is driven his way, we've been getting up for stuff for a long time.

So when you're getting nervous you about your upcoming scene, as ghastly as those nerves can seem at times, feel assured that what you're doing is natural and that you were meant to do stuff like this. That when they say "Action!" or that curtain rises, you're going to tap into something ancient and right and you can just let it happen.

Keep your ego out of it. Perhaps the best way to achieve Trust, and deal with the pressure, is for you to get your ego out of it. If there is no ego in the foreground to take the credit, then there's no ego standing as a target to receive punishment. The ego and the will have a close relationship, but they are not the same thing. An insect has a will, but has no ego. Our egos can direct the will, and that's just where it should be while performing, kept in back, just a tool used to steer your attention.

One way of looking at this is that, if this is a drama, you're there to communicate large concerns about the human condition. You are then like a reporter at the scene of a plane crash, and only a jackass would fuss about how they're personally coming across in the face of so much meaning. If it's a comedy, and there isn't any monumental statement being made by the piece, then it's pure fun and you're like someone at a costume party. How sober and important can you take yourself if you're dressed up like a banana? You're in a state of silliness. Give it up.

So, the event is everything. Either you're overshadowed and have to respectfully step aside, or you're part of a lark and somber self-interest is absurd. The ego will never be removed, that is a faulty notion, but, while you're acting, it must be convinced to remain unobtrusively in the wings.

Aspire, but lighten up. Before you go on stage you ought to be clear that nothing truly bad can happen to you. No bones can get broken, no relationships demolished. The worst thing that can happen is you'll be disappointed or embarrassed. Big deal. Welcome to life. How you relate to what you call failure is completely within your control, so change what you think of as failure.

Know that taking it lightly will give you your best chance at success. Yes, you have to perform under pressure. That's real. But I doubt anybody's forcing you to do it. If you're really so worried about embarrassing yourself, why are you parading around in front of people in the first place? If it's all so grave, why don't you go out and live something serious in real life instead of playing in fiction?

On the other hand, while there's virtually no down side, there is the possibility to educate and transform. There is the chance that something about the human condition will get communicated, and possibilities opened for someone through this understanding; or, even if it's just a little diversion through entertainment, it can give someone a moment of healing freshness. These things are wonderful.

STAY JOYFUL

Connect to your passion. Through whatever difficulties and distractions that arise surrounding a particular production, and no matter how much torture you've gone through working on the part, while you're doing it — the performance itself — you ought to stay in intimate contact with the driving force that brought you into this pursuit in the first place. Connecting to your passion will infuse your performance with the excitement that comes from watching someone who loves their work.

Let the performance come through you. It may be hard to believe, but the greatest thrill you can have is when you have the greatest getting away from yourself into the purpose and meaning of the part. When you do that, it connects you to the big forces.

Denzel Washington said that just before he shot the scene in *Glory* where his character is whipped, he got down and touched the ground. This was on location and the ground where they were was in the south where slaves had been kept. Jenna Boyd in *The Missing*, just a child, was asked if it was cold on location and she said it was, but that she didn't want to wear a big down coat because the little pioneer girls back then didn't get to wear coats like that.

Practice your Craft, but also get out of the way and let it come through.

Be creative, not comfortable. What is joyous and thrilling and worthwhile is rarely comfortable, and what feels good may be exactly the wrong thing to do. Security is comfortable, Truth challenging.

Be inventive, not clever. Always be open to finding a new way of doing things while you're doing it. Maybe you won't find anything new, but just being open to the possibility will put sparkle in your work.

Inventiveness is aliveness; it comes with a sense of fun. Not restless, but never resting. Inventiveness seeks to make the presentation better, while cleverness is what you do to make yourself more liked. Cleverness vastly overrates itself and makes you like every other person trying to be clever. Being inventive and true to your humanity is being what you are — unique in the history of the universe.

Rumi again: "If you could give up cleverness and tricks, that would be the cleverest trick of all."

SUMMARY

Direct Your Performance Concentration

Ignore every thought not beneficial to the performance. You should not battle self-consciousness or extraneous thoughts directly, just keep willing your attention onto Craft. Your observable behavior will only be affected by those thoughts you relate to.

Types of thoughts permissible while performing:

1. **What's happening?** Your most specific response to the most specific nature of the Moment (includes the thrust of what's said).

2. **How close am I to getting what I want?** The status of your current Objective.

3. **How can I better get what I want?** The perfection of the means you use to get the Objective.

4. **Stage Thoughts.** The technical execution of the piece. What you can't make unconscious and still fully serve The Theatrical Event.

Improvise

Stay open. You have to take in everything that happens. You have to believe that, no matter the odds (or what you've read in the script), you can get what you want. You must believe in the possibility that the events could unfold in any fashion. You must risk your sense of self.

Abandon the myth of control. You should distrust the internal voice that judges. Fear favors what is safe and it will lie to you about what is the best choice when it's only the safest choice.

An actor should know their personal acting issues and how to harness them for the good of the performance.

chapter 4

Obstacles to Acting Well

Your biggest obstacle to acting well is that you don't really want to act well. I know that probably sounds crazy to you, and you're saying, "Lie! I am a born performer! I live to charge onto that stage, take the light on my face and move the hearts of thousands." The problem is you want to do it on your terms, and it doesn't work that way. You ride the bull, the bull dictates the terms.

You know the bull I'm talking about. You've had to deal with it your whole life. Your earliest childhood memories are when it raised hell. Your first scary movie. That time you got so embarrassed in front of everybody. I remember what happened to me when my sister found the mystery prize, gold egg at the Easter egg hunt instead of me. My family has taunted me about it ever since.

We all have wildness in us, and if you act right, you're going to rile it up. So, faced with getting on the back of that big, crazy beast, naturally you're inclined to say, "I believe I'll ride the little donkey instead." Even when you think you really want to take on the monster, all it has to do is flinch a little to remind you how much trouble you're going to be in if it releases that power, how this whole thing has the very real possibility of making you look out of control and incompetent and messy and vulnerable, and all those things you dread to reveal. So, in that moment, you chicken out and find a way off.

Here are the ways you avoid the rough ride and what you can do to hang on (and publicly get your butt kicked):

Self-consciousness. Self-consciousness is when you watch yourself being watched so you can monitor and judge what you're presenting. It's failing to engage with the imaginary events because you have a preoccupation with the frightening or self-aggrandizing event of yourself acting.

Self-consciousness causes a lack of focus, the appearance of distractedness, a shallowing: a generalizing of your behavior without impulsiveness or spontaneity; things don't fully get done; there can be a kind of glassy-eyed look. At its worst it results in the cardinal sin — breaking — with that sick grin and laughing, or looking over at things that aren't in the imaginary world. Don't you dare.

Cure: Will yourself to keep your attention on what's happening around you right now, and allow the only exception to this to be if it's important stage business. Postpone your praise or punishment till it's over.

Cliché. This is when you put forth an idea of how a person might be represented, absent your full personal and present experience. It's where your desire to express your own personality is your priority, and your chief concern is to come off as clever, charismatic or deeply emotional, without going through the frightening, self-forgetting process that might, in truth, actually make this happen.

With Cliché, you might take on a personality reminiscent of an anchorperson on a morning show, and the quality of the words take on an excessive importance and become presented in what is thought to be a reasonable, romanticized, or charming way. Yick. The things you do aren't really being done, your feelings not left alone to be really felt.

Cure: Give up the act — it ain't that great. Surrender to what is, and not what you think it should be, and make it more important that the audience have a good time than whether they're impressed by you.

Muscular tension. This is when your physical habits restrain you and cut you off from your full emotional access and expressiveness, particularly prone to occurring with heightened emotion. This is a learned behavior of resisting free expression in order to lessen its magnitude, because your free opinions or feelings were made taboo. Demonstrating suppressed emotion is also a signal of submissiveness, a plea for pity that you need something, but are frightened to assert it.

Watch how free an infant is to cry. It's really quite impressive. A toddler tastes something sour and the shudder goes through their entire body. That's what you aspire to. But because you've found that your expressiveness can attract unwanted attention, you train yourself to ground that responsive charge fast.

Muscular tension will show itself in locked, repetitive gestures and, when emotional, clenching the teeth, growling and a pent-up quality, sort of like you're constipated.

Cure: Leave yourself alone. Retrain old habits through vocal and physical work. Stay fluid and in motion and make your imaginative connection so strong and your connection to the moments so tight, that you have to give up restraint. Convince yourself that you have to give it all up because there is no tomorrow.

Lack of assertiveness. This is a failure to fully commit. It may include demonstrations of submissiveness, distress and helplessness, and poor follow-through. Having been conditioned from a very early age that assertiveness is, by itself, punishable, it may be difficult for you to trust that reaching directly for what you want won't be met with immediate disapproval. Also, to really reach for what you want 100% leaves you open to 100% disappointment. The poet may say, "'tis better to have loved and lost, than never to have loved at all," but you're heart doesn't go for that. It says, "Better not to really ask, than to ask and get turned down." So you consider it a better strategic move to place some of your bet on not getting what you want. This way you know, either way, you'll come away a winner of some kind, even if the win is for how accurately you predicted how you were going to lose.

Lack of assertion causes poor follow-through and may sometimes be seen as the gesture of slapping one's leg after an assertion or bailing out at the end of an assertion with an upward lilt, as if asking a question, sometimes and even with an ad lib of "okay?" As in: "Leave me alone... *okay?*"

Cure: Get tough and be uncool. Oh, and get over the idea that anybody cares how pitiful you are.

Aloofness and cynicism. This is the minimizing of relatedness to the significance or strangeness of events through an attitude of superiority or disinterest. It is adopting the strategy that if there is no investment there can be no loss; if there is no surprise, then everything can remain stable in this comfortable, albeit crumby, world view.

This stance comes with sneering, snippiness, affected boredom, and generally acting like everyone who is upsetting you is either an idiotic child or a lunatic.

Cure: Go for the height of the meaning. Get over the idea that sincerity is for losers, and risk getting roughed up. Sure you can always not care, but isn't there enough time for that when you're dead?

Rushing. This is skipping over moments to avoid being affected by your full contact with the events and emotions. It is the strategy of being a moving target, of getting rid of the hot potato, a dash for the cover of offstage by getting it over with as soon as possible.

Actors rushing will fail to execute as they should and skip too quickly past important moments, saying lines like they're trying to get them over with, and inorganically interrupting themselves while speaking, leaping into the next sentence without finishing the thrust of what they were saying.

Cure: Will yourself to give each thing its due, and stop acting like it's okay to be a scatterbrained twit.

Blanking. This is when you disappear into an absent state, causing you to constantly second guess yourself, to phone in a mechanical presentation, and to forget your lines, blocking or purpose for being on stage. It's camouflage by vacancy, presenting a non-person who won't attract attention and only marking time in the now as the mind races around inside your skull. It's a "deer in the headlights" fear response.

Actors blanking will have the quality of just saying lines: they forget their lines, sometimes vocalizing an "uh" in an inorganic way not heard in normal connected speech, as a way of stalling and trying to get their bearings.

Cure: Engage the survival response that doing anything is better than doing nothing, because, while you're acting, there's no place to hide. Fight through it in the moment, and, again, don't allow yourself the nincompoop option.

Intellectualizing. This is a preoccupation with the use of language and how isolated thoughts are being presented. Given that Western society places such a huge emphasis on the intellectual process, "the left brain," from the earliest age, you're likely to try and use this much prized tool to negotiate your way out of a frightening experience. This is especially the case when there exists the illusion in acting, unlike other arts, that what is taking place is an intellectual conversation. There may be a great deal of analyzing and appraising before the show begins, but make no mistake, *there is almost no intellectual activity while acting*.

The misguided effort to clearly transmit ideas can result in adopting an approach where your reasonable brain tries to appeal to the reasonable brain of others. This causes you to constantly question others about whether they are understanding you, offering points for them to take into consideration rather than driving truths into them, and results in a thinning of the voice, a punching of words artificially and displaying excessive, pantomime gesturing.

Cure: Prioritize the primitive Action. If the other person's brain is affected by you, fine, but try to vibrate their backbone.

Formality. This is a controlled, depersonalized, protective stance you take that does not allow either sensitive contact or direct expression. It may take the form of politeness or a stance of sophistication. This is in the same vein as the make-no-false-move mindset of Self-consciousness and Blanking, and in the appeal-to-reason style of Intellectualizing.

Formality can cause primping behaviors inappropriate to the emotional value in a scene, as when a woman in the middle of pleading for her child's life or insisting to be ravaged by her lover takes the time to neatly place a hanging piece of hair back behind her ear.

Cure: Go animal. Make the meanings in your work more important than whether you keep your mask intact.

Confusion and bewilderment. This is when you affect puzzlement, astonishment, amazement or disbelief about events in order to limit the experience to the issue of your understanding them, rather than really being rocked by them emotionally. It also serves to reduce your appearance of vulnerability. Muscular Tension is usually involved in that it results in tension in the forehead and eyes. This defense strives to buffer the sharp vividness of actual experience through a haze of intellectual interference, making the main issue an event's reasonableness, rather than its raw, emotional impact on you.

Get this, Brainiacs — by about age three you've pretty much seen everything this world can throw at you. After that, it's just a matter of degree. There are even those who say we came into the world with a full knowledge of it already, and that we're only being reminded when exposed to something new, but in any case, you've long ago met with every kind of disappointment, loss, and exhilaration, every type of human cruelty and kindness, and there are only variations now to be learned of its scope and situation. Wondrous and deserving of your intense curiosity, yes, but there's almost nothing all that puzzling or bizarre. That's just an act you put on so it doesn't hit so hard.

This state will cause a squinty tension in the eyes, and can have the effect of thinning your voice up into the head, as with falsetto. It sometimes causes a shaking of the head in disbelief, as if saying "no," and this is probably just what it means, you're saying "no" to accepting the fact that this event is taking place.

Cure: Be awed or horrified, not tied up in crappy mental states. Whether you believe it or understand it or not, plug into how you *feel* about it. Say "yes" to everything.

Anticipation. It is a natural animal function to habituate experience and anticipate what's going to happen, scanning ahead so you can brace for approaching traumas. Also, you tend to resist being surprised because you don't want to look disoriented and not "with it." The result is deadened acting. Because you've rehearsed, your body will start to respond to what it knows will be the next in a sequence of events in a way a character in a fiction couldn't possibly know what was about to happen.

Anticipation will reveal itself in obvious ways; such as wincing before an explosion, or, less obviously, automatically sitting in a chair without going through the organic process your character would go through to choose where and when to sit. Maybe you'll back off on your intention at the end of a line, because you know the other character interrupts you here, falling into "cue-to-cue acting." Remember: *Surprise is the life's blood of acting.*

Cure: Stay in the damn moment. That and trick yourself into believing that, this time, it's going to go differently.

Self-generating. This is where you want to give an emotional performance, but you either lack the trust that you'll be able to get there organically or you don't want to go through the frightening experience of having out-of-control emotion swelling up and hitting you out of nowhere. This kind of acting is, in its extreme, what you think of when you think of bad Method acting. That indulgent actor tortured by emotion, but, as you watch them, you're not really sure why, just that they seem to be having a good time taking a bath in their own feelings. It's inauthentic and egocentric, and because you might have become an actor to express emotion, you may have the mistaken idea that, because you are feeling something, it means you must be acting well, whereas the truth is that acting is all about doing, with feeling only being a byproduct.

Self-generating can be seen in sudden flares of emotion that seem to come out of nowhere, and a self-conscious monitoring of one's emotional life. It can have something of the look of hysteria, because both are conditions of people caught up in their own world who ought to be slapped.

Cure: If you work off of what's in front of you right now, and how you feel about that thing immediately, it's impossible to Self-generate.

Sentimentalizing. This is kin to Cliché and Self-generating, and it's where you're veneered more by the notion of going through an experience than truly having an experience. Like Cliché, it's trying to present yourself in a way you'd like to be seen, in this case as deep, romantic and wise. As with Self-generating, it is using canned and controlled feeling as a substitute for the real unfiltered stuff.

It's striking the pose of someone in a mood, maybe glum, maybe smug, but self-contained with nothing new allowed to affect you. The sentimentalizing actor might take on the air of a poetic soul, oh so appreciative of life and its quirks and their feelings about things, often with a distanced, ironic view.

When sentimentalizing, an actor will veer into the presentation of romantic values within the text and away from the plain message of the Action. They'll smile a wry smile to themselves and cast back to nostalgic pictures in their heads; they might offer a glib, reassuring hand with a tone something like they're tucking a child into bed. Before you organize a mob to hunt these people down and kill them, you should know that a lot of good actors have a little of this quality, and it has served many in the theater, where you interpreted this quality as their appreciation for the stature of the text, rather than the coward's mask it usually is.

Cure: Get real. Don't build a temple to emotions, use them to do work in the world. Know that no matter how dear or elevated the event or the value being expressed, it is still something fleshy and impactful within the moment.

Pushing. This is where you try to force out more intention than is truthful or required for a given moment. It is kin to Self-generating and Lack of assertiveness in that it is born of a desire to do more than is organic and not risk the vulnerability necessary for really reaching out to affect the world. When you push, you blast with a general shotgun, rather than zero in with an intimate and specific laser.

Pushing actors will shout in a way that sounds hollow, and they can have the quality of a child whining, acting the victim, and having a general tantrum.

Cure: You can't Push if you're working to specifically affect the world and move the central core of someone else's humanity.

Disassociation. This is one of the worst impediments to quality acting and one of the most difficult to correct. You nurtured this human talent at an early age and it gave you the ability to lie well, for which you were hugely rewarded. Such a good child who can relieve their parent with a believable "Everything is fine, Mommy."

Dissociation is when there is a break in the assimilation process, a disconnect. This is not the same thing as denial or shock, which may be stages of an energized effort to fully process an event, even as it expresses itself by the active holding off of the dread reality. Dissociation is a mechanism that enables you to disengage from the reality of the event altogether. Apparently, they have a class at the CIA in how to improve this natural ability so that agents can beat a lie detector test. Dissociation, also called "compartmentalization," allows you to go to work on the day a loved one has died, or to dispose of bodies after a disaster. It enables people of conscience to commit atrocities. Sometimes you hear boneheads say, "I could act. I act all the time in life and nobody catches me." That's being a good liar and actors should actually be bad liars, like very young children, because they're so connected to the truth.

Artists must never dissociate. Soccer players can't use their hands, you can't use your ability to cut off. In some sense, dissociation runs against the very purpose of Art. If your character has to work under the pressure of emotion, perhaps even wishing to hide their true feelings, unlike life where you have the ability to cut yourself off, you must call upon the strength to do it in the face of that emotion, with the feelings crackling right at the skin, using an Action. You may have to do Actions that are difficult to perform because your character's desire is to come across in a way that is at odds with your inner life. You may be affecting elegance to appear aloof in front of someone you despise, or demonstrating cheerfulness to be encouraging even though you're aching with sadness, or acting flirtatious to hide your terror. But you can't take the easy way out and do as you might actually do in life and break with the impulse at its root, using the mechanism of dissociation to disconnect you from your feelings. In this way, you must be clear that, in acting, you are to depart from the way it's done in real life.

You are to be fully connected at all times, nothing cut off, everything mixed together with everything. Even if you're acting the part of a disconnected character, you don't play it disconnectedly. Dustin Hoffman shows this in *The Graduate*, as opposed to a less effective portrayal of the same type of character by Adam Sandler in *Punch Drunk Love* (yeah, I know, comparing just about anybody to Dustin Hoffman isn't really fair). Maybe you'll portray a character's deadened response by making an adjustment, and that adjustment might be extreme, so that when your character kills a human being, you substitute the feelings you'd have if you were killing an insect. But the reality of that adjustment will be fully connected to and in no way are you to be dissociated. You intensely relate to the killing of a specific insect.

Cure: Like the doctor's advice to the guy who shows him a particular movement and says, "Doc, it hurts when I do this," I have this to say about dissociation: Don't do that. Stay connected, constantly seek your opinion at its most vivid and play the moments. Sit tight on the bull.

Our studio in Santa Monica.

chapter 5

Ways of Doing Things

The following is a list of adverbs that are actable. Not all adverbs are, remember. While someone watching might describe a behavior as being done angrily, triumphantly or confusedly, the person doing that thing isn't trying to render it this way; they aspire to do it harshly or tauntingly or straightforwardly. People in life don't try to make themselves more emotional or more of a mental condition (such as guilt, disbelief or embarrassment); they try to be more effective. In this way, you never want to do something using an adverb that expresses an emotion or a mental condition.

Also, while some of these adverbs are actable, they describe behaviors only consciously performed this way when a character is intentionally putting on an act, as with acting pitiful, or when someone takes on a manner that they know will be offensive, as with being obnoxious. When you describe the methodologies your character uses, you want to do it in a way they themselves would describe them. For instance, it's possible for someone to know and take pride in how they're being obnoxious, but they are much more likely to think of it as being truthful. Unless it's done as a joke, nobody who is being grandiose would call it that. They would say they're being elegant and expansive; it's only because they're describing a new sofa this way, and not the Sistine Chapel, that we who are outside watching, and judging, call it grandiose.

You can use this list to imagine and isolate the ways your character operates in the world. After you have a feel for who they are, scan the list and try and envision whether, if you were them, you'd ever use a given approach for getting something you want. Once you determine you'll be using a particular adverb as your character, you can then practice your Actions with that adverb, perhaps by doing a Mirror Action (doing something you might do that way, under similar emotional conditions, but for an objective you create out of a fantasy close to you, rather than your character's objective in the scene).

There are many redundancies in the meanings of the words here, but they are included for the sake of nuance and because words will strike different people differently. Every actor should have a good thesaurus for just such a purpose.

Abandonedly	*Artistically*	*Callously*
Abjectly	*Assiduously*	*Calmly*
Abrasively	*Attentively*	*Candidly*
Absolutely	*Audaciously*	*Capably*
Academically	*Augustly*	*Capriciously*
Accommodatingly	*Auspiciously*	*Carelessly*
Accurately	*Austerely*	*Carnally*
Adamantly	*Barbarously*	*Casually*
Adeptly	*Bawdily*	*Categorically*
Adroitly	*Bearishly*	*Cattily*
Adultly	*Beguilingly*	*Caustically*
Aesthetically	*Belligerently*	*Cautiously*
Affably	*Beneficently*	*Cavalierly*
Affectionately	*Bestially*	*Ceremonially*
Agilely	*Bewitchingly*	*Charmingly*
Agreeably	*Blandly*	*Chastely*
Airily	*Blankly*	*Cheekily*
Aloofly	*Blatantly*	*Cheerfully*
Ambiguously	*Blithely*	*Childishly*
Amiably	*Bluntly*	*Chivalrously*
Amicably	*Boisterously*	*Clearly*
Angelically	*Bombastically*	*Clinically*
Animatedly	*Boyishly*	*Coarsely*
Annoyingly	*Bravely*	*Coaxingly*
Antagonistically	*Breezily*	*Cockily*
Archly	*Brightly*	*Cogently*
Aristocratically	*Brusquely*	*Coherently*
Artfully	*Buoyantly*	*Coldly*
Articulately	*Cagily*	*Comfortably*

Compassionately	Decorously	Eerily
Complacently	Definitely	Effectively
Comprehensively	Deftly	Effortlessly
Concisely	Deliberately	Effusively
Concretely	Delicately	Elegantly
Condescendingly	Demonstrably	Eloquently
Confidently	Demurely	Emphatically
Congenially	Derisively	Enchantingly
Conscientiously	Despicably	Endearingly
Conservatively	Destructively	Energetically
Consolingly	Devilishly	Enthusiastically
Contritely	Devotedly	Enticingly
Copiously	Diabolically	Erectly
Coquettishly	Daintily	Erotically
Cordially	Diligently	Erratically
Correctly	Diplomatically	Esoterically
Courageously	Disagreeably	Ethereally
Courteously	Disgracefully	Ethically
Coyly	Dismissively	Evasively
Cozily	Dispassionately	Evenly
Crassly	Disrespectfully	Evilly
Crazily	Dissolutely	Exactly
Creatively	Distantly	Exotically
Creepily	Distinctly	Expansively
Crudely	Diversely	Expeditiously
Cunningly	Doggedly	Explicitly
Curtly	Dominantly	Extravagantly
Cutely	Dramatically	Exuberantly
Cuttingly	Drily	Facetiously
Cynically	Drolly	Faithfully
Daintily	Duteously	Fancifully
Darkly	Dutifully	Fashionably
Dashingly	Dynamically	Fastidiously
Debonairly	Earnestly	Fawningly
Decently	Easily	Fearlessly
Decisively	Eccentrically	Feebly

131

Feistily	Funnily	Heatedly
Ferociously	Furtively	Heedlessly
Festively	Fussily	Heinously
Fetchingly	Gaily	Hellishly
Feverishly	Gallantly	Helpfully
Fiendishly	Gamely	Heroically
Firmly	Garishly	Hideously
Flagrantly	Garrulously	Highhandedly
Flamboyantly	Gauchely	Histrionically
Flashily	Gaudily	Hoggishly
Flatly	Gawkily	Honestly
Flatteringly	Generously	Honorably
Flauntingly	Genially	Hotly
Fleetly	Gently	Humanely
Flippantly	Glibly	Humbly
Flirtatiously	Glumly	Humorously
Fluently	Goodheartedly	Hungrily
Fluidly	Gracefully	Hurriedly
Forbiddingly	Grandly	Hypnotically
Forcefully	Gravely	Icily
Forlornly	Greedily	Idiotically
Formidably	Gregariously	Ignobly
Forthrightly	Grimily	Illicitly
Foully	Grotesquely	Illustratively
Frailly	Guardedly	Immaculately
Frankly	Haggardly	Immaturely
Fraternally	Halfheartedly	Impartially
Freely	Handsomely	Impeccably
Frenetically	Hardily	Impertinently
Freshly	Harshly	Impetuously
Frighteningly	Harmfully	Impiously
Friskily	Hastily	Impressively
Frivolously	Haughtily	Impudently
Frostily	Hazardously	Inanimately
Frugally	Healthily	Incapably
Fulsomely	Heartlessly	Incessantly

Inclusively	Jollily	Madly
Incompetently	Jovially	Magically
Inconsiderately	Jubilantly	Magnanimously
Inconspicuously	Judiciously	Majestically
Indecently	Justly	Maliciously
Indefatigably	Keenly	Manfully
Indelicately	Kindheartedly	Mannishly
Indifferently	Lackadaisically	Massively
Indiscreetly	Laconically	Maternally
Indubitably	Laggardly	Matter-of-Factly
Industriously	Laudably	Maturely
Infallibly	Lavishly	Mawkishly
Inflexibly	Laxly	Meanly
Informally	Lazily	Mechanically
Inimically	Lecherously	Meekly
Innocently	Legitimately	Mellifluously
Innocuously	Lethargically	Melodiously
Inoffensively	Lewdly	Menacingly
Insanely	Liberally	Mercifully
Inscrutably	Licentiously	Merrily
Insincerely	Lightly	Messily
Insolently	Lightheartedly	Methodically
Insufferably	Limply	Meticulously
Insistently	Listlessly	Militantly
Intellectually	Logically	Mischievously
Intensely	Longingly	Mockingly
Intimately	Loosely	Modestly
Intrepidly	Loudly	Momentously
Irksomely	Lovingly	Monstrously
Ironically	Lucidly	Monumentally
Irresistibly	Ludicrously	Morbidly
Jadedly	Lugubriously	Mundanely
Jauntily	Luridly	Mysteriously
Jeeringly	Lustily	Nakedly
Jocosely	Luxuriantly	Nastily
Jokingly	Lyrically	Naturally

Naughtily	*Plainly*	*Rakishly*
Neatly	*Playfully*	*Rapidly*
Nicely	*Pleasantly*	*Rationally*
Nimbly	*Poetically*	*Raucously*
Nobly	*Poignantly*	*Raunchily*
Noiselessly	*Pointedly*	*Realistically*
Noisily	*Politely*	*Reasonably*
Nonchalantly	*Pompously*	*Rebelliously*
Normally	*Ponderously*	*Recklessly*
Noticeably	*Portentously*	*Redoubtably*
Oafishly	*Positively*	*Regally*
Obdurately	*Poutingly*	*Relentlessly*
Obediently	*Pragmatically*	*Repulsively*
Objectively	*Precisely*	*Reservedly*
Obliquely	*Primly*	*Resolutely*
Opaquely	*Prissily*	*Respectfully*
Oppressively	*Properly*	*Resplendently*
Outrageously	*Proudly*	*Responsibly*
Paternally	*Prudently*	*Reverently*
Pathetically	*Publicly*	*Rhythmically*
Patiently	*Puerilely*	*Ridiculously*
Peacefully	*Pugnaciously*	*Rightly*
Peculiarly	*Punctiliously*	*Rigorously*
Perfectly	*Punitively*	*Ritually*
Perniciously	*Purely*	*Robustly*
Persistently	*Purposefully*	*Romantically*
Pertly	*Quaintly*	*Rosily*
Perversely	*Queerly*	*Roughly*
Pessimistically	*Querulously*	*Royally*
Petulantly	*Quickly*	*Rudely*
Piously	*Quietly*	*Ruggedly*
Piquantly	*Rabidly*	*Ruthlessly*
Piteously	*Racily*	*Sadistically*
Pithily	*Radiantly*	*Salaciously*
Pitifully	*Radically*	*Sanctimoniously*
Placidly	*Raffishly*	*Sanely*

Sarcastically	*Slickly*	*Straightly*
Sardonically	*Slovenly*	*Strangely*
Satanically	*Slowly*	*Strictly*
Saucily	*Sluggishly*	*Stridently*
Savagely	*Slyly*	*Stringently*
Scandalously	*Smartly*	*Strongly*
Scornfully	*Smoothly*	*Studiedly*
Secretly	*Smugly*	*Stuffily*
Securely	*Snarlingly*	*Stunningly*
Selflessly	*Snootily*	*Stylistically*
Sensationally	*Snugly*	*Suavely*
Sensibly	*Soberly*	*Submissively*
Sensitively	*Sociably*	*Subtly*
Sensually	*Softly*	*Subversively*
Sentimentally	*Solemnly*	*Suggestively*
Serenely	*Solicitously*	*Suitably*
Seriously	*Somberly*	*Sulkily*
Severely	*Soothingly*	*Sullenly*
Sexily	*Sordidly*	*Supportively*
Sexually	*Soulfully*	*Supremely*
Sharply	*Soundly*	*Surely*
Sheepishly	*Spitefully*	*Surreptitiously*
Shoddily	*Splendidly*	*Swankily*
Showily	*Spontaneously*	*Sweepingly*
Shrewdly	*Spryly*	*Swiftly*
Shyly	*Staidly*	*Sympathetically*
Silently	*Starkly*	*Tackily*
Simply	*Staunchly*	*Tactfully*
Sincerely	*Steadfastly*	*Tamely*
Skeptically	*Steadily*	*Tartly*
Skillfully	*Stealthily*	*Tastefully*
Slackly	*Sternly*	*Tauntingly*
Slatternly	*Stoically*	*Tautly*
Slavishly	*Stolidly*	*Teasingly*
Sleazily	*Stormily*	*Temperately*
Sleekly	*Stoutly*	*Tersely*

Thoroughly	*Valiantly*	*Waspishly*
Tidily	*Vehemently*	*Weakly*
Titillatingly	*Vibrantly*	*Weirdly*
Toughly	*Viciously*	*Whimsically*
Tragically	*Vigorously*	*Wholeheartedly*
Tranquilly	*Violently*	*Wholesomely*
Trenchantly	*Virtuously*	*Wickedly*
Tritely	*Viscerally*	*Wildly*
Truthfully	*Vivaciously*	*Winningly*
Tyrannically	*Vividly*	*Winsomely*
Uninhibitedly	*Vociferously*	*Wistfully*
Unrecptively	*Volubly*	*Wittily*
Urgently	*Vulgarly*	*Wretchedly*
Vacuously	*Wanly*	*Wryly*
Vaguely	*Wantonly*	*Zealously*
Vainly	*Warmly*	

chapter 6

Table of Characters

The following is a list of archetypal characters, sometimes called Stock Characters, which appear in literature, along with their usual characteristics, methodologies and Life Drives. These have many, many variations with regards to their ethics and cravings.

You can go down this list and ask yourself if your character might fit a particular type, and if you do strike upon one that seems to be close, I strongly recommend you embrace this model as a way for you to fulfill your role and give the audience a good show. Whether we've come to know these archetypes because we've learned them culturally or, as some would have it, they're hardwired into us or actually exist objectively in the universe as types, it doesn't really matter. Playing a Stock Character gets an audience on board and running with you as soon as they click into who it is you're playing.

Try and imagine where you've seen this type of character and who you've seen play it especially well. Copy them shamelessly. I probably shouldn't even have to say this, but applying yourself personally and fully within the confines of an archetype, and yes, even imitating how a master has played that archetype, is no less artistic than confining yourself to a tenor sax and imitating a master's technique.

1. **Addled Professor**, a brilliant, enthusiastic specialist who's kind and nonjudgmental and almost completely out of touch with the ordinary world; they know this and it saddens them how their social ineptitude limits their ability to connect with, and help, the ones they love; can be impatient and sharp with others in their profession. Straightforward, intense and sincere. [Life Drive: to discover the new.]

2. **Adventure Hero**, a jocular, dashing and physically skillful daredevil and impresario; vain, irresponsible but kind, they easily accept physical discomfort, even death, as the price for their freewheeling lifestyle; so open, they can be deeply wounded, although loath to show it, and only really are made angry by poor sportsmanship. Passionate, elegant and to the point. [Life Drive: to have fun.]

3. **Alley Cat**, sensual, smart, proud and ruthless, they dread poverty but enjoy a challenge as a way of exercising their gifts; may explore sensitive feelings, but know all the time they'll be returning to their pragmatic, cutthroat world; very good at adapting to circumstance. Impersonal, casual and severe. [Life Drive: to be cozy.]

4. **Autocrat**, officious, paranoid, heartless and humorless; they insist on a tight ship and maintaining the status quo; they are vain and will act the part of a sensualist, but actually are asexual and almost completely ungratified by physical appetites; may have a secret life that involves something from their isolated childhood; courageous in their passion. Proper and firm. [Life Drive: to prove they can impose order.]

5. **Bohemian**, a sweet, kooky, sensualist; a lover of art and culture; eccentric in habit and dress, they live outside the system and operate on a different wavelength, perhaps partly as a result of drugs; they think of themselves as very savvy and, depending on the context, this may or may not be true; very loyal, often bonding for life with a like-minded mate; they sometimes have an authentically remarkable talent. Open, inspirational, elegant. [Life Drive: to be different.]

6. **Bonehead**, think they operate on a higher plane than others and are irresistible to the opposite sex, but, in truth are widely considered an ass; they easily hold forth, assuming the role of teacher and confidante; and can either tend towards playing a tough guy or an elegant man of the world; loyal, they do in fact have grit and will come through in a pinch. Suave, expansive, straightforward and heartfelt. [Life Drive: to be revered.]

7.   **Brute Hero**, a nonintellectual realist who is outrageously strong and tremendously bold; they enjoy isolation and are driven by naked self-interest, but have a wistful sentimentality and a fondness for glory that might lead them to pursue a noble cause; has a phenomenal capacity for consuming volume. Impersonal. [Life Drive: conquest.]

8.   **Bum**, a good-natured, irresponsible loafer who cares nothing for status and lives for intoxication, fun and comfort; can be easily lead because, for them, any place is as good as another; they have an average, if unused, intelligence, and a slight, wistful taste for beauty. Open and innocent. [Life Drive: to be without pain.]

9.   **Bumbling Helper**, enthusiastic and educated for their trade, they are crafty and capable, but their anxiety to please tends to undermine confidence; they like to be as close as possible to the most powerful person (can be either the good guy or the bad guy), prone to putting on airs. Open, earnest and flamboyant. [Life Drive: to be necessary.]

10.   **Carouser**, uninhibited, rude and fun; with large appetites and strong staying power, they are unromantic and totally fine with themselves; can be dangerous because, knowing they can take a punch, violence is always an option for livening things up; tend not to be close with anyone, but will offer friendly advise; usually have an ordinary profession. Expansive and plain speaking. [Life Drive: to celebrate.]

11.   **Casanova**, a jaunty, witty libertine, who is effortlessly excellent at their chosen profession, and very good with the opposite sex as long as they aren't challenged; while always ready to celebrate and enjoy the joke that is life, they do have a tinge of sadness, feeling themselves lacking in substance; and, having much kindness, may do secret, charitable work. Open and casual. [Life Drive: to be useful.]

12.   **Cheap Snob**, stupid, vain and heartless, they put on airs and try to get the respect of powerful people who, because of their low class and obvious self-interest, usually have only contempt for them; vicious gossips who like to stir things up, they are easily offended and given to exaggerated shows of injury. Flat, nasty, elegant and proper. [Life Drive: to be included with the elite.]

13. **Cold Expert**, arrogant and driven, they are brilliant in their field, but unsophisticated in dealing with people; given to soaring enthusiasm or, vulnerable to insult, tantrums and pouting. While almost totally without sentiment about human concerns, they can be very romantic on other topics. Fastidious out of efficiency, not vanity, and what little humor they have is dry. Matter of fact and absolute. [Life Drive: to be the best.]

14. **Crazy Witch**, a clever and powerful wild-eyed force of chaos who knows they are completely awful and love it; have a volcanic temper and are very vengeful. Playfully sarcastic, silly and sickly sweet, monstrously brutal and wild. [Life Drive: to be the worst.]

15. **Damaged Loner**, a bruised and jaded romantic, they think of themselves as hopeless misfits, often due to an affliction that's been exaggerated in their minds; tend to live in isolation, but may latch onto a mate to whom they give themselves completely and unwisely; repressed, but may be promiscuous; often an addict and suicidal. Straightforward and earnest. [Life Drive: to share themselves.]

16. **Dark Saint**, a grim realist, although at heart a romantic; hugely compassionate and deeply pained because of the impossibly high standard they hold for themselves, and will fight mightily and with abandon against agents of inhumanity; may have a dry humor or none. Plain speaking and intense. [Life Drive: to make the world better.]

17. **Demon**, vibrant, cruel, clever, and fun, these predators enjoy having an impact; completely lacking in empathy (can be dangerous psychopaths), enjoy their comforts, but are in no way a slave to them and can bear pain easily, they either have no regard for authority or an active hatred; still and all they really want to be liked, glorified actually, and will pout if punished. Open, free and charming. [Life Drive: to be the center of excitement.]

18. **Ding-a-ling**, a good-hearted simpleton, often physically attractive, they are quite obtuse, may have lived in isolation or had little education; they are spunky and can be provoked to bull-headed anger; liked by all but the most stodgy. Open and earnest. [Life Drive: to be embraced.]

19. **Dissolute Aristocrat**, broken down from years of debauchery, they have a wry sense of humor and are intimidated by no one except those who are completely pure of heart; will hold forth on the necessity of a life with romance, but at bottom are pained by self-contempt for their wasted gifts. Elegant and casual. [Life Drive: to be free.]

20. **Diva**, a manic-depressive, aristocratic and sentimental egomaniac; they will alternately plead for sympathy and give orders, over-sexualized and prone to tantrums, often has an addiction that helps debase them so that they can feel martyred. Elegant, expansive, imperious and coquettish. [Life Drive: to be special.]

21. **Doofus**, a good-natured, clumsy and eccentric clown; confident and opinionated and prone to launching into ill-conceived projects, they are very sociable and have a very loose sense of personal boundaries. Forthright and absolute. [Life Drive: to be remarkable.]

22. **Effete Brat**, stunted from privileged over-indulgence and a terror that the surrounding power could turn against them, these frightened children have adopted infantile, silly behaviors to show they've dropped out of the competition; desperately lonely, they will cling to things non-threatening and virginal, and can be either vicious, out of total egocentricity, or kindly, because they are at heart romantics. Grand, earnest and nasty. [Life Drive: to be treasured.]

23. **Elegant Villain**, a powerful, cruel and visionary force, they are pained and lonely as the only one of real talent surrounded by the ordinary (for this reason they may try to share themselves with a hero in whom they feel a kinship of the talented). Capable of romantic feelings, although the contempt they have for such common things tends to make them view these urges from a distance. Absolute and elegant. [Life Drive: to make everything cold and peaceful.]

24. **Enthusiast**, a big personality; warm, theatrical, with a dry sense of humor and a passionate interest in the topic of romantic love; they will complain freely, but have a passionate love of life and insist others do so as well; loyal and protective, they have a deep

respect for tradition, revering the old, yet will jump in and try what's new. Plain speaking, flamboyant and sincere. [Life Drive: to embrace life.]

25. **Feisty Hero**, small in stature, but big of heart, these idealists have tremendous endurance and may have remarkable strength as well; will take insult at being discounted, but capitalize on being underestimated; feeling themselves the underdog, they are especially prone to helping other underdogs. Straightforward and sharp. [Life Drive: to meet challenge.]

26. **Grouchy Helper**, skilled, stubborn, and loyal to the death, they think of themselves as realists, but are in truth sentimentalists; always put upon and misunderstood, they are prone to being teased and, depending on circumstances, can respond to this with either grudging joy or bitter anger; given to eccentric tastes or personal habits. Blunt. [Life Drive: to be effective.]

27. **Hired Gun**, a jaded realist and addicted gambler who will go whichever way the wind blows to their advantage; has contempt for the pretensions of the visionaries and the wastefulness of the sadists with whom they often work (if pushed, may tip toward the good guys out of a grudging admiration for the effectiveness of people who have better integrity). Flat. [Life Drive: to be near the action.]

28. **Humble Joker**, a cordial, attractive Everyman, with a witty humor that includes a wry certainty in their own ability to screw up whatever comes their way; they are quirky, but favor blending in, and therefore tend to be conventional in appearance; being sarcastic, they are fair game for the sarcasm of others. Casual and earnest. [Life Drive: to make people happy.]

29. **Ice Royalty**, judgmental, vain, self-involved control freaks who think of themselves as earthy, sexy, good sports; they are great cosmetic homemakers and hosts; extremely defensive at perceived humiliation, and may break down on occasion and play the misunderstood child. Proper, sassy and severe. [Life Drive: to be admired from afar.]

30. **Innocent Hero**, an honest, sensitive, heart-on-their-sleeve person who strives to do the decent thing, but, favoring enthusiasm over sophistication, can blunder into complicated situations and do more harm than good; self-confident and stubborn, yet humble and tends to be religious. Plain speaking. [Life Drive: to meet their destiny.]

31. **Insecure Punk**, a vain, possessive bully who will go to desperate, often vicious, lengths to prove themselves a leader, but people only respect them out of fear for their insane volatility, or their position of nepotistic power; gullible, and may have a skill honed from hours of desperate practice. Flip and wild. [Life Drive: to be feared.]

32. **Jaded Hero**, a sharp, pragmatic survivor with a dry humor and a sense of style; they are often successful in fringe, but legal, professions (e.g. gambling, private detective), and have strong integrity and loyalty, but are fundamentally isolated; have a deep romanticism that gets them involved in desperate causes. Casual, plain speaking and brutal. [Life Drive: to be effective.]

33. **Kindly Mother**, robust protectors who are plucky, but anxious, and a constant moral support; may be quite cantankerous with their mate, but usually only gently critical with child figures; they are focused on, and bashful about, youthful sexuality. Sincere. [Life Drive: to nurture.]

34. **King Thug**, brutal and crude, these tyrants often hold sway over large numbers by sheer force; their desire for possessions is only to symbolize their power the better to keep it, and they seek the total destruction of all obstacles; family bloodline is very important to them. Blunt and harsh. [Life Drive: to consolidate power.]

35. **Know-it-all**, cocky, petty, insensitive ass who must always be the center of attention; they can be volatile and even nasty, but, if truly cornered, will give up the front and humble themselves like a child; not totally dislikable because they do have a loyal, good heart, quick to forgive. Grand, flip and earnest. [Life Drive: to be admired.]

36. **Loyal Comrade**, like a German Shepherd; serious and deeply principled, they take care of business, either waiting diligently or

coming to the rescue; although realistic and knowing the ways of the world, they remain essentially innocent and are often socially shy. Up front, proper and passionate. [Life Drive: to be honorable.]

37. **Mad Scientist**, a visionary, isolated megalomaniac, they appreciate fine machinery, such as the killing machines they employ (e.g. a shark, a bomb, a psychopath) and relate to people as insects; may be childlike and silly, or totally grim. Imperious and flip. [Life Drive: to create paradise.]

38. **Misanthrope**, an agitated, bitter and socially inept loose cannon who feels compelled to confront everyone on their inadequacies, and, even when trying to connect out of loneliness and a genuine regard for people whom they respect as earthy, they inevitably alienate due to their grotesque insensitivity; rarely can hold a job equal to their gifts. Matter of fact, sarcastic and brutal. [Life Drive: a moment of peace.]

39. **Miser**, sour, paranoid and scheming, these hermits hate risk, but love to accumulate, and, fancying themselves very clever, find tremendous joy from getting over on others; massively greedy, they may or may not be lustful or gluttonous. Nasty and open. [Life Drive: to win at amassing wealth.]

40. **Nerd**, an expert at science without giving the talent much thought; they are romantic, with a rich fantasy life, and very much wanting to be hip, but their lack of social sense makes this impossible except in the opinion of other nerds or those who find this weakness endearing; egocentric and yet essentially timid, especially with authority. Open, casual and earnest. [Life Drive: to be remarkable.]

41. **Noble Hero**, a deeply principled person, with an open availability to learn; has a dry humor and a sharp mind, usually cultured and family oriented; they can find themselves pent up by the confines of their disciplined life and heavy conscience. Direct and gracious. [Life Drive: to do what is correct.]

42. **Noble Mentor**, worldly, educated and with a philosophical nature that often extends to the quirky, these natural guides are committed to the struggle against evil and will hold out to the death in their loyalty; tough, impatient and even a bit callous, yet they deeply love their students. Open and plain speaking. [Life Drive: to serve a good cause.]

43. **Nut**, a smart, ambitious, insecure and fundamentally straight-laced kook who can present an attractive persona, although they are actually quite socially inept; enthralled by glamour, they are prone to reckless schemes; kind, yet with a dominating, childlike self-interest. Open, gracious and wild. [Life Drive: to be in the spotlight]

44. **Odd Detective**, a brilliant, student of the universe with a humble good heart; usually rumpled or eccentric in dress, very much a creature of their habits, they have a wry, good-natured sense of humor and conventionalism that leads them to operate within the system; worldly, but fundamentally nonjudgmental. Honest and offhand. [Life Drive: to see what's hidden.]

45. **Ogre**, a powerful, self-righteous world unto themselves; absolute in their habits and firm in their desire for personal stability, they deal with all difficulties by using maximum force; can be sentimental and curious. Blunt, harsh and open. [Life Drive: to maintain order.]

46. **Ordinary Folk**, decent, earnest, curious and helpful, these dear souls are model citizens who take pride in being without airs and think of themselves as savvy, when the fact is they are quite unsophisticated. Sincere and cheerful. [Life Drive: to make the world nicer.]

47. **Pariah**, fragile shut-ins for whom life is a war; terrorized into a grim embrace of their hopeless condition, they still bravely continue to aspire and, with rich fantasy lives, are hugely romantic; not unintelligent, but backward from a lack of experience in the world. Plain and earnest. [Life Drive: to prove themselves worthy.]

48. **Passionate Predator**, dynamic, sexual, regal, possessive and competitive, these primal beings always burn for what is out of reach; very socially aware and extremely calculating, but also impulsive and reckless. Sincere, elegant and wild. [Life Drive: to have everything.]

49. **Poetic Fool**, a good person with a huge, romantic heart, but not much intelligence; conventional and given to being either in soaring romantic ecstasy or crushed heartache, they see themselves as plucky and will make a show of soldiering on against dramatically exaggerated circumstances. Earnest and passionate. [Life Drive: to share themselves.]

50. **Pompous Fool**, refined and conscientious and given to holding themselves out as grand impresarios and connoisseurs of everything, they are easily embarrassed and capable of tantrums due to their deep insecurity, but are good-hearted and self aware enough to recognize the truth of their own idiocy. Sophisticated and direct. [Life Drive: to be thought elegant.]

51. **Powerbroker**, a sophisticated opportunist adrift among their meaningless pleasures, embracing brutality to prove what a bitter joke life really is, and filled with deep self-loathing for their own lack of an inner core; they can be led, half-knowingly, to their own destruction for the chance of one moment of something real. Elegant and casual. [Life Drive: to have the best.]

52. **Prig**, cultured, rule oriented and snobbish, they are a functioning member of society, rigid in their, sometimes eccentric, habits; vulnerable to flattery, and longing to be embraced by the powerful; basically good people with insecurity; often a hypochondriac. Proper, elegant and absolute. [Life Drive: to be necessary to the important.]

53. **Quiet Sadist**, psychopathic, wry and cruel, these aimless murderers, while not interested in comfort, have some sense of style, and may take a job as a henchman for the basic pay and steady supply of victims; can be extremely clever and adept. Impersonal and casual. [Life Drive: to do damage.]

54. **Rich Slug**, an aristocratic, ruthless megalomaniac who, lecherous and hedonistic, fancies themselves masters of good taste; they will wear a jovial mask of humility, while winking to themselves all the while, and can have true sentimentality for objects and nostalgia; extremely controlling. Gracious and absolute. [Life Drive: to acquire power.]

55. **Righteous Idealist**, a childish, egomaniacal visionary playing outside the system or directly against it; they are highly disciplined and willing to suffer deprivation, but at the same time, selfishly crave fine things for themselves; vindictive and not nearly as secure as they insist everyone believe them to be; nonconformist, but prim. Romantic and intense. [Life Drive: to reveal the truth.]

56. **Rogue**, flamboyant, and highly skilled at survival; they can become teachers of worldliness, either to exploit the student or to bask in their admiration; may have varying degrees of sentimentality and real goodness, from a lot to none; so sure in their own opinion of themselves, they can affect humility. Flamboyant, sincere and open. [Life Drive: to have romance.]

57. **Sad Sack**, gloomy, nearly affectless, moist-eyed realists who have, all but for a twinge of wistfulness, given up on life; extremely good-hearted and fair, they will try to be helpful, even aspire for themselves, but really know pretty much the whole way that it will go unnoticed or blowup in their face. Plain. [Life Drive: to get through it.]

58. **Scalawag**, a carefree prankster, charismatic and adept at various practices, they love to mix it up and stick it to the high-and-mighty; enjoy pleasures, but aren't slaves to creature comforts, and have a deep, unselfconscious humanity that can make them especially passionate toward a given project. Open. [Life Drive: to have fun.]

59. **Schlemiel**, a grumpy, selfish, panicky egomaniac who is ambitious and resourceful, yet highly prone to failure, either because of their consistent bad luck or terrible social skills; given to putting on airs, they will take pride in both their accomplishments and their status as world-class losers. Passionate and flip. [Life Drive: to be special.]

60. **Searcher**, an isolated nomad looking for what will take away the inner torment; everything, including their own romanticized past, is probed for its possible usefulness to the quest, and discarded immediately if it shows no promise; capable of deep feeling for others, but rarely will they sacrifice the cause to be with them. Casual, absolute and earnest. [Life Drive: to find the secret.]

61. **Sheltered Angel**, beautiful and innocent, they are often kept in isolation, perhaps because of actual captivity, but possibly due to tremendous privilege or extreme shyness, they have a rich romanticism and are passionate, but are dutiful and live in fear of the dominant figures around them. Open and earnest. [Life Drive: to have romance.]

62. **Spirit of Youth**, open, romantic and childlike, they are hungry for experience and very loving, but also scheming, volatile and tend to be self-involved; they are quick to idolize and surprised when someone doesn't know exactly how they feel; refreshing and can cause a lot of trouble. Sincere and straightforward. [Life Drive: to have it all.]

63. **Spunky Helper**, a crafty, scrappy, hard head and lover of adventure, they are eccentric, socially awkward and will try to keep a low profile; valuing loyalty above all else, they will attach themselves to those whom they idolize and feel need them. Straightforward. [Life Drive: to back up a hero in a pinch.]

64. **Survivor**, a grim, highly skilled pragmatist; without affectation and a dry, bitter humor; very clear that they are out for themselves, but can be dragged into a good cause, partly out of a grudging sentimentality, but mostly for the secret joy they have in exercising their talent for performing well under stress. Direct and brutal. [Life Drive: to come out on top.]

65. **Sweet Fool**, childlike, kind, romantic and spunky, they have a curiosity and physical clumsiness that frequently causes mishaps and tends to be irritating to pompous authority; may have a deep unrecognized loneliness; if roused to anger they can actually be quite dangerous. Sincere and innocent. [Life Drive: to be helpful.]

66. **Sword of Justice**, a no-nonsense righter of wrongs who often defies authority that is seen as an impediment; self-confident, sarcastic and can be vengeful and savage, they have friends, but rarely can sustain family; may be innately suave or conventional in style; magnetic to the opposite sex. Direct and brutal. [Life Drive: to bring justice.]

67. **Transcendent Person**, having seen through the game, these peaceful souls now only want to provide comfort for those still caught up in it; capable of a full range of feelings, including anger, but it's anger as at a child that is loved; may be totally lighthearted or with wistful sadness. Honest and straightforward. [Life Drive: to give comfort.]

68.   **Troll**, an isolated misfit who clutches whatever objects they perceive to be of value; they are clever and enjoy exploiting being underestimated; have a deep loneliness that leads them to develop an alter ego as a companion; may have a physical deformity. Blunt, silly and earnest. [Life Drive: to be safe.]

69.   **Troubled Outsider**, an intelligent old soul, cleverly aware of how things operate and convinced of themselves as a hopeless case; with a dry humor, they yearn for romance in a grim world, and, while low-dominant with nothing to prove, can get in over their heads due to their huge sense of decency. Plain speaking and sarcastic. [Life Drive: to do what's right.]

70.   **Visionary**, a driven, sophisticated and conscientious person, usually in a socially aware profession, sometimes the arts; they make an effort to live a balanced life, but if it isn't out of obligation, they actually only indulge in recreation and social activities because they know it will make them better for their work; while happy when in the thick of the job, on reflection, they know they can never do enough. Open, plain speaking and graceful. [Life Drive: to make the world better.]

71.   **Waif**, an innocent child on its own and at loose ends; they tend to idolize people and be enthusiastic, but may be paranoid from past abuses; they are hugely romantic and seek a refinement they don't possess by putting on airs, will fight wildly if their dreams are threatened; may be sexual or asexual. Open and earnest. [Life Drive: to belong.]

72.   **Weasel**, mean, cunning, lustful opportunists who are arrogant and enjoy taking risks, but are obsequious to power and will tend to play for pity, quickly acting wounded by injustice, even when injured by those who were only defending themselves; may harbor grudges, yet will surrender them for self-interest. Solicitous, wild, cold and vicious. [Life Drive: to get more than anybody else.]

73.   **Wild Child**, scrappy, resourceful, and deeply lonely, they hate feeling vulnerable and look for every opportunity to prove they are not to be threatened, attacking before they can be attacked; truly soft-hearted and companionable, they are looking for a protected place to make a home. Direct and nasty. [Life Drive: to be safe.]

74. **Wise Observer**, a sardonic witnesses, dispassionate in the face of both great calamity and good fortune; they consider themselves realists with complete self-interest, but in actuality have great compassion for humanity and a true sadness at their own failure at finding meaning in their life. Elegant, sarcastic and blunt. [Life Drive: to see what happens.]

75. **Worldly Friend**, wise, loyal, capable persons who enjoy their creature comforts; full of grace and humor and, while they usually will advise moderation and the long view, knowing that life is temporary, they will also jump in to join in what is reckless. Open, casual and plain speaking. [Life Drive: to live with dash.]

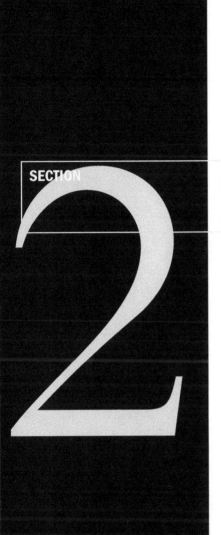

PRINCIPLES
FOR THE ACTOR

chapter 1

Work on Self

KNOW YOURSELF

It's said that the magnificent ancient Greek culture was based on two principles: Nothing too much (more on that later) and Know Yourself. As an artist it is your absolute, non-stop homework to study your own humanity. It's the only real way to improve your sense of Truth and your appreciation for the Universal. Know the world by how it exists perfectly in yourself.

Knowing yourself improves your base of analysis for work on characters.

As the subject of your study, you must accept yourself exactly as you are at this moment, a work in progress. Live life affirmatively and begin to deepen yourself; feel your will to live, feel your harmony with Life; lucid, joining in, let each wave wash you a little further up the shore.

Here's a good clue as to who you might be. What are those things you're doing when you especially have that feeling that you shouldn't be doing something else, where time flies, and you feel intensely alive. It could be you even feel a little scared that you could be in over your head. Maybe you don't listen to it or you can't believe it's true, but there's a little voice inside you saying at such times, "This is the real me!"

Come alive. It's time to live while you're alive. Get out from behind the mask you've built to conform to external definitions of who and what you are. Sure, society's been doing its best to make you like everybody else, but you have to fight the good fight and be more of yourself, even when you can't say what that is.

You're going to have to face yourself some time. Why not now? If you're honest with yourself, then maybe you'll become less afraid of how your honesty will reveal your hidden selves to others. How can you be appreciated if you don't let yourself be known. Great people (your audience) are happy and supportive to see you just as you are right now.

I'm not saying it won't be frightening. You're going to have to constantly say goodbye to the world you've always known. If you look at yourself truthfully, you'll probably have to recognize yourself as the real reason for your limitations, and you won't be able to lay the blame off on somebody else anymore. While blaming has no positive effect on the world, it does give you the rotten luxury of feeling you're right, and when you give that up it can mean losing your identity and the illusion of safety it's always given you. It may mean there's still some grieving to do. You're going to have to allow the unexpected into your life, and naturally, you are going to have to fight your desperate desire to cling to your illusions.

Moving toward maturity is always difficult because of the fear you have that you'll miss out on your old pleasures, and those potential pleasures you have to grab before they're taken away, sometimes called the "scarcity mentality." There's also dread that, if you aspire to something, you'll be disappointed, so it's better not to get your hopes up.

Every great thing makes you uncomfortable at first. By definition it's unfamiliar and, besides that, you don't think you can live up to it. But then again, what worthwhile thing have you ever done that wasn't uncomfortable at first? It's only after you've taken it in as your own that you can possibly value it.

Of course you feel safer with mediocrity; it leaves you in peace, undisturbed. It's only when you give up that image of yourself that you prized so highly or that safety net you thought so dear that you can set yourself free. Free for greater pleasures you have yet to conceive of.

And how do you get there? You know the answer. Love. Touch the will to live. Trust the miracle that you came into being. Feel how Life delights in Life. It can put you in the mood to risk a lot and spur you to commit everything.

NURTURE CONFIDENCE

Believe in yourself. You want to cultivate bravado, pluck, élan, pep, dash. In French, *je ne sais quoi*. To carry yourself with a buoyant elegance, a spontaneous ease. To increase this possibility you should feed your creative esteem by being your own friend and supporter in every way you can. You need to always accentuate the positive.

Believe in your work. You should aspire to ever more excellence of craft and effectiveness. You should connect to the great power of your being in service, to feel yourself used to educate, inspire and communicate something about people to people.

Expand your comfort zone. You'll gain strength, courage and confidence every time you face your fear. Use fear as a positive energy to work through challenges.

EXPERIENCE

Learn about the World. To hold a mirror up to nature, as you've been charged with doing, you should learn everything you can about the world you intend to represent. You'll learn about the World from first-hand exposure (travel is especially good for this), by reading or watching recorded material, and from having conversations with others. Impressions are experience. Someone who watches a documentary on Moscow, or who talks with someone who has lived in Moscow, has an experience of Moscow.

Sharpen your senses. Be a person on whom nothing is lost. In order to experience the World, the apparatus to receive the World should be as available and clear as possible, therefore "Nothing too much." Excess in anything clouds your faculties and dulls your participation.

Grow more cultured. All the arts are related and the basic principles within them are the same, so if you study any of the humanities it's going to be of benefit to your acting.

You don't have to be exceptionally intelligent to be an actor, but you should be cultured. You should have some knowledge of the history of the theater, the great plays, as well as the important works in film and television. You should have an appreciation for the culture you inhabit.

Don't take the limits of your vision for the limits of the World.

IMPROVE YOUR PHYSICAL LIFE AND SPEECH

Get relaxed. Relaxation is fundamental to everything. You can use meditation, visualization, hypnotic suggestion, or any technique available to habituate a sense of ease in how you operate. Performance experience is helpful. If you've been in front of an audience and made it through with being booed or pelted with anything, you're more inclined to be relaxed the next time.

Free the body. You should be comfortable in your own skin and have easy, comfortable movement. Your body should be an open medium of expression. Aspire to be the perfect transmitter of impulse, just like a baby.

Use the Alexander Technique. Fredrick Mathias Alexander was an actor who developed a technique for using his body and speaking more effectively on stage. Since then it's not only been used by actors to better their performance, but also bicyclists, gymnasts, and secretaries at their keyboards. The truth is this technique is applicable for virtually every use of the human body.

The basic technique is quite simple: you should lengthen your neck and have full breath. The best way for you to experience this is to have an expert practitioner lay their hands on you, but you can get a little experience by following these instructions:

Tilt your chin forward so that your neck naturally lengthens; keeping this extension of the neck, lift your head so that your eyes go to the horizon line. The head should float easily on top of your neck. There's a separate vertebra, the first one down from the skull, that tends to get locked; ease up there. The shoulders should drop naturally. It's as if you were suspended by a wire coming from the top of your head. Breathe fully, but easily, pushing out the belly using your diaphragm on the inhale, and with a widening of the back; go wide around the top of your chest as if holding up a band that's wrapped around your chest, up under the armpits. Release the breath and continue to easily get length in your neck.

Maintain a good physical condition. The demands placed on your body as an actor and the endurance you may need can be extreme. For this reason it's wise for you to be ready to perform by staying in good shape.

Flexibility is an excellent quality to consistently improve. It provides overall, healthy conditioning and prevents injury.

Free the voice. Of course, you should go to a proper speech teacher and get yourself a proper speech CD that you can use to drill with.

Just as with the body, the voice should be an open medium of expression. Purity should be maintained with emotion and there should be a consistent clear tone.

You can imagine the voice coming from a room in your stomach and the sound issuing from the perfect center of that room and, if you were holding a pencil in your mouth, the sound should go out over the pencil. You can feel the proper placement in your mouth when you communicate a simple yes by going "Um-hum." That's pretty much where your voice should come from.

Develop good diction. Good diction means that each word can be understood without distraction. You should have undistorted elocution and pitch, and an appreciation for standard usage.

With respect to your personal speech patterns, I hesitate to advocate in every case that you homogenize your speech to standard. One of those proper speech teachers I just recommended for you might be aghast at this advice, but I think a unique quality or slight accent can make a performer especially interesting and give flavor to your speech, provided it doesn't interfere with intelligibility and you can do a standard American accent if it's called for.

Having a pronounced foreign accent can limit the characterizations available to you, and even a light foreign accent is much more limiting than an American regionalism for an American piece. Even if not explicitly stated in the text, however, as long as it doesn't distort the truth of the piece, an authentic foreign accent can set someone off as exotic, and can be used nicely for something romantic, disquieting or comedic.

The best advice I can give an actor with a foreign accent is for them to either remove it altogether or keep it subtle, and be ready to perform Standard American at a moment's notice.

Cultivate stage skills. The large variety of skills that you could possibly be called upon to use precludes a list that could reasonably be maintained at practiced fingertips, but there are some obvious skills you can be acquainted with, such as singing, dancing and various forms of combat.

Of course, even this is dependent on the kind of parts you're likely to be playing. If Musical Comedy isn't something you'll want to perform, tap dancing maybe won't be at the top of your list. If you don't see yourself venturing into Shakespeare, it would probably be better to know how to use a side arm than a sword.

The most important element in this area is to have that basic, good conditioning, including flexibility, so as to be able to work on what is needed for a role as quickly as possible.

Persevere

Yes, like every other motivational speaker, or fortune cookie, I'm going to tell you to persevere. If you don't want to act, don't act; that's your business. I'm just telling you that, once you've started the process, you might as well go all the way. If you're going to do it right and honor this ancient art, you've got to press through.

DON'T QUIT

Stay in motion. A primary law of physics is that objects in motion tend to stay in motion, and those at rest tend to stay at rest. Don't stop. Even if you're limping, you're still walking. You fall, you get up.

If you're a true artist it doesn't matter what happened the day before; it doesn't matter how tired or emotionally battered you are; it doesn't matter how many extraneous or pessimistic thoughts run through your head; you keep your eye on the goal and do what you can from right where you are.

When you're on stage it's like wrestling a gorilla. You don't quit when you get tired, you quit when the gorilla gets tired.

Drive the body, not vice versa. Strength is a matter of the made-up mind. If you're going to push through any real difficulty you have to make your mind run the body. Never let your lazy body tell the mind what to do. Your body will always want to quit. Know that you can do your best work even when you don't feel like it.

Don't over-think, do. Slip a little into your unconscious, be a little impulsive, stop calculating and jump; feel your life pulsing forward, telling you what's good and useful; accept the simplicity of it all, the honesty of it all; dread troubles less, have faith. Find a way for yourself or make one.

EMBRACE FAILURE

Fail forward to success. You can't be great if you never fail. Thomas Edison said, "I have not failed ten thousand times. I have successfully found ten thousand ways that will not work." Let's say you make a decision that turns out to be wrong, and you have to go back and do it over another way. You'll probably still be further along than those who stalled on making that original decision. While they're hesitating because they're afraid to look inferior, you're busy making mistakes and becoming superior.

Difficulties are messages. It's Truth showing a little bit more of itself and, in this way, there's every chance it's going to reveal an opportunity. Opportunity's favorite disguise is trouble.

You can rate how mature you are by how much embarrassment you can take, and if you're never embarrassed, it means you never take any chances. And you really shouldn't feel embarrassed by your failures, anyway. To admit you were wrong and made a mistake is only saying that you're wiser now than you were the moment before. You're only a failure if you don't learn from the experience, or you blame somebody else, or you quit. If you're doing it right, you'll probably see a lot of failure, because it's the constant companion of success. Don't worry about failure: worry about the chances you miss when you don't even try.

Use failure. What you call failure is entirely a matter of how you take it. It can often be converted into a bracing tonic by simply changing your attitude from one of victim to one of fighter. You can either make yourself miserable or you make can make yourself strong. The amount of work will probably be about the same.

Obstacles build in you a capacity to overcome them; they develop your dormant talents. You won't get better by playing it safe, you're going to have to go out and risk getting knocked on your butt, and, in the long run, it's hard to say whether the successes or the failures are going to do you more good. Perhaps the best thing in the world for you right now is a kick in the teeth. It can strip away false values, like the insanity of conceit, show you where you're ignorant and where you're strong. It'll introduce you to yourself. It can show you what you're really made of and what you really want. It's only through struggle that you get a sense of your own dignity, and besides, there's no real glory in winning if it's easy, is there?

A man named Frank A. Clark said, "If you find a path with no obstacles, it probably doesn't lead anywhere interesting."

PRACTICE HARD AND WELL

There's a methodical way to practice so you get the most out of your time. I offer here some basic tips, some repeated from earlier, some painfully obvious.

Want to get better. You should have the clear goal to get better at what it is you want to get better at.

Make mental models. Keep visualizing how you want to perform. Increase the elements within your visualizations to include more factors and greater finesse with old ones.

Be aware of what you're doing. As you do the thing you're practicing, put your attention on the details of what you're doing, and consider the value in doing it this particular way.

Get feedback. Seek out people you trust to evaluate your progress, take note of what they say and change your behavior as necessary.

Practice consistently. Your practice should not be haphazard and subject to whim, but regular and sacrosanct.

The great musician Vladimir Horowitz is supposed to have said, "If I don't practice for a day, I know it. If I don't practice for two days, my wife knows it. If I don't practice for three days, the world knows it."

Me & Jeff Goldblum
at his place.

chapter 3

Develop Good Work Habits

BUILD SELF-DISCIPLINE

Organize the basics. You will increase your habit for self-improvement by getting your act together and organizing yourself in the smallest of ways. Clean your desk, your bag, your files, whatever gets messy, on a regular basis. Make yourself take the time to put things back where they belong after you use them. The act of organizing yourself both sends you (and others) the right message, and trains you in making decisions about what is and isn't important.

Make and stick to a schedule. Write down your appointments somewhere and keep to them.

Keep your agreements. If you say you're going to do something, do it. If you say you're going to be somewhere at a specific time, be there without fail. You have to develop the discipline, and the ethic, not to just say you're going to do something because you think the person at the time wants to hear it at the time.

Favor honesty over harmony.

Finish what you start. Or as Baltasar Gracian said, "Don't just stalk the prey, make the kill." This, of course, will often be required of you in the keeping of your agreements, and there are certain personality types that have a particular problem with "closing the circle." Maybe it represents death to them. Maybe it means, by doing this particular thing for real and finishing it, they are making a statement that in all ways in their life they are going to put away childish things.

Welcome correction. Criticism can be painful if you're already so hard on yourself that the least little suggestion that you might not be perfect triggers your internal self-punishment. This can make you seek to defensively fight off the criticism through justification, invalidating the source, or negotiating the terms of the critique so that it can be softened.

Epictetus said: "When criticized, remember to relax and accept that this thing may well be true from this other person's perspective, but that they do not know you in full. Otherwise they wouldn't have mentioned only this one item among your many other faults."

Take on more responsibility. So long as you're willing to maintain your agreements, volunteer to do more work. Make yourself exercise that muscle for organization on the boundary of your comfort zone.

Don't always have to be entertained. There just might be more to life than filling every possible moment with an enjoyable diversion. Do you really think the person who passed the most time without discomfort wins? Consider what will contribute to your well-being and, therefore, bring you peace of mind.

Do what you have to do, so you can do what you want to do.

FOLLOW A STANDARD

Be professional. You should have work habits that don't intrude on the work of others. You should always be early, never late, and do what you say you're going to do.

Be prepared. Do all that stuff about acting well that I told you.

Check your personality. Maybe the best advice about personality in the work environment is not to have one. Having friends and making friends is wonderful, but you should always be clear about why you're there. You shouldn't vent anxieties and discontent at work, whether concerning personal matters or those about the production, and you shouldn't gossip or indulge in factionalism. Bite your tongue.

You should feel free to offer a good idea if it's appropriate, but you must be very sensitive about this and, when in doubt, keep your mouth shut. You shouldn't require a disproportionate amount of time or focus, or talk about your performance unless it contributes to the success of the production.

Beyond this, you shouldn't brag, complain, or judge too much, but you should be involved and enthusiastic and considerate: What will help?

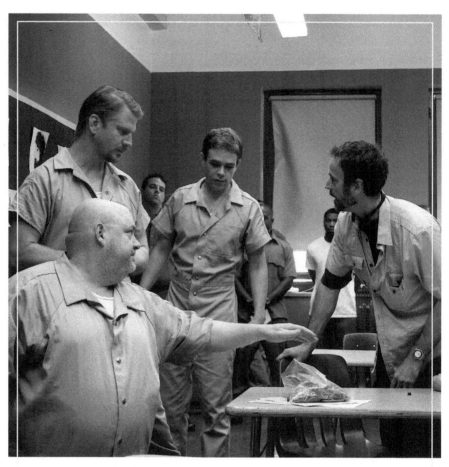

On the set of In Northwood,
with Dash Mihok (tall blond),
Pruit Taylor Vince (bottom),
Nick Stahl and me.

SECTION

3

HOW TO GET A JOB

I'm not going to spend a lot of time on this topic (although I imagine some of you have flipped straight from the table of contents to this page); this is a book on how to be good at acting, and isn't meant to be one of those fine publications on "How to get an agent" or "Market yourself in Hollywood!"

I will say this, though — show business is like a mystic pyramid, and there are throngs trying to get to the king's chamber. That's where Brad Pitt and Angelina Jolie presently sit, I suppose (although by the time you read this they may have been displaced by somebody else). You can get lucky and push on just the right brick and a wall will open, or you can scrape and scrape at a spot where you think you can break through to a path that leads to a higher chamber. You can befriend someone who knows part of the way, or you can seek out an expert (such as myself) who'll give you skills you can use to your advantage. But like all success, it's going to come down to the old A, B, Cs: Ability, Breaks, and Courage.

chapter 1

Reasons You Get a Job

- **You're a star.** You can get hired if your name gives the production a stamp of authenticity and gets people to pay to see the show because you're in it.

- **You have buzz.** Even though your name doesn't bring in paying customers, the powers that be will put you in a role because they think your star is on the rise and they want to associate themselves with your momentum.

- **You're connected.** If you know someone who can help you get hired, perhaps a relative, they might do you the favor of making it happen. That's always nice.

- **You're the right type.** You can book the job largely on the fact that you're so physically and temperamentally right for a part.

- **You're lucky.** Being in the right place at the right time can lead to getting you work.

- **You can act.** You're just so damn good you can't be denied.

- *Old Theater Story:* A production of *Hamlet* is holding an open casting for the lead, and an elderly Jewish man shuffles onto the stage. The director calls out from his seat in the house, "Sir, we're not reading for the smaller parts just yet, come back next week when we're having the auditions for Polonius." To which the old man replies, "I'm here to audition for the role of Hamlet." The director shares a smile with the producer who is sitting next to him, and he says, "Okay. Go for it." The old man turns to the side for a moment, and there comes over him a transformation. It's remarkable. He steps to the center of the stage, now having become the tortured, young prince, and he launches into the classic "To be or not to be" soliloquy. He is amazing. Everyone stops what they're doing — people come out of the box office and from back stage to watch. Everyone's crying, totally blown away. He finally finishes and the director, wiping his eyes, says, "You have the part! You have to do this part for us. But, sir, my God, how did you do that?" The old man, who has now returned to his normal, slumped-shouldered self, just shrugs and says, "That's acting."

Be Seen and Be Good

If you can get yourself seen and, when you do, you knock it out of the park, you'll have a career as an actor. That's it. Getting yourself seen, however, requires you to have the skill set of a producer, so you'll need political savvy, tenacity, and the brazenness to sell yourself the same way you would if you were selling any kind of product, and selling yourself as a performer may be more difficult than selling a shoe or a rug cleaning service because to hold yourself up as worth buying can strike you as egocentric, and this is commonly felt to be in poor taste. Also, the thing that brought you into acting almost certainly is a highly charged primitive passion, fraught with ambivalence, so to brag about it and recommend it and put a big sign over it that says, "Buy This!" might not feel comfortable.

Trade favors. What successful people know is that much of how the world works is by trading favors: "You scratch my back and I'll scratch yours." If you think you can do a decent job as an actor, then don't be embarrassed to ask for a favor that might get you a job. Look the person in the eye and acknowledge that you're asking for a favor, not charity, and that you to intend to repay them with interest.

If you were a qualified chef, I doubt you'd be embarrassed to ask for investors to open a restaurant. So, walk right up to that acquaintance and ask for an introduction to that agent, or call that person you know has access to an opportunity to read for a part you're right for, and do it with the clear understanding that, when you get into a position to help them, you will. You'll get their script to a director you know (now that you're successful), or you'll work on their project for less than your usual quote, both because you're honorable and it's the right thing to do, and because that's the way it's done and it won't be worth having your reputation suffer if you don't repay the favor.

171

Get close to what you want to do. A good, general recommendation for the pursuit of any occupation is to get near the work. Put yourself near the real deal as it's happening. I'm not necessarily suggesting you toil for years as an extra, but then again, you're more likely to be in a position to get yourself seen from there than if you were selling insurance in Idaho. If you want to launch yourself from a sitcom, hang out in comedy clubs or with sketch player outfits. If you want to do film or theater, volunteer to work at film festivals or in a theater, and for the love of God produce your own projects!

You can get near the business by interning for an agency or a casting agent, or working in some capacity in production. Any place you are that there could be an opportunity for you to step up and say, "How about giving me a shot?"

Audition well. You have to commit to every audition as if it were a full-blown performance, putting in as much work as you possibly can. You have to be as good as you can be, every time. It doesn't matter that the room is not conducive to being creative — you can play your instrument whether it's in a field or a concert hall or in a rented office. It doesn't matter if you're totally wrong for a given part or you know someone else has a lock on it — you have to take every precious opportunity to shine as bright as you can so that you'll be thought of as good and word will get around and you'll get hired in the future. I know many, many stories, such as my own where I was given a part without having to audition because I had done something they liked while auditioning for a part I didn't get. I cast Dash Mihok in my film strictly because I saw a copy of his screen test for a part he didn't get.

Auditioning typically has a very heavy psychological component, and will affect different actors differently depending on their temperament. There are actors who are good auditioners, but, like some fast sketch artists, they never improve their performances beyond what they show in the first audition. There are also many fine actors who need time to develop a performance because, for them, it's a layering process that requires a period of gestation. Just know that, if you are in this last group, you will then be dependent on having a reel that can be seen and is strong enough to overcome your limitations for auditioning, and even then, you face the short-sightedness of judges who, if they can't hear the exact dialog read, can't imagine how you might do well in a specific part.

Give it your everything every time. There is a story told of how acting legend, and powerful person of the theater, John Gielgud went to see a play because he'd been told a young actor performing in it was interesting. Mr. Gielgud went unheralded to a matinee and this actor evidently felt the hour too early or the audience too sparse in number to render in his best work. I gather this lack of effort was clearly noticeable, because the story goes that, following the play, Mr. Gielgud sought out this actor backstage and told him, "Young man, you will never participate in any production with which I am associated."

Don't require permission to act. Nobody wants the responsibility of validating you as an actor. It's like dating. You're more attractive if you seem like you have other options. You have to walk in to an audition the way you'd want a doctor to walk in and audition for an operation you needed. Not trembling, hoping you like them and approve of their plans for your surgery, but giving you the sense that they're assured of their competence and believe themselves capable of delivering the best possible outcome. You want the sense that they'll go on doctoring whether or not you choose to use them or go with someone else.

CONCLUSION

Acting is a performing art and it needs to be done with the intention that an audience will be watching, but this is not to say it's only validated by you getting paid money for doing it. Purchase price, by itself, has nothing to do with what is or isn't art. You can act in a class or for charity or for something freely posted on the Internet, and it could be among the finest acting there has ever been. I recommend you nurture and find your passion for acting without requiring the external approval of financial reward. As it so happens, a love of acting, free of those kinds of strings, tends to make your work better and all the more likely someone will want to pay you for it.

So, fight like a demon to get seen if you have to, but when you actually start acting, I suggest you let it be for the fun of doing it. Don't worry so much about whether you get cast from a single, fragile opportunity; it's more likely by giving up caring so much about whether or not you get it that you'll get it. Oh, Life.

Photo credit: Michelle Pattee

Me & Sam Raimi.

4

ASPECTS
OF ACTING

On the occasion of needing to meet the following day with a class of my students for one-on-one evaluations, I developed an outline for the basic factors involved in the Craft of acting, the better to specifically address how each student had been progressing. I found these elements laid themselves out for me in a group of three with each defined by three features. Fascinated by the symmetry, I found I could do the same with the subject of Talent. Pressing on, I created similar abstracts for the motivations to act, the inherent fears that arise from acting, and the problematic responses a person can have to these.

For what it's worth, I offer these bare-bones outlines to help you evaluate where you currently stand with regards to these characteristics, the better to target where you'd like to improve.

TALENT

A. Imagination
   1. **Depth**
   a) Degree of Emotional Connection with the Imaginary

   2. **Presence**
   a) Degree of Affinity for the Imaginary

   3. **Impulsivity**
   a) Degree of Free Exchange with the Imaginary

B. Killer Instinct
   1. **Grace**
   a) Tendency to Increase Focus with Stress

   2. **Smarts**
   a) Ability to Make the Theatrical Event Work

   3. **Goal-Oriented**
   a) Strength and Clarity of Purpose

C. Enthusiasm
   1. **Showmanship**
   a) Ability to Communicate with an Audience

2. **Sensationalism**
   a) Inclination to Embrace the Amplitude and Purity of Imaginary Meanings

3. **Adventurousness**
   a) Zeal for the Intense

D. The Foundations of Talent: Involvement, Vision, and Passion

CRAFT

A. Concentration
   1. **Awareness**
      a) Attention to the Significant, Distinctive Features Arising from All the Imaginary Events

   2. **Personalizing**
      a) Quest for an Ever More Specific Opinion About Imaginary Events

   3. **Focus**
      a) Exclusion of All Thoughts Unrelated to the Theatrical Event

B. Investment
   1. **Aspiration**
      a) Association to Imaginative Events at Their Greatest Degree of Meaning

   2. **Assertion**
      a) Projection of the Will

   3. **Receptivity**
      a) Processing Everything

C. Poise
   1. **Simplification**
      a) Eliminating All That Isn't Useful

   2. **Execution**
      a) Tending to the Task at Hand

3. Trust
   a) Belief That Everything Will Unfold As It Should

D. The Foundations of Craft: Specificity, Intention, and Ease

MOTIVATIONS TO ACT

A. The Desire to Have an Impact
   1. **Need for Affirmation**
      a) To Be Known

   2. **Narcissism**
      a) Gratification from Exalting Self

   3. **Personality Type: "Exhibitionist"**
      a) Attention Seekers

B. The Desire to Live Imaginary Circumstances
   1. **Need To Express**
      a) To Have Catharsis

   2. **The Wish to Play a Role**
      a) Gratification from Modeling a Different Personality

   3. **Personality Type: "Escapists"**
      a) People Who Live in Fantasy

C. The Desire for Exhilaration
   1. **Need to Experience Thrill**
      a) To Get an Adrenaline High

   2. **The Wish to Be at the Most Intense Place**
      a) Gratification from Transcending the Ordinary

   3. **Personality Type: "Adventurers"**
      a) Thrill-Seekers and Romantics

MOTIVATION PITFALLS

A. Exhibitionist's Pitfalls
    1. **An Inclination to Watch Oneself Being Watched**
        a) Less Attentive to What's on Stage Than What's in
           the Audience

    2. **Prone to Fakery to Maintain an External Perspective**
        a) Hesitant to Lose One's Self By Really Doing Things

    3. **A Wish to Be Thought Well of as a Personality**
        a) Reluctant to Disappear into a Role or Appear "Unlikable"

B. Escapist's Pitfalls
    1. **Gravitation Toward a Personal Issue**
        a) Pushing for a Particular Emotional Quality and Luxuriating
           in Emotion

    2. **Imitation of a Model Inappropriate to the Part**
        a) Recreating an Image from Childhood That Is Untruthful
           for the Character or Un-Aesthetic in Its Expression

    3. **Disregard for the Audience**
        a) Oblivious to or Resentful of the Discipline Needed for a
           Clear Communication with the Audience

C. Adventurer's Pitfalls
    1. **Lack of Discipline**
        a) Intentionally Unprepared In Order to Increase Performance
           Stress

    2. **Disregard for Artistic Considerations**
        a) Not Relating Imaginatively or Communicating with the
           Audience

    3. **Uninspired and Impatient**
        a) Dissatisfied, Looking Ahead, Guessing and Assuming

FEARS IN ACTING

A. Fear of Rejection
   1. **Doing Something That Will Turn People Away**
      a) Abandonment and Isolation

   2. **Offered Something That Will Be Disregarded**
      a) Invalidation

   3. **Sought-for Approval Will Be Denied**
      a) Disappointment

B. Fear of Disapproval
   1. **Doing Something That Will Bring Punishment**
      a) Painful Consequences

   2. **Incurring Severe Judgment**
      a) Shamed

   3. **Being Stigmatized**
      a) Hopeless

C. Fear of Being Unprotected
   1. **Leaving One's Self Open to Attack**
      a) Defenselessness

   2. **Attracting Unwanted Attention By Doing Something Vivid**
      a) Without Camouflage

   3. **Failure to Foresee Danger**
      a) Blindsided

D. The Fear of Exposure
   1. **Revealing the Disowned Self (Qualities of Silliness, Anger, Pain, Fear and Sensuality)**
      a) Public Image Invalidated

   2. **Showing Disorientation**
      a) Condemned for Incompetence

3. Revealing What One Feels to Be Important
a) Judged as Weak and Stupid

E. The Fear of Emotion
1. Experiencing Certain Emotions Perceived as Toxic
a) Adverse Associations with Certain Feelings

2. Opening an Internal Pandora's Box (Cataclysmic Rage, Bottomless Grief, Crippling Terror, Mindless Joy)
a) Loss of Self

3. Being Emotional Means Losing the Argument
a) Wiped Out

F. Summary of Fears: All Fears Are Fears of Power
1. Being Out of Control
a) Looking Vulnerable and Undefended

b) Looking Disoriented and Incompetent

2. Getting Into Trouble
a) Being Unlikable

b) Failing to Do What Is in One's Best Interest

3. Loss of Self
a) Invalidating a World View

b) In–The–Moment = Death

DEFENSE MECHANISMS AND PROBLEM RESPONSES

A. The Responses to Fear of Rejection
1. Hesitancy
a) Looking Ahead for Danger or Lagging Behind to Monitor the Experience

2. Over-Concerned with External Reactions
a) Wishing to Appear Clever

3. Resentment at Having to Ask for Attention
a) Disrespect for the Audience

4. A Feeling of Isolation
a) Loneliness Causing Depression

B. The Responses to Fear of Disapproval
1. Playing It Safe
a) Doing Less to Risk Less

2. Lacking Assertiveness
a) Demonstrating Submissiveness (Distress and Confusion)

3. Over-Concerned with Being Pleasing
a) Inauthentic

C. The Responses to Fear of Being Unprotected
1. Judging the Correctness of Responses
a) Going Slow to Allow Censoring of Impulses
b) Deadening and Suppressing Responsiveness

2. Tentativeness
a) Guessing and Interpreting Moments Instead of Living Them

3. Blanking
a) Avoiding Vivid Behavior

4. Fear of Vulnerable Positions
a) Increased Anxiety with Increased Impulses

D. The Responses to Fear of Revelation
1. Adjusting Behavior In Order to Conceal
a) Slowness Used to Slow Responsiveness

2. Reduced Willingness to Experience Surprise
a) Minimizing Relatedness to an Event's Specialness

3. Avoidance of the Deeper Self
a) Minimizing Relatedness to an Event's Significance

4. Fear of Vulnerable Positions
a) Increased Anxiety with Increased Impulses

E. The Responses to Fear of Emotion

    1. **Monitoring Responses for the Quality of the Emotion**

        a) Cautiousness and Self-Consciousness

    2. **Disengagement from Imaginary Events That Call Upon a Deep Response**

        a) Disconnecting from People or Things

    3. **A Feeling of Danger**

        a) Dread

F. Summary: Fear Seeks to Hinder Full Acting

    1. **The Unconscious Will Push for the Safest Behavior**

        a) Fear Makes People Lie to Themselves

        b) Solution: Take Risks

    2. **Most Defense Mechanisms Require Time to Work**

        a) The Intellect Requires Time to Calculate

        b) Solution: Trust Your Craft and Act Before You Think

    3. **A Preference for States That Make the Actor Feel Unaffected and Safe**

        a) Confusion, Amazement, Detachment and Minimizing Circumstances

        b) Solution: Relate Big Emotionally

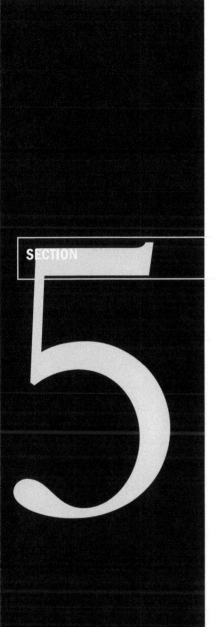

ACTING TIPS

chapter 1

Staging

BLOCKING FOR THE STAGE

Be seen. Your blocking for the stage must address the problem of being seen. The stage is either "proscenium," with the audience in front only, "thrust," with the audience on three sides, or "theater-in-the-round," with the audience on all sides. Each has their own challenges, and it's never possible for everyone to get the best view all the time, but the view should be varied so that the audience as a whole is accommodated.

Project a widening focus. You should find opportunities to open up the angle of your body toward the direction of the audience. This means there should be a tendency to use your hand on the upstage side, whether you're right- or left-handed: if you go to one knee, it should be your downstage knee; if you gesture to indicate a reference to someone or something at a different location, if possible, that location should be in the direction of the audience.

Opportunities should be found to do things in relation to the blocking that require your character to turn out in the direction of the audience, or getting out from behind people, creating better visibility for yourself. This is called "cheating" because it is a cheat on the truth of natural reality.

Bounce dialog off the other characters. With your Action firmly established, and still keeping anchored to the other character or characters who are the object of that Action, there may be times you can shift your gaze away and out, opening yourself up, as long as the Action isn't one that currently has to be driven into them. You can do this when describing something being visualized or for parenthetical statements: "You've got to help her" (then, looking out, as if visualizing her) "she just sits there by the window all day" or "You've got to help her" (then, turning out, expressing how beyond you it all is), "God knows she won't listen to anything I say."

Use the Fourth Wall. One possible way of opening up to be seen by the audience is to create an imaginary reason to look in the direction where the audience is seated. Turn and look out at the landscape, perhaps through an imaginary window. Maybe you can relate to something on the fourth wall, transparent to them, such as a mirror, or a fireplace. Only in very rare stylized presentations should any invisible object be actually touched, at which point it becomes "pantomime."

The direction of the audience can be used for "thought lines." This is a placement of your gaze directed at the horizon line when your character is working out a problem in their head.

Find a safe place to look. You may want to avoid looking directly into someone's face in the audience when you look out in that direction, because if a particular face snaps into focus it can be disorienting for both of you ("Oh, my God, it's uncle Ned!"). You might want to examine the theater space beforehand and find places where you can look when the house is full where you can be sure there won't be a face, such as an exit sign or the edge of a banister.

Talk to the back of an actor who's facing the audience. One of the best blocking schemes you can have is when one actor is speaking to another actor's back, with the downstage actor throwing their dialog back over their shoulder: in this way, both faces are seen. Of course, there'll be a logical choice for which of the two characters would be more prone to consistently look at the other character, and this should be the person upstage.

Spend some time with your back to the audience. Having said all this about being open for the audience, there is nothing wrong with having your character spend some time with their back to the audience, particularly when used for theatrical effect. It's come to be considered provincial to always be excessively open to your audience, sometimes dismissed as "community theater–style acting," and there is a completely valid stage value in having one's back turned toward the audience.

There should be times when the full back is presented, whether as a simple moment that adds variety to the blocking, or as a strikingly theatrical moment where the audience is kept in suspense by not being able to see you and read your expression. Let's say you've just been told your spouse wants a divorce: you can immediately give your back to the audience and they will be kept hanging, unsure of how you're taking this, until you turn around and reveal that you are, in fact, smiling.

Sense the balance of the stage in its entirety. While major blocking schemes are usually the responsibility of the director, it might be helpful for you to have some sense of the entire picture being created on stage.

Too much bunching up in a particular area of the stage for too long or too often is usually to be avoided, and every area of the stage should probably be used eventually. If there are a lot of people on a lit stage at one time there should perhaps be an effort made to keep them spread out enough so that it doesn't seem that there's an obvious emptiness in part of the room.

Have justification for movement. There's the old chestnut about the actor who, when told to go to a particular spot by a director, asks, "What's my motivation?" to which the director snaps, "Your paycheck. Now move!" Motivation is in fact a very serious issue for you; it's just that you shouldn't depend on a director to supply it. The director may want you to go to the window because there's some particular stage picture they have in mind. Whatever their reason, it's going to be your job to execute what is required and make it look natural.

The best motivation for a movement is a task. It could be picking up something or putting something down, it could be straightening something or cleaning something, it may be to inspect something curious. A cross to the window might be motivated by an interest in the weather because there is an upcoming event for which rain would be bad. The task needn't be completed; maybe your character goes to do it and then is interrupted. It isn't even necessary for the audience to know exactly what the motivation is, for that matter, only that they feel that you, as the character, know your motivation, and that it unfolds truthfully.

Another justification for movement might be that your character has an impulse that causes a rush of energy that is expressed in movement.

This movement can then carry you to exactly where the director wants you to go. It might be some external event that happens to you that creates the impulse, or it might be a new thought that gives a jolt of new energy to justify the movement: "It's always the same with you." (At this point the swell of irritation from the past frustrations energizes a move to the table where your hands are pressed on a chair back) "I'm sick of it."

It might be that the energy to motivate a move comes from an impulse after your character has finished speaking and the Action is expressed physically. You have, in a sense, run out of words and must finish the thing you were doing with its physical expression.

Look first where you're going. This might seem an odd recommendation, since it is fundamental to normal movement to look where you're going, but you're going to have to deal with anticipation and the non-reality of things as lived within imaginary reality. You're usually going to know exactly where and when you sit because, unlike your character, you've sat there many times at this precise moment in rehearsal or production. You have to therefore be sure to let your eyes move to where you're going to sit or at whatever you're going to touch, even if it's just for a fraction of a second.

Speak and move at the same time. This is another odd suggestion on the face of it, given this is what you always do in real life, but on stage with the awful fear that you might do something wrong constantly haunting you, it's very possible you'll try to box everything up in to manageable units. Over and over I see an actor say a line, then pause, then do their activity, such as sit or set something down or pick up a book, and then, and only then, do they deliver their next line. Let it flow together, easily, fluidly. Live, my child.

PROPS, COSTUME, AND THE SET

Know about the things you use. It's your responsibility to be thoroughly knowledgeable about the costume and props you're going use. Not only in the obvious case where your character is intimately aware of their personal property: even when you're playing someone who's unfamiliar with a prop, you'll need to know exactly how to deal with it so you're in control and don't get thrown off guard in such a way as to interfere with the smooth running of the production.

Walk the set! It's highly recommended that you check the placement and condition of your costume, personal hand props, furniture you use and the surfaces you're going to be touching as close to curtain time as possible. I say surfaces you'll be touching because there may be spilled water that can be slippery, and because set technicians are particularly fond of their paint and using it to cover over smudges on a set. You, not knowing this paint has been applied, will lean against a wall during the performance and then step away with a lovely stripe of paint on your costume.

There may be a new throw rug that someone thought would be just the right touch to add, and you, again, ignorant of the new change, make your brisk entrance, and have this rug slide out from under you, dropping you on your keister. A costumer may have felt the line of your slacks would be improved if a pocket were sewn shut, unaware that this was the pocket you were using to quickly hide a love letter during a scene.

Practical props will have to be checked early enough for them to be placed, and though the set may be "hot," with everything in the exact location it's meant to be in at the beginning of the show, you can tiptoe around and check things as long as you leave them undisturbed.

Walking the set is crucial if you're a stage actor, because you can find yourself on stage with a house full of expectant faces watching you reach for that gun in the drawer that isn't there tonight, and it just isn't as threatening when you use a ballpoint pen. But even if you're acting in film, where you have the luxury of starting over again if there's a mistake, you might want to ensure a great take isn't lost for some technical reason.

Beware physical objects. Complications must be expected with all costume, props and furniture. Long dresses get stepped on, lighters won't light, and flimsy tables break when leaned on. You should try and consider every possible mishap that can occur with each thing you use, and know that what you don't anticipate might come back and bite you.

Some props are outstandingly problematic and, if they can't be replaced, you must red-flag them and constantly be vigilant to their idiosyncrasies. Cords of all kinds get tripped over, snagged and generally cause mayhem. Phone cords can be the most troubling of these (remember phone cords?), as when, in the middle of a phone call on stage, it pulls out from the wall and you continue with your now absurdly impossible conversation.

Acknowledge and remedy mistakes. Should something go wrong, you have to fix it. This also might seem like the most natural thing in the world, and yet in the adrenaline-charged environment of the stage it's easy for you to go into a kind of panic/denial and ignore the awkward mistake as if it never happened. This then leaves that dropped book of matches, or that bunched up throw rug you just tripped over, as testimonial to the unreality of everything that's taking place.

If something drops, you have to pick it up, and not just kick it behind the sofa or into the wings. If you bunch up the rug, you have to take the time to straighten it. Yes, it may be a pain in the butt, but you have to do as the character would do, or everything that follows will be corrupted in the mind of the audience by this falseness.

Besides, it can be these very accidents that you effectively deal with that gives your audience the thrill of live theater, and they'll feel privileged to have been there the night something went sideways.

Take note of the lighting. While lighting is much less a direct concern for you than props and costume, you should nonetheless have some sense of the lighting on the stage that you're working on. There may be a simple lighting scheme or very involved lighting, but the basic issue is where on stage are the areas that are brightest and darkest. What's mainly of concern for you is how well your face is lit, especially your eyes.

You can use the seam between a bright area and a darker one for theatrical effect, casting a dynamic shadow on your face or revealing brightness at a dramatic moment out of shadow.

STAGE BUSINESS OPTIONS

Enter with a continuation of a physical action. A good technique for conveying the reality of life is to make an entrance finishing doing something that you'd started prior to entering. Come on stage tucking in a shirt, straightening a belt, putting away a pen, glasses, or a handkerchief. Actors don't think about doing this because they're all geared up just for that time when the audience is going to see them, and they don't consider that their character might have actually had an ongoing life offstage. But not you, right? Not anymore.

Your physical action might be chosen first from something that's carried over from a logical prior activity: having just gotten off the train, you enter folding the newspaper you were reading; coming in after a cab ride, you enter putting your wallet away that you had out to pay the driver. The audience needn't even know exactly what it was that was taking place prior to your character's arrival for this technique to give your work that reality of a life lived.

Enter in disarray to display ongoing emotionality. Entering in an unkempt condition can communicate that your character is experiencing high emotion, happy, sad, or angry. This is because a person may not prioritize their appearance when emotionally preoccupied. You can make weak efforts to straighten yourself, and then abandon them, all the more illuminating your charged emotional state.

Women can have imperfect facial makeup, running mascara or smeared lipstick that can even give the impression that the nose area is reddened from upset.

Interrupt behaviors. Another effective way for you to represent real life is to go do something, and then for some reason not follow through with it. This is another thing actors won't think to do because they've set so concretely for themselves everything that they're going to do. People constantly interrupt their behaviors in life, but given that you know at the outset exactly what tasks you're going to finish or not, you'll tend to have none of these false starts. An interrupted behavior might be going to set something down, then not, going to sit or stand, then not, going to take a sip, then not, and here's something actors really tend not to do that happens all the time in life, be about to speak, then not.

Interrupted behaviors are really good at communicating changes of Actions. The original behavior, being part of the original Action, is stopped when the Action changes to a new undertaking. You might be having a casual conversation until your spouse says that they've made a large purchase today, at which point the sip of wine you were about to take stalls, and you then set your glass down and confront them about their spending habits.

In this same way, interrupted behaviors can also function as nifty punctuation moments for the ends of scenes, what are called "buttons." This can be done when the scene ends and, say, your character is left unsure of what or how to proceed with their life now, so you go to do something and then stop, either out of distraction or overwhelm.

WORKING WITH TELEPHONES

Create the reality of an actual conversation. To give the impression that a conversation is taking place on the telephone, when in fact there is no one on the other end of the line, it's really all about just acting well and creating a specific Relationship with whoever is supposed to be on the phone with you. Technically, you have to give the imaginary person enough time to answer the phone or to say what they might say during the conversation, but usually, in order to move things along, it should only be the minimum amount of time it would take for them to do this.

In life we constantly interrupt each other, and you'll seem more real on the phone if you interrupt the other person, or look as if attempting to. When interrupting someone who's speaking, you tend to go louder at the beginning of your sentence, and sometimes you just vocalize the first syllable of your first word and hold, the signal we give each other that an interruption is being attempted.

Another good representation of life on the telephone is to laugh or otherwise respond emotionally to what the person is saying, even if the audience doesn't know specifically what it is you're responding to.

Don't cover your mouth with the phone. It's a good idea to hold the mouthpiece for the phone maybe lower than you would normally, to keep it from blocking projection, but, more than anything, so the audience can read your lips.

Use low numbers on a dial phone. If it's a period piece with a dial phone, it's good to dial an imaginary phone number that is made up of low numbers so you can speed up the proceedings by avoiding the long time it takes for a dial phone to cycle back from the higher numbers to the beginning position.

WORKING WITH ELECTRICAL SWITCHES (NON-PRACTICAL)

Non-practical switches on stage, such as a light switch or a stereo, are in fact useless and a technician is controlling the operation of whatever the thing is. This can present a problem of timing when you seem to be activating it and the timing is off. If you flip a switch and there is a delay before activation, it shatters the reality of that moment.

Cover the switch and look away. It's good to cover the entire switch with your hand and look away so that the audience can't see exactly when the switch has been moved and so you're not seen to be oddly staring at a switch that you're not activating. In this way, if there is a delay in it turning on or off, it will be attributed to your character's absentmindedness.

Don't block the technician's view. Come on now, get out of the way so the technician can see the damn switch and activate whatever he needs to activate when you flip that non-practical switch on stage.

WORKING WITH CIGARETTES

As smoking has become less acceptable in our society, it's become less welcome on stage as well. Maybe it's not your job, but if you want to avoid the gasps of horror and incensed mutterings of outraged smoke-o-phobes in the audience, I recommend adequate ventilation and warning signs in the lobby so it doesn't come as a shock when a cigarette is taken out on stage.

Pull hard on the first puff. Lighting a cigarette, if done hastily, can end up requiring multiple lightings, causing a delay that will make your character look less like the suave detective you intend them to be, and more like Inspector Clouseau. Pull very firmly on the first puff so both you and the audience can tell your cigarette is well lit.

Favor lighters. Matches are prone to malfunctioning, either not lighting at all or throwing off distracting burning pieces, and they also require two hands to operate. If the period and situation allows, it's better to use a lighter.

Have a tray and tap the ash often. Ashtrays should be strategically placed so you won't have to make long trips across the room at inopportune moments in order to remove the ash. Also, a long ash, unless used for effect, can be very distracting for an audience that will become less involved with the story and more gripped by that ash and when it's going to fall.

chapter 2

Film and Television

BE PREPARED

Every film and television program evolves as a function of three stages. First there's preproduction, where preparations are made, assembling the necessary ingredients, such as the script, the actors, the crew, the locations. Secondly, there is principal photography, recording on film or tape the necessary pieces, and finally postproduction, the editing, the adding of sound effects, special effects and music, and so forth.

While you may be involved in preproduction, rehearsing with the cast and the director, and there may be some postproduction work that requires you to go into a studio and dub dialog, in the vast majority of cases, rehearsal time in film and television is very brief, postproduction work minimal, and your only substantive working contact with a production is for the time when you're performing for the camera.

Show up ready to act. Because of limited rehearsal time, you need to be especially self-sufficient in the development of your role. There may be a reading of the entire script with the other actors, personal time with the director for rehearsing specific scenes and rehearsals for the technical aspects of the production with the cameras, but the reality is you should expect to show up on the set and act the part without any outside input. I did four scenes with Virginia Madsen in a movie and the only time we acted together was when the camera was rolling.

It's highly recommended that you do what it takes to become intensely familiar with the script as a whole, because in this way you can remain oriented when scenes are filmed out of order, as they usually are.

Be intensely prepared or go with the first spirit of connection. There can be an awkward stage that arises after working on a part for a period of time, specifically in the development of a character different from yourself. At the beginning of the process there is often a wonderful freedom and intuitiveness, then, with more intensive work, the performance can bog down and needs to be worked through. Once fully constructed, the part then has a substantive quality that the beginning, fresh version in no way possessed, but you might have to go through a difficult stage to get to virtuosity.

In movies, usually without much group rehearsal, you must do the hard work all on your own and be able to smooth out most of the roughness before filming begins.

It pains me to say this, but if there is a shortage of time to prepare, given that film particularly favors a performer with an uncluttered mind, it might be preferable to devote your efforts, not so much toward building a fully three-dimensional character, so much as learning your lines cold, preparing very deeply emotionally, and getting mentally ready to have maximum freedom with the part.

LOVE THE CAMERA

Have a love affair with the camera. That black lens of the camera is your audience of one. That's the only reason you're there and you should know it really has nothing to do with anybody on the set. You can use the psyche you have found effective with any audience you worked for (you might be the kind of actor who likes it a little antagonistic: "I am going to break them down!" or one who connects to them as loving souls), but it's always some kind of intimate relationship.

You should feel that lens gently pulling at you, at your most essential nature, pulling the best from you. You do well to know that, as long as you're honest and true, the camera will support and nurture you.

Stay intimate. With the sense of the single small eye of the camera being your audience entire, you should maintain maximum intimacy with that audience and not slip into old habits of projecting out into a big house.

BE PRESENT

Emphasize being in the moment. When James Cagney was asked what the most important thing in acting was, he answered, "Don't get caught doing it." This is very much the case in most film acting where the style tends to be naturalistic, and, free from the obligation of projecting your performance to the back of a large theater, it's key for you to be relaxed and nuanced, always fluid and relating deeply and continuously.

With work on the stage it's critically important for you to guide the audience's attention through the play, but in film and television an audience's attention is controlled by the editing. Therefore, the emphasis for you shifts from being clear about where your attention is directed, to being truthful and present. The main priority in most film acting is not to look like you're acting.

Don't say much. A general recommendation for all acting, but especially for film is, "Speak as quickly as you can and act as slowly as you can." What this means is that, because being in the moment and telling the truth are the supreme values when you're on camera, it's good to de-emphasize the words. You want to reduce excessive animation, especially in close up, and not feel at all that you have to sell what you're saying.

There are exceptions to this, of course, but for the most part the value of what is said should be minimized and communicated with a powerful sub-textual intent. What's being expressed is projected on a deep, nonverbal level, and the words issue simply and freely out of the experience.

In order to do this, to be fully present in the moment and concentrating on projecting intent, you have to have your lines memorized cold, cold, cold.

Think loudly. The camera, especially in close up, has the ability to capture the process of thinking — so give it a show. Burn those thoughts at a high wattage.

APPRECIATE THE MOMENT OF NEW RESPONSE

Get caught reacting. While being reactive is fundamental to all acting, there are some special techniques for camera work. Reactions are the most powerful aspect of film acting, and particularly that moment when an event touches your character's heart for the first time and changes their life. In this way you want to have a pure response from the event and how it affects you. Film stars have been known to give away dialog to innocently grateful secondary actors who then later hear these lines of exposition droning away on the soundtrack while the camera lingers on the star's soulful reaction.

Delay your response until it's time to speak. There is a tendency for the acting that comes before and after a line to be cut out of the final edit, especially if your role is not a leading one. Therefore, to guarantee that this fresh moment of reacting makes the final cut, you might tend to save important reactions until just before you speak. Let's say the character opposite you says, "Your brother is dead. I'm sorry, we did everything we could." Even though you'd normally begin your response to his death immediately after the first sentence is spoken, in order to make sure your initial reaction makes it into the film, wait until the other character finishes speaking before you begin to have your initial response to the news of his death, just as you start saying your line. Remember to speak as your reaction begins, otherwise there's a good chance that initial reaction will be cut.

You don't have to worry too much that the audience is going to notice this delay and think it strange. Film reality distorts time so much, slowing it down, speeding it up, chopping it apart, that even the most outrageous delays — as with the typical, descending security door that takes forever to close — are usually forgiven, if not completely unnoticed.

Always be responding. This advice on occasionally delaying a response for a major moment is not meant to suggest that you remain blank faced and passive until it's your turn to speak; you have to always be cautious to avoid the major acting fault of indicating your responses instead of really having them. It's good to be reacting all the time, giving the editor plenty of reaction shots of your character while others are speaking. This delayed reaction is only a suggestion for big moments.

USE THE EYES

The moment of reaction is typically the most important aspect of film acting and the eyes are the most important feature to transmit that response. With this in mind, you can have a sense of using your eyes dramatically. By the same token, lapses in concentration are most profoundly reflected in the eyes.

Act with the eyes. For effect you may deny the camera your eyes and then reveal them, or let the camera's movement find your eyes. You might want to know where your eye light is going to be, the specific fixture called a "Tweeny," so that you can catch that light with your eyes, or, less frequently, use the shadow.

Keep your eyes relaxed. It's especially important for those tight close ups to have all the muscles surrounding your eyeballs nice and relaxed. This is where the acting fault of bewilderment, disbelief, and astonishment can hurt you by giving you a squinty, strained quality there. However bizarre the event, let it be awesome, let it be ghastly, but don't filter it with tension in your eyes. Let it in… let it in.

Keep the gaze steady. It's usually preferable to maintain a sense of calm with your eyes. Another old, film acting tip is "Look 'em in the eye and tell the truth." While in life it's normal to look back and forth at both of someone's eyes and down at and their mouth as you speak to them, it's best for you to maintain your the attention on only one of the opposite character's eyes when connecting with them. When you're in frame, and the other actor is opposite you standing next to the camera, it's best for you to look at the other actor's eye that is closest to the lens.

When doing a scene with more than one person, it's usually best to constantly watch the person who is speaking. In this way, the editor has a strong, consistent look to use of your character absorbing what's being said. This means not doing what is normal and looking frequently at the other person or persons also being spoken to, checking in with their reactions to what is being said, unless it's for a singularly important moment where your character would want to see what their reaction is.

Flash looks. On the other hand, it can be good to strategically dart periodic, reactive looks at people and events so that the editor can use these as a way to cut to those people and events, should you sense that that's where a cut would go.

Shift the eye line while the lids are closed. This is an old trick and, truthfully, runs the risk of coming off as a bit corny, but it can still be effective, if used right, to convey enigmatic thoughtfulness. It's when you're looking in one direction and then you close your eyes in a slow blink, and while your lids are down, move your the eye line so that when the lids are raised, your eyes are looking in another direction.

PROJECT A NARROWING POINT OF FOCUS

In the reverse from performing for the large venue of a theater, in film and television, with the camera's individual eye alone as your audience, it's good for you to have a sense of bringing things down to a small point.

Project to the distance of the lens. The amount of your expressive projection depends on the size of the framing. For the most part, with a camera as your audience you're completely freed from a concern for the projection of your performance, and you can simply speak as you would in life to the characters playing opposite you. Beyond this, you might even minimize further to the intimacy of the frame and go less expansive than you normally would in life if you were speaking to someone at a given distance. A rough way to calibrate how much you should project your performance would be to gauge as follows: A Long Shot (three or four full people in the frame) should be done in a style consistent with a theater of twenty audience members; a Medium Shot (from the feet and up) should be done as if for someone ten feet away; a Medium Close Up (rib cage and up) should be done as if two feet from one person; an Extreme Close Up (chin and up) just think out loud, as if the other person can read your mind.

You can learn the size of the shot by asking the director of photography (DP). It's not necessary, and probably isn't advisable, to disturb the director with this question; the DP wants to create attractive pictures so they'll usually be eager to tell you the framing.

Speak to the boom microphone. Another way of modulating your performance is in relation to the volume used, and in this way you might choose to project only to the distance of the boom microphone, which is usually held just out of frame. If you adjust your volume, and the resultant expansiveness of your expression, to the distance of the boom microphone, you'll have appropriately adjusted the performance to the size of the shot.

Don't worry about impractical volume. This ratio of expansiveness to the size of the frame can be used regardless of how far away the other characters are in the scene. It doesn't make literal sense to speak as if the other person is only two feet away when they're supposed to be twenty feet away in the scene being played, but using this lower volume is nonetheless the way you'll tend to be most effective on film in the close up, because, once again, the altered reality through which we experience film, as if it's a dream, allows for this distortion of space in the same way it allows the distortion of time.

Beware of doing things when you feel the camera cut to you. Just as you should be already acting by the time "Action!" is called out, in the case of multiple cameras, you should not suddenly leap into performance mode when you feel the camera cut to you. This can produce tense and unnatural behaviors that are particularly undesirable in close up such as flaring nostrils, widening of the eyes, lifting the eyebrows, or tensing of the mouth.

APPRECIATE THE FRAME

Because framing will vary in size, and because of the different perspectives that different lenses create, you can accommodate these realities to create a more effective film performance.

Work within the frame. You might want to operate in front of the camera as if there is a carpet stretching out in front of the lens and you want to be on it and seen. This means you may need to cheat out from behind people or objects, and perhaps accept bunching up with other performers as part of the necessary reality.

All things being equal, it's good to have your hands in the picture. This may mean that they will need to be held higher or closer to the body than would be normal.

Beware moving out of frame. Although Steadicams and handheld cameras are relied upon for staying close and following the action, you might use caution in moving too quickly to be followed by the camera. This can be distinctly problematic in standing up or sitting down where it's easy to drop or lurch out of frame. One way of controlling this movement is to put one of your feet deep under your chair in order to better ease a descent onto the seat or to rise steadily out of one when you stand.

Moving past a fixed camera can also cause problems because, due to the perspective, the closer something gets to the lens, the quicker it will appear to move. Because of this it is perhaps best to go slower as you get nearer a fixed camera.

Be aware of how you're moving into the frame. Because of the peculiar quality of the lens, when you move into frame, as opposed to when the camera moves to find you, this can have an odd effect, giving this sudden appearance a kind of arch bluntness. If this is the case, you might wish to project a softer affect than might otherwise be used.

Because moving into frame can be so austere, there is a technique for showing less of the face and more of the back of the head at first appearance, moving into frame, then turning to reveal more face.

Werner Herzog described a technique used by Klaus Kinski to capitalize on the odd quality of this lens effect by pivoting into frame. He would stay out of frame, but plant a foot, on the leg closest the camera, in front of the camera in such a way that it required an awkward twisting of the torso to remain off to the side of the lens. Then, on "Action!" he would move into frame, first in three quarters turned away, and then his body would turn to stand directly over the planted foot using a controlled twist from profile to a more full shot of the face.

Don't spend it on the masters. The reality of most film work is that master shots, large framings that include all of the players, are usually done and the entire scene filmed in these large perspectives, but it's very unlikely these large-size shots will be used in the final film for anything but the beginnings and ends of scenes. Because of this, you may want to emphasize different acting values in the wide shots, such as the use of the environment, and save your major emotional work for the tighter close ups.

APPRECIATE SOUND

Avoid looping. You should do whatever you can to help get good dialog recorded at the time the picture is filmed. If, for whatever reason, the dialog recorded on the set can't be used, you'll be asked to go into a studio and loop your dialog, but this is almost never as desirable as getting the actual dialog that is recorded during the scene, because looped dialog will tend to sound just like what it is, disembodied and not of the experience.

Avoid overlapping dialog. Overlapping dialog tends to be problematic when working with recorded sound. While overlapping can be great on stage, when you hear overlapping dialog in a movie, it has often been overlapped electronically later in a studio. Two voices speaking together on tape can compress in such a way as to make the words unintelligible.

Without losing energy or pacing, and still picking up cues, you should allow at least a fraction of a second of silence after another character speaks before you're heard.

Don't make noises that interfere with the dialog. You want to avoid making noises that cover dialog on the soundtrack. Even small noises can ruin sound, especially when using low vocal levels.

Such ordinary things as rattling keys, a closing door, a squeaky chair, or rustling clothing can make it impossible to understand what you're saying. Scenes at meals can be a problem because of the clatter of clinking glasses and silverware and things getting set down.

You shouldn't have to tip-toe and move about gingerly on a set, but you should have an awareness of when not to create interfering noise.

KNOW THE SET

The same basic principles of staging apply when working in film and television and this includes the use of the set as well. An actor should still be eager to "walk the set," although Assistant Directors are even more concerned than Stage Managers that once everything is in its proper place on the set, and it is "hot," that it not be tampered with due to the issue of maintaining continuity.

Study the set. Because of the limited rehearsal time available for film work, it's possible you won't get to rehearse on the set until the day you're actually shooting. You may therefore need to study the set in private, probably while technicians are moving lights around. You may find that the file cabinet sticks, and you can ask that it be oiled; you may find that there is a chair in the way of the window you were supposed to look out, and you'll ask if it can be moved; and on and on.

Familiarity is going to be especially important for you if your character is supposed to be familiar with the location.

Practice hitting marks. You may be called upon to walk while being filmed and then to stop at a specific location, and the technicians composing the shot will want this location to be made definite so they can set focus properly. The camera operator will usually indicate this desired spot on the floor by placing a piece of colored tape there. This tape is of little or no use to you. Looking at the ground when you approach the general area where you're supposed to stop is usually unnatural in the extreme, and a behavior nearly impossible to finesse.

A good remedy for hitting a mark without looking down is to request that a sandbag be placed on the mark (sandbags are common objects on sets because they're used for stabilizing equipment). Having this sandbag will enable you to find your mark by feeling it with your foot, and it won't make noise when your foot touches it.

Another way to locate your mark is to find, or place, two reference points that are high enough to be seen with your peripheral vision, for example a door frame and a light stand, with your mark exactly between these. As you approach these higher, visible marks you'll know when you're getting close to, and then hitting, the proper spot.

WORK WITH PROPS

Use props when possible. Using props can be extremely effective in film. They may have something to do with the location and its inherent activities, such as a toothpick, a rubber band, the label on a bottle, a rear-view mirror, or they may be small personal props such as a watch, a wallet, a pair of glasses, clothing, or a piece of jewelry.

Film favors these small props because they provide interesting, intimate behavior.

Oh, and it's nerve-racking as hell to work with props so you won't want to do it. Acting in the intense, pressure-cooker environment that is life in front of the camera, you're going to want to strip away all non-essentials so you can square up, and take on the serious acting at hand. It can feel a little like waiting to have a baseball thrown at your face, and you're inclined to want to trade lines until the madness is over. You won't want to sip a cup of coffee, you won't want to get a mint out of your purse, you won't want to crumple and toss a piece of paper away.

You need to allow yourself greater overall ease while you're acting, greater command. Rehearse as much as possible with your props.

APPRECIATE CONTINUITY

A film or a television program is a collection of recorded pieces of material that have been edited together to form a coherent presentation. This means that shooting will stop and start, and there may be a separation of several minutes to several weeks between filming what will appear in the final product as part of a continuum. A film shot over the course of three months may on screen represent the events of a single day.

Continuity is an issue because there will be several different versions, takes, filmed of the same event by the same actors, and the editor wants to be able to choose from these different versions. There may be different angles, or different sizes of framing, or different qualities of performance, but it's all meant to look as if one single event has been captured on film.

Do the same physical things on the same moments. If you cross your arms when you first mention "John" in a scene, then every time you subsequently do the same scene you should cross your arms at that same moment. Even in a tightly framed shot, when the arms are out of frame, that crossing of the arms will effect the position of your shoulders.

You can reinvest in the emotional values in the scene, you can alter the levels of intentions and their expansiveness according to the framing of the shot, but you shouldn't change your basic physical movements.

Not only will matching ensure your footage can be used, the editor will likely notice you as an actor who is helping them in their job and this may incline them to return the favor. And an editor has great power to do well by an actor they like.

Don't let matching dictate performance. As important as it is to have all the versions of a scene capable of being used, it is much more important to have an excellent performance. You should be mindful of matching when you can, certainly, but just as certainly you should do what the artistic spirit insistently moves you to do.

As much as an editor likes to have the option to select from every piece of footage in front of them, any good editor is more than willing to accommodate for a brilliant performance.

This is your personal path to tread between the disciplined and the wildly inspired. Just know that should you be given to being undisciplined, you better be pretty sure you're quite inspired.

Create a physical behavior that carries over from the previous scene. A good way to create a sense of continuity is to enter with a continuation of a physical activity logically linked to the previous scene in the story. If the previous scene was a long car ride, you can then be stretching your lower back or straightening your clothes; if the previous scene was a restaurant, you can be brushing crumbs off your clothing or dealing with food in your teeth or putting your wallet away when you enter; if you were outside in the cold, you can create a sense of this as well.

While the truth is that the scene that follows immediately in a continuation in your film may in fact have been shot three weeks ago, or won't be shot for another three weeks to come, you want it to appear as a natural part of a continuum, so you want to have a sense of this and plan to connect them with both your emotional and your physical life.

Know in a given scene where you are in a changing condition. Because of the issue of shooting out of sequence, it can be particularly tricky to perform a developing condition in a film. Some changing conditions might be physical, such as an injury that gets worse or better, drunkenness that becomes more or less sober. It could be a developing emotional condition such as depression or obsession.

A good way for you to establish the level of these conditions for yourself is to practice the condition as it escalates from the least to the most extreme, and with this sense of the progression, establish the degrees of severity for yourself in some way, perhaps with the use of a tape recorder or a video camera. These levels might then be given a number value, say, between one and ten. You then look at the entire script and choose the degree that your condition is affecting you in each scene and mark it accordingly. This number can then be referenced for when a scene is to be done and rehearsed.

Rehearse the last thing done. At some point, relatively close to when actual shooting is to be done, it's a good idea to thoroughly go over what has just happened prior to this scene. If you can get together with the other actor or actors who might be in that prior scene for a rehearsal or an improvisation, so much the better, whether it's an actual scene where the lines from that scene can be run, or one that was implied, though never actually written and the lines are ad-libbed. At the very least, revisit it in your imagination for yourself.

KEEP A GOOD OUTLOOK

It's just acting, do your work. Sometimes amid all the madness and expenditure and the sense that what's being done is being recorded for history, you can feel extremely pressured. Don't. The entire apparatus and all of the personnel are there to simply record an event. It might be a big event with explosions and stunts, or it might be a subtle event where your character goes through a small, personal transformation. Good acting is good acting and you just need to rely on your fundamentals and trust yourself.

Let it go, but fear no retake. Upon hearing the word "Cut!" you'll wait to hear how the scene was received. Maybe you're one of those actors who always feels they can do it better if they have another chance, and you must be willing to trust the eyes of others and surrender and move on. Maybe you're one of those who upon hearing "Let's do it again" winces and fears they will never do a take as good as that one, and you have to learn to believe that you can always do it better, and look forward to every opportunity to have more experience working in front of the camera.

Don't waste energy. While it's rare to work on a play for twelve hours straight, a workday on movies can easily be that long, or longer. Because of this, and because during this time you'll be performing the material that is actually going to be seen in the final product, you should conserve your energy on the set.

It's easy to be social, and there may be the excitement of acting in an interesting location with these creative people, and it's getting toward the end of the day and you've been snacking a lot, because the Craft Service table with all those snacks is constantly beckoning you, and then they call you to the set for your important scene, and, as you're walking there, only now does the exhaustion hit. Too late, Grasshopper. You should have been saving yourself all day.

chapter 3

Comedy

There is no fundamental difference between performing a drama and performing a comedy. On the other hand there is a huge difference — not fundamental, but huge. You have to make people laugh. And there are all kinds of laughs. The tickled giggle of silliness or the warm chuckle of sympathy; laughs where people fall backward with a hoot of amazement, or laughs where they fall forward in agreement and recognition; laughs where they don't actually laugh, but are wonderfully amused, and laughs where they make a lot of noise, but it comes from the throat and afterwards they don't recommend anyone go see that show.

Comedy will tend to veer further stylistically from naturalism more often than drama, and, because of this, if it's broad enough, it can forgive a performance missing in the values you get from a truly quality performance. I'm guessing, and hoping, that along with the laughter you'd like some delight and gratification to go along with what you're presenting and that requires you do the only kind of acting there really is, good acting.

HAVE A SENSE OF HUMOR

Know what's funny, but don't try to be funny. Part of what makes a comedic performance funny is the feeling the audience gets that you have a sense of humor and that you're using it. It often hurts comedy if you work too hard for a specific laugh, as opposed to creating an environment of humor. You ought to convey a feeling that you're using your sense of humor in a way that it takes in the entire show, not just joke by joke.

With comedy you should give the impression that, even if you're playing someone who is unhappily the brunt of a joke, everything is bathed in the light of humor.

Have a light, human touch. While comedy should be as fully fleshed out and lived through as drama, you ought to nonetheless have a sense that what's being conveyed is the humorous side of life with an appreciation that it's a silly, ironic or satirical angle taken on the human condition. The piece may have genuine depth, but comedy's function is to render the sparkling highlights off the surface.

By the same token, there ought to be a loving and charitable wink at what makes people tick. Comedy might be an angled approach, skewed with a kind of distance, but you have to maintain closeness with the beating heart of what it is to be human. Much of what makes a situation comedic is the tension between the artificiality of manners, obligations and expectations of society, and the true nature of the people trapped within these constraints. In order for comedy to be gratifying, you have to communicate compassion and respect for your character's universality.

Athene Seyler said it well: "Have a fastidious ear and a simple heart."

Play up to the audience, but don't be afraid of anything. It's your responsibility to aspire to the highest level of the sublime, and with comedy this is no exception. The sense of humor can be considered one of our higher attributes, and it needn't be exclusively witty or ironic humor: even the most lowbrow humor can have something exquisite in it. You should extend the best of who you are and seek to take the audience into your confidence.

And it's perfectly all right to assault them, insist they respond, hit them where it hurts. Just as with all acting, comedic acting should be fearless. That is, there should be no lengths to which you won't go to be more effective. You have to be ready to be totally free, even spectacularly outrageous. There's something wonderfully theatrical in seeing someone willing to go to extravagant lengths for the sake of pure silliness.

BE CLEAR AND VIBRANT

Be heard! Beyond timing or wit, this might be the most important tip of all for comedy. Obviously it's vital for comedic moments that are based on the witticism of the words themselves, but it's also key in having an audience humorously inclined that they not be put off, struggling to hear the dialog and made unhappy that they're missing something.

It's crucial that your audience hear each word of the dialog. Of course, this is not to say that you should shout through your performance, only that you use enough vocal projection and clear enunciation so that what you say can be heard without effort.

If you're no longer getting a laugh on a line where once you did, this is the first place to look. And if the joke line can be heard, next you should check to see if the set up lines are being heard. Intelligibility is also essential for the feed lines and don't mistakenly think of these as less critical because the laugh doesn't immediately following them. The wit of the joke or the humorous character trait revealed has everything to do with the context the feed line provides.

Keep the pace dynamic. You should be as relaxed as possible, but use as much energy as the part can contain. Responses, if not the cues themselves, should be vigorous, quick and reactive. There should generally be an increasing escalation of tone, a constant topping of the last moment played. A pause or dip in your intention, which might be just a bit of a stumble in a straight drama, can destroy the pacing in a comedy that is necessary to make it work.

Dynamic pacing by itself communicates to an audience that they are in the hands of a performer who is assured, and this assuredness allows them to relax and enjoy the show. It also gives a sense of momentum, and this momentum creates a kind of tension that the audience will pleasantly release through laughing.

Escalation, like everything, can be carried to an extreme and I've seen sitcoms that I just know were coached by sitcom specialists who had the actors escalating inorganically like screaming meemies, trying to top each other with such manic intention it obliterated their humanity, and hence, any real humor.

Maintain the rhythm. It is especially important to keep the rhythm of a funny line. When delivering funny dialog it's usually good to keep the rhythm of the line consistent through the last word.

Also, listing things or laying out a series of some kind can be funny if the rhythm is consistently maintained: "I come home, I open the door, the dog is in my chair." In *The Odd Couple*, Felix asks Oscar why he's evicting him from the apartment: "What is it? The cooking, the cleaning, the crying?" To which Oscar responds, "I'll tell you exactly what it is. It's the cooking, the cleaning, the crying." If the actor playing either Felix or Oscar breaks up the rhythm of that list it will lose the humor. I have no idea why.

USE CHARACTER ADJUSTMENTS

The vast majority of comedy is based on character, and what makes a character funny to an audience is mostly their disproportionate reactions, both too big and too small.

Exaggerate something small. If your character cares too much about something the audience knows isn't that important, there is comedy in this discrepancy. It might be caring too much about someone's admiration, or a desperate competitiveness, or becoming incredibly upset because of losing an object that is purely symbolic.

In *The Four Seasons*, an expensive car cracks through the ice on a frozen lake and sinks and it's played for humor as the owner, the actor Jack Weston, goes to his knees and cries, "My Mercedes!" We laugh because we know it's just a car. It wouldn't be so funny if there was a puppy in it and a little boy going, "Rusty!" as it sunk in the lake. Well, maybe some of you sick bastards would find it funny, but not us nice people.

Minimize something significant. Another character adjustment is to undervalue something for which the universal response should be greater. If a slob treats an enormous mess as if it can be tidied up with a few casual efforts, or a drunk relates to mortal danger as if it's a simple inconvenience.

Undervaluing the significance of events will often style the comedy as dark by portraying a character as callous, as when someone discussing their painful divorce is interrupted by a cad and asked if they will please pass the salt, or a sleazebag treats a funeral as an opportunity for a romantic pickup.

FINESSE THE JOKES

Punctuate laugh lines with small activities. Upon finishing a punch line, it's effective to do an activity of some kind so that the joke isn't just hanging there in space. These activities can be continuations of something that was interrupted by your delivering the line, as when you're going to drink some coffee as someone else is delivering the set up line, you pause, the cup poised by your mouth, say the joke line, then sip your coffee. Maybe you're looking for something — a paper on your desk or in one of your pockets — you stop, say the line, then continue your search.

The behaviors can be whole new activities that you start after the joke line is said, often with the quality that your character has just been distracted by something or struck with an idea that pulls them away from waiting on the joke. For example, you're involved in a conversation in a restaurant, you say a joke and then suddenly spot the waitress and go to call her over, perhaps you're even unsuccessful in getting her attention. Or you say the joke, then act as if you just remembered you need to call someone and, holding a finger up to indicate to the other character that they have to hold their thought for a moment, as you go for your phone.

This continuation behavior helps take any preciousness off a joke and often demonstrates that you accept such absurdity as the norm of life. You can see this technique performed by stand-up comedians who, upon saying a joke, will then continue with, "But, you know," even though they never finish that sentence of that pretended new thought. Some stand-up comics do it by puffing on a cigar or taking a sip of a cocktail.

If you don't have any dialog after a laugh line, you can still create this sense of continuation by having your character go to speak, then stop themselves, perhaps with a shrug or in firm determination not to say any more.

Sometimes it's enough to simply punctuate the laugh line with a relaxed, wistful half turn of your head.

Don't do anything after a joke. There is also the possibility that the best thing to do after a joke is absolutely nothing, actually freeze. This is the case in much of what is called "deadpan humor." You may be playing a character who has a flattened affect and, after a joke line, you do nothing but hold with the sense that you have nowhere to go, and as if staring at them or straight out is as good as anywhere else to rest your baleful eyes. Or you might be playing someone simple minded, in which case you're holding on them is a hopeful waiting on their response.

It might be good to hold after a line because it's clear from the context exactly what your character would be thinking in that moment, and you don't want to interfere with the audience projecting it onto you.

Sell the other guy's joke. Key to making a laugh line work can be how you respond to it on stage, and to do that you have to be clear if your character registers the humor in it or not. On the television show *Friends*, the character of Joey, something of a simpleton, more often than not didn't know that what was being said was funny, while the character of Chandler almost always did. If your character doesn't get the humor, you nonetheless need to respond to the moment, perhaps simply nodding as if it's normal conversation, or with a behavioral: "How's that, again?" or a shrugging, "Oh, well, whatever that means." Possibly your character finds what's been said or done only outrageously idiotic or rude, and you'll express this value behaviorally to the offender or seek the sympathy and mutual agreement of others around you. This is the work of the classic "straight man."

If your character appreciates the joke, you might freely laugh at it (which, by the way, you may do even if you're the one saying the laugh line, surprised as you are that it came out of your mouth), or your character could suppress the laugh for the sake of good taste. You might understand the humor in a quip even as your character finds it singularly unamusing, told as it may be at their expense, In this case, after the joke you might have a behavioral response something like: "Ha, ha, very funny." or "Do I look like I'm in the mood for your jokes?"

chapter 4

Playing the Lead

What I mean by the Lead is that your character is someone the audience can trust to relate to things with a universal sensibility, the way they ought to be related to, and because of this, we will live through your character empathetically.

A Lead character isn't necessarily the star or straight looking. This term (and I do wish there was a better one) can be confusing because it doesn't mean you're the main character. Richard III is clearly the main character in that play, but hardly a "Lead" in the way I mean it. A Lead character could be playing a secondary role or even a very small part. In this way it's also not to be confused with a "leading lady" or "leading man" type which has typically referred to someone good looking and on the bland side. The Lead, in this way, could be played by someone who is clearly what you'd call a character actor (Dustin Hoffman, Philip Seymour Hoffman, etc.).

I wish I could use the term "hero," but that too isn't quite right either because the type of character I'm describing is very capable of doing unheroic things. Sometimes they'll do predominantly unheroic things, and even the role that is technically the villain might embody characteristics of a Lead — they're just gotten trapped on the wrong side of an issue.

The Lead character knows what's what. You may have a quirk as the Lead, you could be germ phobic or smoke or not like cats, but, whatever the quirk, you know how wrong you are for doing it or how weird you are for feeling this way. We are meant to connect with the Lead, live vicariously through them, have catharsis when they have catharsis. We are expected to feel badly if something bad happens to them, even if in some ways they deserve it. A Lead character has a sense of humor, even though they may be of the type that never laughs out loud or even rarely smiles. A Lead has their full ethical faculties and a maximum of empathy. When they do something cruel, they know it's cruel and feel the bitterness of it. Oh, they'll do it, just as I'll dig a splinter out of my hand with a needle, hurting all the way, because I know it must be done, or even bang my hand against something, hurting myself, because I'm angry. A Lead character feels pain whenever one of their brothers or sisters in the human condition feels pain. They feel for most species of animals, too.

The actress playing Rosalind in *As You Like It* must understand this when she says the critical things she does to Phoebe, like, "Sell while you can, you are not for all markets." Because, no matter how unpleasant Phoebe may be, Rosalind has to appreciate her own cruelty and so deliver her line with a wincing subtext ("I hate to say this, but you need to know it for your own good.") as she criticizes Phoebe's looks. Otherwise, we'll think Rosalind is a bitch. Not a Lead.

You can do all kinds of terrible things and get away with them, maintaining your position as our Lead, as long we get that you know how terrible they are. There's a heartbreaker scene in *The Champ* where the has-been prize fighter viciously berates the little boy so he'll stay away from him and no longer be contaminated by the boxer's bad influence, but we know it's killing him to hurt the boy this way. William Holden playing a tough bank robber in *The Wild Bunch* kills one of his own men because the man's been wounded and fallen from his horse. He executes him flatly and without a moment of hesitation, yet we feel he appreciates the weight of what he's doing, that this boy could be his own son, but the wound was mortal and he had no choice.

The Lead character may be so totally open and nakedly honest that if you met them in life they would appear alarmingly fragile, as is James Dean in *Rebel Without a Cause*, or Emily Watson in *Breaking the Waves*. A Lead character may leap at the chance to give their life for another, even strangers, or, as described, they may be jaded and do nothing to help someone in trouble because they've cynically promised themselves they're going to mind their own business. Our Lead guy may be one who tries to drink his drink normally as the bully is picking on the old man or harassing the young girl nearby, but he is badly bothered to the core, and he must work to strike a pose of casualness he often can't maintain. You know the type.

Cultures are corrupt, but Art stays in tune. It is amazing to me that over the centuries, the values of our characters in literature have remained so consistent. As whole societies rise and fall with hateful and barbaric value systems, the artists just keep going along getting it right. There are no Lead characters that sustain in any way that don't have basic decency. Name one character in literature we were meant to admire in the last two thousand years who, without recognizing it as a flaw in themselves, abused the weak, chose money over love, was bigoted regardless of someone's character, mocked the pain of someone who's never injured them, and on and on. Evil societies can produce art that has great technique, lovely instrumental music or architecture, but they produce no Lead characters in stories who endure. There are many fascinating types that are fun as hell and interesting to watch, even compelling in a way, like watching a shark feed, but it's not the same as a Lead character. We recognize them to be the best of us.

Talking shop with
my student,
Robin Wright-Penn.

chapter 5

Romance

APPRECIATE PHYSICAL ATTRACTION

Lust isn't comfortable. The impulse of lust is very powerful. People risk losing their families, finances and good name for the sake of a single physical encounter. I'm not saying you, Dear Reader, would ever do such a thing — mercy no, but it ain't one of the deadly sins for nothing. It's never comfortable to have someone wield a lot of power over you, and if you aren't portraying this vulnerability, you aren't representing a true, physical longing.

Never touch casually. When playing a romantic relationship you might consider acting as if there's a charged field surrounding the object of your romantic attentions. You and them are something like two magnets when near one another.

The French have an expression: "Love is in the skin." And so when touching the object of your romantic love, all the feelings associated with this relationship, the elation, the fear, the power, the wildness, these should rise to the surface.

HAVE A SENSE OF ROMANCE

Act like you share a secret. To convey the romantic relationship is to operate as if there is a secret between the two of you. The depth of that secret creates the level of intensity. Two people hiding a surprise party might look similar to a couple having a flirtation.

A man approaching a woman with romantic intentions does so with an attitude that he and she share a secret together. If she wants to encourage him, she responds in kind, if she wants to discourage him, she makes clear they share nothing.

Feel the allure. When playing a romantic relationship you might consider it as something like being near or, actually in, a rapid river. You don't know where the rapids will take you, only that it feels wonderful to be in the river and that it will sweep you away and out of control and you might hit rocks and crack your head open and, God, it's exhilarating. Your character may choose to never to go in the river, because of fear, or they may choose to get out of the river because something practical is making demands on them, but you should always feel the intoxicating pull of the river and wonder where it leads.

NEGOTIATE LOVE SCENES

Do it with contracts. The degree of intensity and nudity involved in love scenes can be quite extreme, and each performer must make a personal decision about what they're willing to do, but it's recommended that the agreement be made firm ahead of time. The Screen Actors Guild deals with this issue in standard contracts. Although, even with these contracts in place before filming begins, I've known actresses who were pressured and cajoled once on the set that they be good sports and more artistic and that it would be fixed in editing so nothing was seen, and how about a little more skin, sweety-baby.

▶ *Story:* I did a movie with an actress who fell for this line of argument, and then at the premier for the film, instead of being able to enjoy her success in what was a lovely performance, she was mortified that her parents had seen her pubic hair up there on the big screen.

Choreograph the boundaries. Let's be honest, given men have never been fully domesticated, in the vast majority of cases it's going to be the woman who is concerned about being compromised. Unless it's a gay love scene, of course, and then those same guys who were so eager to go for broke with a woman suddenly can become less freewheeling and artistically enlightened about having somebody else's tongue in their mouth. In any case, here's how you want to present this issue to a frisky co-star.

Tell the guy that he should recognize that, more important than copping a feel off of you, is whether both of you look authentic doing the love scene. That his image as a lover won't be helped if the audience gets the feeling that you're repulsed by him, so it's in his interest that you feel safe. Tell him it doesn't matter how he thinks you should feel, that this is the way it is, and if he makes you feel embarrassed about it by rolling his eyes and so forth, all this will do is make you feel worse and you'll be even more repulsed by him. Therefore, the love scenes should be choreographed in the same way a fight scene would be, with everyone feeling so comfortable with what is going to happen that you're able to fully commit to it unselfconsciously and make it look real.

There should be discussions about the limits of what will be touched and how, and these discussions allowed to be very technical. A neutral area of the body can be used, the calf, say, to demonstrate the degree of pressure that is acceptable.

KISS WELL

Know your kiss. As with a love scene, the nature of the kissing should be agreed upon beforehand by the players. There are all kinds of kisses: delicate romantic kisses, thrilling to the slightest touch, escalating delirious kisses, kisses to consume the other person and kissing as a surrender to be consumed.

Keep lips loose. Just as relaxation is good in all acting, so it is for kissing scenes. Loose lips move more easily and so show more while kissing. Dragging a kiss across the face is a nice effect.

Directing Nick Stahl
and Olivia Wilde on the
set of In Northwood.

chapter 6

Difficult Dialog

There are special problems you have to face when you take on material that is awkward, either because it is heavily stylized, involving subject matter that a modern audience finds hard to relate to, or the writing just plain stinks. In either case, the bottom line directive for you is to make it work.

KNOW IT

Make it your own, backwards and forwards. The best technique for dealing with difficult dialog is for you to be absolutely sure of what you're saying and what it means. The words should be thoroughly paraphrased so that you're completely confident in your comprehension of the meanings in the text. Every emotional value should be fully explored and personalized so that nothing is unclear.

Most of what is thought of as bad is, in fact, only material that requires some extra work. Fear of the material might make you tentative, and this will make any challenge more difficult to overcome. If you really know what you're saying and how you feel about things, even if there are words or turns of phrase that the audience doesn't fully understand, the fact that you seem to understand them, and it comes natural for you, helps bridge an understanding to the audience by bringing the material to life.

▸▸ *Note:* I find the version of *Hamlet* that Mel Gibson directed very illustrative of comparative acting techniques. You have Alan Bates playing Claudius in the classical, external style, very crisp and presentational, clear in his Actions, and with no real feelings going on in himself.

This acting style probably requires that you have an understanding of the play to fully appreciate what's going on. Then you have Mel Gibson as Hamlet, emoting within the part, but really just reciting the lines, something like a poetry reading with emotion where you have to forgive the stylized way he's speaking and, in this, you fail to understand much of what's going on because you can't tell what he's doing. Then you have Glenn Close who acts in the style I personally favor, and it doesn't even seem like she's doing what you think of as Shakespeare because it's so lived in and real, and the meanings in her dialog seem perfectly clear.

JUSTIFY IT

Be someone who talks like this. The best way to do virtually anything you have to do as an actor is to justify it in such a way that it never even occurs to the audience as anything but inevitable, and this pertains to stilted or difficult dialog as well. You can create a character who expresses themselves in a way that excuses them speaking in a manner that is awkward, dithering, arch or melodramatic. There are such people. I've met them.

Excuse it because of diminished capacity. Another way to justify your character saying something that is phrased awkwardly is to establish a condition for them under which they might speak this way.

You might be forgiven for expressing yourself badly because you're excessively emotional. Maybe you're unable to frame what you're saying well because of your elated giddiness or your sputtering frustration. It could be you're off your game because you're so struck by a mind-blowing event that you're not fully attending to what you're saying.

Other mitigating conditions you could use to justify not speaking perfectly might be fatigue, perhaps as a result of illness, or the influence of a mood-altering substances. These have been known on occasion to make the most articulate of people sound like baboons.

COMMIT TO IT

Sometimes the situation you find yourself in with cumbersome dialog can't be helped, and, instead of taking half measures, which might actually call extra attention to it, you should jump in with such a strong commitment that you will suspend judgment because of your degree of reckless enthusiasm.

I'm reminded of a piece of advice from the classic *Elements of Style*: "If you don't know how to pronounce a word, say it loudly. Why compound ignorance with inaudibility?"

LESSEN IT

Use a behavioral subtext that appreciates the problems with the words. When delivering a line that may seem too melodramatic or stilted, you can ease the brunt of the dialog by addressing it as if your character themselves feels the same difficulty with what they're saying. You can say a line in such a way that you make it clear that you know you're communicating it awkwardly.

Some subtextual meanings to lessen the impact:

> ▸ "I know this sounds silly, but…"
> ▸ "This isn't how I want to put this, but…"
> ▸ "I'm going to just say this however it comes out…"

AVOID UNINTENTIONAL LAUGHS

It's difficult to return from having had your audience laugh in mockery at what you meant to present to them as solemn and profound. Suicide is an option, of course, if there's a letter opener or something like it close at hand on stage, or if you think the orchestra pit is deep enough to kill you when you do your swan dive into it, but why not do what you can to ensure they never come out of the show and start laughing at you in the first place?

Reverse the tips for comedy. All those things you do to try and get laughs? Don't do those. Don't maintain the rhythm, break it up; don't top the other character, go under what they last gave you with less intensity; don't do little casual activities after a line. It's not great, but if it's really bad, you can even maybe be a little hard to hear in a moment. Perhaps enough so they can get most of it, or all of it after a moment of processing, but sort of soft so they don't get smacked with that big, purple turd of a line right away.

chapter 7

Superstitions and Etiquette

STAY LUCKY

The theater has taken on many superstitions over the centuries and, without judging the unreasonableness of these things — oh, hell, let's judge it — they're insane! But it's all part of the fun of show business. So let's make ourselves aware of these traditions and rituals, and perhaps observe them in the name of good taste or to honor our heritage or to humor the old codgers we happen to be working with.

Don't wish someone good luck before they act. This is perhaps the most well known of stage superstitions because it calls for a reverse wishing of bad luck to occur, sending a performer off with the classic "Break a leg!"

Don't whistle. Whistling anywhere in a theater is considered bad luck, but especially in the dressing room. The remedy for the offending whistler is to go outside the theater, turn around three times and ask to be let back in.

It's considered especially bad luck to whistle the song "Three Blind Mice."

Don't say "Mac★★★★" or any lines from it while working. This particular play by Shakespeare's has come to be associated with bad luck and, while those who are very superstitious find it disconcerting even being around a production, it's thought especially unwise to say the name of this play outright during working hours. The common, substitute reference is "The Scottish Tragedy."

Also, speaking any of the lines from this play while working on another is highly discouraged, but, if done, speaking lines from any other Shakespeare will help reverse the bad luck.

Flowers have powers. It's bad luck to receive flowers before a play and good luck to get them afterward. At the end of closing night, it's thought to be in good taste for the director or the leading lady to receive flowers that have been stolen from a grave.

Real flowers are bad luck on stage and fake flowers should be used instead.

Be careful with makeup. Knocking over a makeup box is bad luck, and if powder is spilled it's curative to dance on it. Also, makeup boxes should not be cleaned out, and it's bad luck to use a new grease paint on opening night.

Three candles are bad luck. It's bad luck to have three candles on stage, or actually anywhere in a theater (the closest person to the shortest candle gets the curse).

Avoid knitting in the wrong place. It's bad luck to knit while to the side of the stage or on stage. Do it back in the greenroom, Granny.

Beware two reflections. While on stage, you shouldn't look at another actor in a mirror so that both of your reflections can be seen at the same time. It's worse luck for the person closest to the mirror.

Kiss the hem of your garment if you trip. If you trip over the hem of your dress, robe or cape, pick it up and kiss it, blessing the fairies who tripped you.

Caution with some colors. Yellow is a bad luck color for ties, vests or hats and it's terrible for a clarinet.

Blue should be matched with some silver for good luck.

Leave a light on. This superstition really maintains its unquestioned hold. A light should be left on in the theater, specifically on stage, because a dark stage attracts the ghosts of those who have acted there.

Throw a piece of coal to christen a new stage. To bring good luck to a new theater, someone should stand on stage and throw a piece of coal into the gallery.

Avoid saying the last line or the tag line before opening night.
It's good form not to actually say the last line of the play, or the line for which the play is most known, prior to opening night.

Keep your shoes off the dressing room counter.

BE RESPECTFUL

We leave now the realm of superstition and move to issues of basic manners. The truth is, if you follow the "golden rule," being tidy, discreet and dependable, you'll do just fine. Here, however, are some extra cautions.

Don't bother an actor who is preparing. You should exercise maximum sensitivity when it comes to interrupting another actor who is warming up for their performance. Even if they seem to be in a casual state, going about routine business or, say, stretching, this may be part of their ritual and you should give them a wide berth.

Don't mess with another actor's personal property. It is considered bad form to touch another actor's things, both personal objects and the things they use while acting. If something has to be moved, of course, it can be delicately placed to the side safely and otherwise left undisturbed, but another actor's personal items should never be used without permission.

It might seem a minor thing to reach over and take a piece of gum that another actor would certainly not begrudge, but it's more an issue of an actor maintaining a private, preparatory space, with a mindset that includes ritual, and this should not be tampered with.

The other actor might have a fascinating personal prop or costume for their character that you'd like to examine, but repress this desire and even asking for permission to handle it is perhaps being a kind of pain in the ass.

Don't go through the lobby if possible. It's considered bad form to exit or enter through the theater lobby and this should always be done through the stage door if possible.

Don't show yourself in costume when not performing. It's disruptive to an audience's experience to see any of the actors in costume or makeup prior to the show or during intermission. After the show, it's less a matter of being disruptive and more an issue of just lacking class.

Don't use props or prop furniture when not acting. Of course if you're on stage and waiting for the production or a rehearsal to begin you can sit on a prop chair or a sofa, you just shouldn't be very comfortable about it.

Don't put anything but props on the prop table. Regardless of how tempting it might be to use the surface for just a moment, keep the prop table sacrosanct.

DON'T SHARE UNWANTED INFORMATION

As in all nice society, if there is any doubt, it is more discreet to say nothing, and if you can't be kind, be vague.

Don't discuss reviews in front of another actor without permission. Many actors don't want to read or hear anything of reviews while they are in the run of a play, or even anytime thereafter.

This is regardless of how good the review is considered to be, and even if there's a huge enlargement of it in the lobby. Some actors just have a policy to ignore all reviews. They consider the bad ones terrible and the good ones not good enough.

They might fear that a good review will point out a quality or specific moment in the production that they will then become self-consciousness about and ruin.

It's best simply not to mention reviews in any way to an actor. If there's something artistic to be gleaned from them, the director can address the issue as part of their notes.

Don't discuss who will be in the audience in front of another actor without permission. Many actors don't want to know who is in the audience. Not entertainment industry people or reviewers, not their friends and family, and not even your friends and acquaintances who they don't know at all. They don't want the audience personalized in any way.

232

NOTES ON CHARACTER ADDITIONS

Here are some notes for how to be more effective executing some Character Additions. These tips aren't, of course, meant to be a substitute for intense and thorough study of the actual conditions as they exist. You'll want to uncover of all the details you can, including the underlying causes for the behaviors, and not just the behaviors themselves.

▶▶ *Note:* Sometimes actors feel hesitant to study certain conditions at locations they consider out of bounds, such as hospitals or drug rehabilitation centers, for fear of being seen as voyeuristic or exploitive. This fear is undeserved and the reluctance has to do with a core issue you might have to overcome in order to adequately portray these conditions. In the vast majority of cases, people living the situations you might be sensitive about, or people who work with them, welcome intense study by actors who will then better depict what is their day-to-day reality. They know honest exposure can only serve to lessen misconceptions and stigmas associated with some of these conditions. To do justice to playing those realities you feel squeamish about studying, you probably have to deal with the fact that you personally keep people like this at a distance because they disturb you, and so it's your projection of how you would feel being watched by someone aloof and prissy like yourself.

chapter 1

Accents

ACQUISITION OF REGIONALISMS

Get coached and drill. There's no substitute for going to a professional accent specialist; but at the very least you should get a CD made by one and drill, drill, drill. There are CDs for most major accents.

These CDs come with study sheets to help you master pitch and stress and the diction of particular pronunciations.

Determine the point of resonance. It can be very useful to determine where in the mouth the basic placement of the accent is generated. This is called the "point of resonance." Standard American, for instance, is placed in the center of your mouth; if you pinched your cheeks it would be the point where your fingers would meet. The point of resonance for proper English is right where your teeth meet. If you have an ear for accents, this sense of where the accent is centered is almost all you may need to execute an accent and keep you on the mark.

Get someone with the accent to read all your lines. It's great if you can find someone with the desired regionalism to read all of your exact lines of dialog so you can hear and study exactly how those words are pronounced.

Get a catch phrase that sounds like the right accent. It can be helpful for you to have a particular phrase that typifies your desired way of speaking so that you can then use this phrase to quickly tune up and lock into the accent.

USAGE

Don't let an accent dehumanize your character. There is a tendency for accents to appeal to your conventionality and you should be cautious not to fall into caricatures. No matter what eventual character work is done, you have to seek the full humanity of the role, and your initial approach to the accent should be as if you yourself had been raised with this way of speaking.

Be intelligible. With rare exceptions, the audience should understand everything you say, word for word,

Be consistent. Probably the biggest danger in doing an accent is being inconsistent.

There should be a consistency among characters from the same location (this is really a director's issue to determine and make clear to the cast).

Let Intuitive Embodiment nuance the physical life. You may find that the accent will affect you in such a way that you start to have a shift in your physicality, specifically as it relates to speaking. Beware caricature, by all means, but allow a legitimate influence that might emanate from the accent.

IMPEDIMENTS

Stutter or stammer. A stammer is when an individual gets stuck at the first sound of a word, and a stutter is when the first sound of a word is repeated, often with a kind of palsy of the lower jaw. For those who have them, stammers and stutters will tend to happen on specific consonant sounds and increase in severity under stress, as when you're trying to assert yourself.

Knowing the type of stutter or stammer your character has, you can mark the specific sounds in your script and plan for each occurrence. With an increase of the emotional intensity, you can plan to have more consonant sound combinations emerge as problematic.

▶▶ *Note:* Lawrence Olivier, in *King Henry IV, Part 1*, established a stammer on Ws for his character Henry Percy (known as "Hotspur"), so that when he is wounded in a swordfight, and knowing he is about to die, he says (speaking of himself), "Percy, thou art food for" — and his stammer trips him up so he can't say his last word. It is then up to the man who's killed him, Prince Henry, to finish: "For worms, brave Percy."

Lisps or whistled Ss. There is the typical lisp where the "s" sound is replaced by more of a "th" sound, and there is a lateral lisp where the "s" gets pressed by the back sides of the tongue and is pronounced more as a "sh." A "whistled S" is when there is an actual slight whistling made behind the front teeth when an "s" sound is pronounced.

These types of conditions need not be marked in your script because, like accents, they are continuously present in the way your mouth is used, regardless of whether an "s" appears in any of the words.

Nasality. Nasality is created when there is a kind of hollowing of the roof of the mouth, so affecting the sound of the voice that there is extra resonance up into the nasal cavity. Typically the more pronounced it is, the further back in the throat. The most extreme nasality commonly occurs with forms of brain damage and in this way may be associated with some diminishment of a person's affect. It also commonly present in people who have a hearing loss.

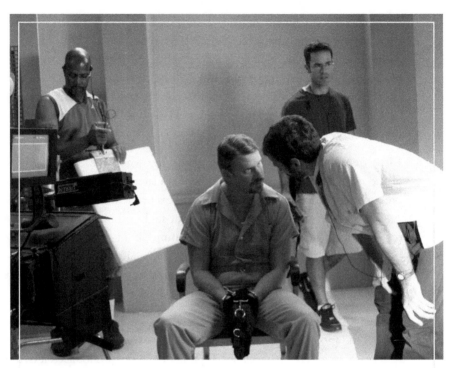

Directing Dash Mihok.

chapter 2

Pain

Move away from the area of the pain. Often actors make the mistake of collapsing into and grabbing the area of pain, when in fact the true behavior is for the rest of the body to flex and stretch and try to move away from the area of pain. It's as if this painful spot were to be avoided by the rest of the body. An exception to this might be sudden gripping pains such as heart attack where there might be an effort to compress the pain, to crush it in order to contain it.

Create the sadness and upset that comes with pain. An important value for you to create for the condition of pain is to have an emotional condition running that is consistent with the degree of discomfort. This is an aspect that often gets missed, and can be extremely effective in selling the quality of the pain your character is experiencing.

TYPES OF PAIN

All of these types of pain may evolve and blend into each other to varying degrees.

1. Sharp Pain. Sharp pain typically comes on quickly and will cause the body to react without any thought whatsoever. There is a feeling of being attacked. It makes the eyes go wide. This type of pain causes a sudden inhalation, hissing through clenched teeth, and loud, high-pitched vocalizing (screaming). After the initial rush of panic, there will be quick, shallow breathes. The area of pain demands intense intention, and a kind of openness to take any available option to get away from it.

In many different circumstances, this is the first type of pain you feel.

2. Stinging Pain. This type of pain is often referred to as "burning," and might resemble a milder form of sharp pain, but it is its own kind of pain and can express itself at times as even more extreme in its discomfort. This type of pain is given to being located across a thin surface, or with pinpoint specificity, and causes a kind of cringing reaction, and may narrow the eyes.

3. Gripping Pain. Gripping pain will tend to cause groaning type vocalizations. The breath is held, then there's gasping. Gripping pain especially causes the sufferer to squirm and writhe as if to find a posture that will lessen the discomfort. The attention given to this type of pain may be less on the specific local and more on the quality of the event.

Gripping pain is often associated with attacks that come in waves. At the peak of the wave the pain commands complete attention and, in the extreme, the eyes may roll back in the head and fainting can occur. There may be desperate disbelief at the peak of an attack. When the pain eases off, there is relief and, while fear remains, a kind of elation that the awfulness has gone away. An urge to speak may also arise, in the form of venting — either to talk about the experience, or as an attempt at self-reassurance, which might include prayers.

4. Ache. Aching pain often throbs. Aching pain causes a build up that results in moaning type vocalizations and heavy, regular breathing. This type of pain brings on depression and dread, and there can be a kind of internal collapsing, a demonstration of surrender. The attention of the sufferer of this type of pain almost seeks to avoid focusing on the specific area.

Ache is the type of pain that usually remains and fades away slowly at the end of injury episodes.

SPECIFIC MALADIES

A. Headache

Fix where the headache is located and how painful is it. You should determine the specific areas of pain, such as the temples, the base of the skull, or the inside corner of the eyes, and rub or press these areas.

There is a sensitivity to stimuli so you can squint at light sources and wince at sudden noises.

Migraine or cluster headaches can be awesomely terrible. These types of headaches are among the worst pains known and can be felt as a cavalcade of every type of pain of erupting at once. *See* Attacks.

B. Breaks and Sprains

Sharp pain, then Ache. These injuries begin with Sharp Pain and then, after a while, Ache comes on; if there is a re-injury, which is very prone to happening, there is again Sharp Pain, perhaps even worse than when first injured. You should have tentativeness in dealing with the affected areas, a submissive quality even. The area will stiffen with swelling in time.

If a cast has been applied, there probably will be itching underneath, and, as the duration of the cast lengthens, you'll want to create more agitation, impatience and depression associated with it.

Stinging pain with ligament tears. If it isn't a full blow out or major event injury, tears of the ligaments can be felt as stinging pain.

C. Gunshot and Stabbing

Know something really bad just happened. The initial response to sudden wounds of this type may be numbness and frozen shock, a dull feeling of dread, knowing that something awful has just happened, but not feeling the actual pain or being fully aware of the true severity of the injury. With gunshot wounds it can feel more as if one has just been hit with a hammer.

The initial sensation of pain from a gunshot may come as extreme stinging or as huge ache.

D. Burns

Have a feeling of being wronged. Burns cause sharp pain or stinging pain that is followed by an overall feeling of dread and fear. With severe burns there is no sensation because the nerves have been destroyed and only later do sharp and stinging pains begin of a very high magnitude.

chapter 3

Attacks

(heart attack, appendicitis, epilepsy, etc.)

PRECURSOR SYMPTOMS

Feel something strange is starting to happen. The symptoms that arise with the beginning of the particular type of attack should be created (*see* Infection). There can be cramping and twitching, which you can indicate by massaging the affected area. There is likely sweating, which can be created by wiping sweat from the forehead, upper lip, and neck. There can be a feeling of overheating or a chilled clamminess.

The beginning of most neurological conditions (migraines, epilepsy) starts with what is called an "aura." This is a kind of sickly high and includes sensory disturbances, such as blurring, flashing lights or tunnel vision that you can create by squinting, excessive blinking and rubbing your eyes as if to clear them out. With severe headaches one eye may be affected much worse than the other. Auditory problems of pounding, roaring and even deafness can be created by holding your ears or intentional yawning as if to clear pressure. Smell and taste may be involved, with either sharp smells and a bitter taste or the faint smell of burnt wood. You can create this by snorting, pinching the nose or swallowing.

There can be nausea, either severe or just queasiness with a sense of rising and falling in the stomach.

ONSET

Intensify precursor symptoms. Depending on the type of attack the pain will either be Sharp or Gripping or a combination of both. *See* Pain.

The individual becomes consumed with their attack and there might be either a slackening of the mouth or a clenching of the jaw. At the extreme, the eyes may roll up.

AFTER THE ATTACK

Feel that something traumatic just happened. After an attack you should create the maximum emotional values associated with something as alarming as this having happened to you, and perhaps a feeling that you avoided something even more terrible.

Create unconsciousness or death. If the character goes unconscious after the attack you may simply want to initiate a deep daydream, transporting yourself off into an active fantasy with peaceful values. To create the illusion of death depends on the technical circumstances of the production. If there is only a limited time that you will be required to maintain the illusion, you can hold your breath. If this is impossible, you'll then want to fill the lungs as much as possible without having the stomach appear to rise, probably by widening the chest with your concentration on the area just under the armpits. The duration that the illusion needs to be held will also dictate whether you can choose to keep your eyes open, and this is probably preferable unless the extended passage of time would force you to blink.

SPECIFIC ATTACKS

A. Seizures (epilepsy, brain tumor, etc.)

Onset. The onset of an epileptic convulsion is usually a brief period of flashing lights in the visual field and a flopping sensation in your stomach.

Attack. With the classic, "grand mal" convulsion, which can be caused by a number of things, there is a sudden and complete loss of consciousness. During this you fall to the ground and jerk violently and rhythmically, guttural sounds are made and a clacking sound that emits from your throat.

A smaller seizure, a "petite mal," is so subtle that when it happens no one may even be aware it's taking place, not even the person having it. With this type of seizure there is just a simple blankness of your expression and a fixed stare, as if you are lost in thought, and there may be a slight twitching of an area in your face or arms.

With what's called Focal Epilepsy you may or my not lose consciousness and there is a twitching that starts in a small part of the body and then spreads and intensifies.

▶▶ *Note:* **There is an unusual and rare condition known as Temporal Lobe Epilepsy. With this you have an aura of only a few seconds and then there is a sudden onset of bizarre behavior, perhaps angry or laughing. *See* Psychosis. There can be a strange chewing movement of the mouth associated with this condition. There may be an extended period following the episode that is called a fugue state where you change your entire life, perhaps moving to a new location and establishing a new identity. Afterwards there is amnesia.**

Post seizure. Following a convulsion there is often normal sleep or a return to consciousness with disorientation. The mood tends to be deep upset, the backlash of your fear, perhaps weeping, depression and irritability. There can also be shame and embarrassment, the feeling of having made a spectacle of yourself, all the worse for having no memory of it. And, if your character knows they are given to seizures, all the feelings associated with living with this condition will rise up in you.

B. Heart Attack

Onset. The beginning of a heart attack may just be a feeling of being ill at ease. The first physical symptom is a sense of tightness in the chest. There can be varying levels of Ache-type discomfort in your neck, jaw, back and stomach, but especially common is a bad pain in your left arm, which you can create by gripping and massaging. The onset may also include a shortness of breath, dizziness, sweating, chills, nausea, and fainting.

Heart attacks can be brought on by a rise of blood pressure and this can happen because of emotional stress, exercise, or eating.

Attack. Heart attacks may be very slight or among the most traumatic physical experiences that can happen to you in so short a time.

C. Giving Birth

Onset. When a woman begins her labor her water breaks, which can be experienced as a gushing or a trickle. There is usually a harmless, bloody discharge. The low abdomen begins to feel Gripping Pain cramps and there are twinges of a backache. The onset can vary greatly in severity.

The labor. The labor itself is a Gripping Pain cramping that comes in waves with shortening pauses between attacks of longer and longer duration. There is the feeling you have to make a bowel movement.

D. Appendicitis

Onset. An appendicitis attack starts with a vague feeling of Ache discomfort around the navel that worsens to become increasingly Sharp Pain localized to the lower right part of the abdomen. This area will be sensitive to pressure that causes a Sharp Pain. Fever and nausea may increase with possible vomiting.

Attack. The attack is an increase in Sharp Pain. If the appendix ruptures, there can actually be a lessening of pain as the pain becomes less localized to the lower right and the abdomen swells.

After an appendix ruptures an infection quickly develops that can be lethal. *See* Infection.

E. Kidney Stones

Onset. The beginning of a kidney stone attack can be a twinge that feels as if you've pulled a back muscle. This then increases in tightness to clearly become way beyond any pulled muscle you've ever had.

Attack. Kidney stone attack is considered one of the worst possible pains. An alarmingly violent, Sharp and Gripping pain combination that, as with only the most severe pains, induces automatic vomiting.

chapter 4

Infection and Poisoning

(fevers, parasites, snake bite, etc.)

BASIC SYMPTOMS

Pain. *See* 2. Pain. All types of pain are possible at the location of the wound. A general Ache is common, as is a pounding headache and cramps.

Fever. Fever causes the symptoms of overheating, as if you're trapped in a sauna. There is a burning sensation, specifically the face, which can be flushed, and there is sweating. The feeling of overheating can alternate with chills, and the feeling that you can't bundle up enough and the teeth may chatter.

▶▶ *Note:* **You can only indicate a fever but, if you're willing, you can actually give yourself the chills. I did this for an episode of *ER* by using ice packs and the air-conditioning in my trailer — oh, and no breakfast or lunch.**

There may be a dry mouth, from dehydration, and you can create this by having difficulty swallowing or through a weak smacking of the lips. Fever may cause a ringing in the ears, even a roaring in the ears, and there may be dizziness and difficulty focusing that you can show through squinting or excessive blinking.

Fever causes a feeling of being dazed, with a sense of unreality about things. With severe fever, something over 105 degrees, there can be delirium. *See* Psychosis.

Fever will tend to increase at night, where sleep is fitful and dreams are disturbed and given to nightmares.

Exhaustion. Sicknesses of this type usually will cause an overall exhaustion, drowsiness and a tendency to fatigue easily. This exhausted condition can be created with heavy eyelids, deep, heavy breaths, an inclination to position yourself as close as possible to a sleep posture, even if socially inappropriate, and a desire to try to keep conversation brief.

Nausea and vomiting. There can be Gripping-type pain in the abdomen, cramping, and a swollen or flopping feeling in the stomach. There is a hesitancy to move and with no appetite, even a worsening of the condition in the presence of food or the prospect of eating.

When the nausea worsens to include vomiting, it usually begins with excessive salivation, the mouth hanging loose, perhaps causing you to spit; the nose also will tend to run. The actual vomiting gives a small sense of panic at an ongoing, out-of-control event. The vomiting itself can be created offstage with sounds of water spilling and even onstage with the subterfuge of a hidden cup you spill. Following the vomiting there ought to be an indication of a bad taste in your mouth, swallowing with a grimace, and having a coated tongue. There should also be a sense of having overexerted your stomach muscles. Dry heaving, where little or nothing is coming out of an already emptied stomach, causes an especially bad taste in your mouth and pain in your stomach muscles.

Stomach gas may be part of nausea and this can be created by belching and perhaps having small vomits that only get so far as the back of the throat and then are swallowed again, with Sharp Pain and a bad taste.

Hypersensitivity of all senses. *See* Headache. An infection-type condition causes hypersensitivity, as with a headache, and might include a tingling, needles-and-pins sensation in your head, coupled with an overall sense of numbness, where any type of pressure is painful.

In some extreme cases, as with the rat poison strychnine, too much stimuli can set off a fatal convulsion. *See* Seizures.

Swollen Glands. With infection and some poisonings there is a swelling of the glands, particularly those closest to the sight of the areas most affected. These major gland clusters are located in the groin, the armpits and neck, and under the jaw. These areas can become very painful, Ache type of pain, and this causes stiffness and problems with movement or swallowing.

The emotional impact of illness. Sickness generally affects the emotional life making you depressed. You may tend to be grumpy and irritable, or you might have a flattened emotional line, as if on automatic pilot. On the other hand, it's possible for some people when sick to feel like they are on vacation and in this way you could have a buoyant mood.

SPECIFIC AILMENTS

A. Flu or Head Cold

Flu versus a cold. A flu can be distinguished from a cold in that a cold will not cause a fever, and a cold will usually be considered less debilitating than the flu. A cold will typically begin with a sore throat, then go on to cause congestion of the sinuses, and end in congesting the chest with a cough (*see* Bronchitis). The flu remains in the throat and chest with less congestion. The classic cold will be three days coming on, three days present, and three days leaving; the flu, on the other hand, can often be of a short duration, more than four days being less common. A cold, unlike the flu, will cause heavy sinus congestion, and the headache from a cold is often related to this congestion, whereas flu's headache feels more associated with the fever.

Sore throat. The first symptom of a cold or flu is usually a sore throat that causes particular Sharp Pain and difficulty swallowing.

Sinus congestion. Sinus congestion will cause a headache in the forehead and around your eyes. Your speech will become nasal, and the nose will become clogged or run, which you can create by blowing your nose, or dabbing and wiping. It can be shown that the condition has been present for a period of time by acting as if the nose is raw and sore from this.

The ears might be clogged and pressurized and you can create this symptom by gaping the mouth as if to clear them.

There might be sneezing, which starts with a slight tickle between the eyes, a watering of the eyes, a deep, slow inhalation, and then a burst of expelled air, which may be vocalized as something like, "Choo!" or "Snee!"

Bronchitis. Bronchitis is a congestion of the bronchi that causes an Ache type pain in the high chest, and may include the center of the back. You can create this condition of pain by arching your back as if in an attempt to relieve the pressure. There will be a cough, either a dry, hacking cough that causes Sharp Pain in the upper chest, or a productive cough, which, because of its wet sound, will be much more difficult for you to reproduce. Bronchitis can cause a wheeze that you can create through a panting breathiness and a whistling that can be a vocalizing "hee." Wheezing may come with a kind of weak feeling that requires pausing for the episode to subside.

Pneumonia. Pneumonia happens when bacteria exploit your depressed system because you're suffering from a cold or a flu, setting up an infection in your bronchi and lungs. Pneumonia creates extreme or extended conditions of fever and exhaustion. It causes a deep Ache in the chest and sides, and there may be Sharp Pain with coughing. There can be wheezing fits or coughing fits that, because of the serious distress to the lungs, are extremely alarming to the sufferer.

If bad enough, pneumonia will kill you from weakness and drown you in lung fluid.

B. Poisoning

Food poisoning. Most food poisoning will have the same symptoms as stomach flu, without the fever, and include terrible diarrhea and vomiting, including a lot of dry heaving.

Hangover. A hangover is essentially the same as food poisoning because it really is just poisoning by excess alcohol, but there is typically more of a headache. Also, you may want to respect the theatrical convention associated with a hangover that there's particularly painful oversensitivity to stimuli, and this may be set off all the more through having the smells or sight of food, or especially alcohol, elicit gagging or more vomiting.

Toxic agents. Poisons that are used to kill people intentionally are often neurotoxins (*see* Animal Bites), which paralyze the breathing, but those that kill upon inhalation — gases used for warfare, for example — typically cause bleeding in the lungs that drown the victim.

Execution in the "gas chamber" was done with cyanide. Cyanide poisoning stops the ability to metabolize oxygen, which causes difficulties breathing and a feeling of suffocation; death occurs as a result of suffocation. There is irritation to the nose, mouth and throat, a headache, weakness in the extremities, and a rapid loss of consciousness.

C. Animal Bites and Stings

In poisonings from animal bites and stings there is the issue of whether they are hemotoxins (blood poisons) or neurotoxins (nerve poisons). Some snakebites contain both types of poison. Both hemotoxins and neurotoxins can cause the response of nausea, cramps and vomiting, headache, weakness, and fever, with sweating, thirst and dizziness, which may include blurred vision.

Hemotoxins typically cause more pain, whereas some neurotoxins may hurt very little, then kill you, but of course with both there is usually vivid pain at the sight of the bite or sting itself, Sharp Pain first, then Ache, and, additionally, there can be a numbness and a tingling around this area and great radiated discomfort to the nearest cluster of glands.

Hemotoxins. Hemotoxins are closer to symptoms of standard poisonings and include diarrhea.

With the exception of the coral snake, most poisonous snakes of North and South America, such as rattlesnakes and cottonmouths, are predominantly hemotoxic.

Neurotoxins. Neurotoxins can produce symptoms of paralysis such as difficulty breathing and swallowing, with a feeling of a swollen tongue or throat and causing excess salivation, loss of coordination, slurred speech, and drooping eyelids. They can also cause convulsions (*see* Attacks), and either drowsiness or anxiety and restlessness.

Poisonous snakes of Africa, Asia, and Australia are predominantly neurotoxic, as are the stings and bites of poisonous insects and poisonous animals in the sea, such as lionfish, urchins, and sea snakes.

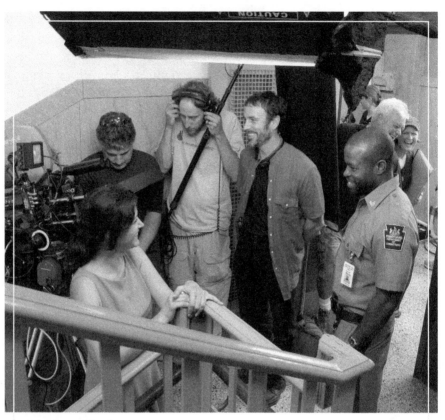

On set with Shoreh Ahgdashloo,
Tariq Trotter, and crew.

chapter 5

Blindness

EYES

Use dark glasses (cheater). Of course, the easiest way for you to deal with the issue of blindness, with respect to your eyes, is to wear dark glasses, which is both realistic and eliminates the necessity for you to do any work with your eyes. This also enables you to actually look around without shattering the illusion of blindness. Ultimately, however, it is better to not hide behind sunglasses, at least not all the time, and to create the behavior that will sell that you're blind with your eyes.

Keep the eyes out of focus. You should give the impression of sightlessness by not focusing on objects and keeping a glazed look to your eyes. This can be done by focusing on an imaginary object that floats in the air four to six feet in front of you. After a while the out-of-focus state can be maintained without the need for an imaginary object.

Avoid a fixed stare. You should avoid any tense fixing of the eyes and keep a loose gaze so that your eyes drift about easily. Your fear of being seen to be sighted can make you want to hide your eyes by looking up into the ceiling or into the floor. No, no. The stage ain't no place to hide.

Choose to either droop the eyelids or open them wider. It's good to convey that there is something not right with your eyes by either choosing to have the eyelids either partially closed, droopy, or opened a bit too wide.

MOVE BY TOUCH

Feel your way with eyes closed, and then recreate the experience with eyes open. A good exercise to work on the reality of blindness is to close your eyes and move about an area feeling your way, then to open your eyes, go back to the same starting point and try to recreate the exact same experience you had with your eyes open.

Appreciate familiar locations. Adjust the movement of a blind character to convey that they are areas that they either know well or not at all. Caution should be taken here because there is the theatrical reality that your character mustn't seem periodically sighted to the audience, and, even in reality, with the most familiar of locations, frequent periodic touches are used for reference.

Practice with a cane. The blind use a very specific cane, which is folded up in a very specific way, and this will have to be practiced if you're going to use a cane. The blind typically use the cane with tapping and a short sweeping motion. The arm moves the cane in front so that it rarely exceeds a separation of a yard at the tip, and often the wrist waves so that the tip only covers an area one foot in width with occasional tapping to establish the ground surface.

ACCENTUATE HEARING

Feel the sound environment. You should, as a blind person, accentuate the sense of hearing so that you tune in more acutely to the sounds of your surroundings, and allow for this sensitivity to create movements of the head and body in response to noises and vibrations.

Aim the ear to the sound. A good way to convey blindness is to direct the ear toward a sound, specifically someone speaking, so that one of your ears is pointed at the mouth of the speaking person. This is especially important for creating blindness on stage where a full ninety-degree profile should usually be shown to the character speaking opposite you. This is because, to some seats in the theater, looking even within a seventy-degree angle of the speaker's face may appear as if the blind person is looking directly at the speaker and making eye contact as if normally sighted.

254

chapter 6

Nervous System Impairment

(spinal trauma, cerebral palsy, MS, etc.)

The following symptoms generally address issues of the nervous system with the exception of the higher brain functions, and in this way, these conditions may, even in their extreme expression, in no way diminish your mental functioning.

PARALYSIS

No sensation. You have to keep the area that is meant to be paralyzed totally relaxed and without a hint of movement. This can be difficult to maintain because a loss of concentration even for a moment can result in an automatic reflexive movement. You need to be especially mindful when you're dealing with small objects. Watch your sneaky little toes as they go to dart into an oncoming sock.

Curling because of damage. Nerve damage often causes a tightening type of disposition wherein there is a kind of curling inward: the hands will curl the fingers in toward the base of the palm and the wrists bend; the elbow bends so that the hands come up to the chest or armpits; the toes curl and the feet turn inward, pigeon toed; and the knees bend. As part of this condition the head may be held back with an elevated chin because of a tightening in the neck, and one or both shoulders may be raised.

If there's little damage, this type of curling may only be very slight. In cases of total loss of sensation, such as with a severed spine, there is probably no curling at all.

Have a loose, swinging leg. Slight nerve damage may cause you to have a walk where one or both legs never fully straighten and have a loose, swinging quality. Your knee remains partially bent and one or both legs when brought forward have a hanging foot.

SPASMS

Have difficulty holding still. With some conditions, where the internal mechanism for the maintenance of balance is impaired, such as cerebral palsy, there may be a constant movement caused by an effort to maintain a fixed position.

Twitch. There are conditions where there is constant movement, as if the nerves of the muscles are continuously stimulating a contraction. This movement may be consistently rhythmic and have a set pattern, or it might be random.

Spread episodes. You can choreograph a pattern of twitching movements and create patterns within patterns for movement in completely different parts of the body. For instance, a shoulder raises twice and then the mouth gapes once, then, after four shoulder raises, the opposite arm suddenly straightens once.

These patterns of movement can spread to include other areas and this is especially prone to happening with heightened emotional states.

chapter 7

Mental Impairment

(mental retardation, autism, head injury)

This category of symptoms addresses conditions where there is an impact on personality and mental function. Someone with Mental Impairment may have extreme symptoms of other nervous system impairment as well, or nearly none at all.

PERSONALITY

Act like a child. Professionals will refer to someone with a mental disability as "having the mental capacity of a six-year-old." This age reference can give you a concrete approach to creating the condition if you then imitate a child's behavior of a specific age. Of course, doing justice to this condition is not as simple as merely imitating a child at that age by itself. There are additional factors, such as the degree of actual nervous system damage (*see* Nervous System Impairment) and a physical life that lacks the animated vitality typical of a child. There is also the tremendous impact of having sexual development, and the years of experience you've had with a routine that create habits very different than any child would have.

The more your character is a case of being "slow," that is, having a low IQ as opposed to an injury to the brain, the more you might rely on simply recreating a child's behavior and then lessening the energized physical life.

Shallow the personality. There can be a condition by itself known as "affect disorder," and Mental Impairment likely flattens the affect. Affect is what's thought of as the vitality of someone's personality, how openly your responses can be seen. People vary as to how much affect they have and, while some very sharp people may have a very low affect and can be difficult to read, people with damage to the frontal lobe of the brain have a diminished affect that is part of a detachment and a failure they have to process the meaning of events. They do not experience emotional highs and lows. This was why lobotomies were done in the evil old days to damage the frontal lobe and reduce levels of volatility.

A person with frontal lobe damage can discuss topics of large importance without any apparent relatedness to their significance, and to create this condition you can make adjustments to minimize how you relate to events. For instance, when discussing a funeral you might relate as if talking about going to the supermarket.

Monotone. Along with the nasality that may come with neural damage, you may want to flatten out the highs and lows of your speech, maintaining a constant tone and volume.

A low affect with a deep undercurrent. It's possible that the character you're playing doesn't appear to respond to events, yet can be affected on a deep level. This can cause a delayed response so that after a given event it might appear at first as if there's no response at all, and then later comes an upwelling of emotion stemming from the event.

This can especially happen if the elements of the event have some sophisticated meanings, whether it's with uncommon vocabulary or the events have to be considered in relationship to other things.

Total self-interest. Characters with personality disorders brought about by damage may live in an entirely self-centered universe in the same way as young children do. This means they may respond only to those things that they perceive to have an immediate impact on their own situation, whether fearful or gratifying. Everything else they will experience without judgment, like watching a leaf fall from a tree.

In this way there may be absolutely no compunction to respond socially to events, no desire to appear acceptable in a particular way. Your character may be completely amoral and without empathy.

Poor impulse control. People with these personality disorders may be volatile, delinquent, and act out without a sense of appropriateness. They may be excessively talkative, with stream of consciousness prattling or they can be loud and obscene.

Lack of awareness. This condition makes for poor attention, poor memory, poor judgment and poor abstract thinking. It creates a failure to foresee repercussions. It also creates absentmindedness, and you can represent this through poor grooming and incorrect or only partially accomplished dressing.

Speech may be primitive and some words and thoughts must be deeply considered if responded to at all — like speaking a foreign language.

A DEADENED PHYSICAL LIFE

Have a low center of gravity. With brain damage, and a lack of regard for how one presents oneself, there may be a kind of disconnection with the normal vitality of the body, which will cause a slumped looseness to the physical life of your character.

Have a plodding gait. The low center of gravity that comes with this condition makes walking somewhat heavy-footed. It may be there's a flat-footed quality, without bounce, or it might involve the turning in, pigeon-toed effect of nerve damage.

SPEECH

Create nasality. There will be a very strong tendency to have a nasal quality to speech and the degree to which it exists is in direct proportion to how severe the brain damage is.

Have a speech impediment or a thick regionalism. Stammers, stutters and lisps are much more common with people who have disorders of the nervous system than in the general population.

A fantastic element to communicate the condition of Mental Impairment is to do a heavy regionalism. This will establish in your character's basic lack of sophistication.

AUTISM

Autism is its own special category of mental impairment and the condition is still not fully understood by experts. Only recently it was found that individuals thought to be completely stunted and disengaged were in fact quite aware of what was going on around them and could communicate on a keyboard in complex sentences. The condition has a wide range of severity, from total incapacity to a mild form known as Asperger Syndrome. It seems that someone with autism has difficulty accessing their body, as if they are held off in a remote world with a poor connection to this one.

Autistics may bang their heads or grind their knuckles into their eyes, generating flashing lights, to increase stimulation and pull themselves into the here and now.

Repetitive movements. Autistics are prone to engaging in repetitive movements, perhaps rocking, shaking their hands, clapping, or finger twiddling.

Difficulty making contact. It is typically difficult for someone with Autism to maintain eye contact with another person, and relating to other people can cause anxiety. Autistics often have an aversion to being touched.

Obsessiveness. An autistic person is likely to have particular obsessions, both things they invest great interest in and things that they abhor.

An extreme talent possible. Autistics may be what are called "savants," individuals who have a very low ability to function in a normal life, yet have an extraordinary capability in another area such as math or art. This type of person may not be able to dress themselves properly, but will be able to do phenomenal mathematical computations in their head or, upon hearing a song once, play it perfectly on an instrument.

Mental Illness

SCHIZOPHRENIA

Schizophrenia is a condition wherein the psychological behaviors are so profoundly abnormal that they are classified as psychotic. It's unclear what causes this condition, although there does seem to be a significant genetic predisposition — 40% of identical twins with siblings who suffer from the disease will also have it.

Symptoms of damage. *See* Nervous System Impairment and Personality Disorders. Individuals with schizophrenia may have extreme symptoms of damage or nearly none at all.

Delusions. Delusions are when you have specific ideas about people, objects or events that are false. These ideas may be inaccurately drawn conclusions from actual events or made completely out of whole cloth. They are relationships drawn between unrelated things, such as the garbage men come on Wednesday because I was born on a Wednesday and they are trying to signal to me that I am garbage.

Many schizophrenics engage in elaborate, ritualistic behaviors that can seem arbitrary to an outside observer, but are in fact extremely specific to a personal system. It's possible that these rituals are being performed for some lofty reason, to prevent earthquakes, say, but they are much more commonly done for personal safety, maybe to prevent radiation poisoning. Delusions may be based on organized religions, or involve unique mystical beliefs. Physical objects are often deemed necessary as talismans or protective medical devices.

Delusions may involve paranoid conspiracies of complete fantasy, such as aliens from outer space, or they could be based on recognized organizations such as the FBI, or institutions that they themselves actually are in contact with, such as social services.

Hallucinations. Hallucinations are any abnormal perceptions of the five senses. They may be continually occurring, episodic or singular and they may come on gradually and worsen, or they can occur suddenly in full force.

With schizophrenia, hearing sounds, particularly voices, or perceiving smells is very common.

If you're going to create this condition, it's important to know that in the majority of cases, the quality of the hallucinatory reality is recognizable by the sufferer as different from normal reality. In this way, while a schizophrenic may believe a hallucination to have a kind of reality, they nevertheless can tell the difference between a hallucination and what we call reality. Some schizophrenics are able to function rather well simply by willing themselves to ignore their hallucinations.

Make it personal. When you create the realities of insanity it's necessary to make sure that you create all of the behaviors specifically and that you aren't just generally "playing crazy." Even in the most severe forms, the behaviors are either created in response to very specific delusions and hallucinations or by damage to the brain. You have to make sure you create situations wherein you respond exactly as you yourself would respond if this were happening to you.

Be traumatized by the illness. One of the most important factors if you're going to do justice to the condition of Mental Illness is to do the deep, emotional preparatory work. All Mental Illness is traumatizing. In addition to the continuous experience of the hallucinations and delusions, immensely stressful in and of itself, your original life has been fractured and all your relationships destroyed or severely changed.

To do justice to the condition of Mental Illness you'll probably have to work toward the same degree of trauma you would if you were portraying someone in a concentration camp.

MOOD STATES

1. Depression. This state may be profound and lead to suicide or be more superficial and thought of as melancholy. This mood state may be associated with hypochondria.

2. Ecstasy. This state has been described as a dreamlike, twilight state, a sense of all desires fulfilled. It may be associated with religious rapture. This isn't to say it is free of upset and the sense of trauma, but rather something like being miraculously rescued from a terrible death.

3. Mania. This emotional state may be confused with euphoria, but is in fact charged with anxiety. It can create capricious behavior, perhaps pursuing a cause in response to a delusion or hallucinatory command.

4. Anger. This is a hateful state that may have full-blown raging behavior directed at specific individuals or a simmering, malevolent quality.

5. Incoherence. In this state you're rendered incapacitated by too much stimuli or too many associations. It may result in fragmented speech or excessive activity, perhaps ritualistic.

6. Delirium. This state is characterized by acute hallucinatory episodes and may have a sudden onset and then recovery to normal. This state may be created by non-schizophrenic pathology such as fever delirium or post-traumatic stress, as can be caused by battlefield experiences.

7. Catatonic. *See* Chronic Types.

CHRONIC TYPES

The types of schizophrenia listed here may overlap and blend.

1. Simple Schizophrenia. This is the most common form of the illness and is often the case with people you see living on the street. They may have few symptoms other than those associated with Personality Disorders and are generally passive.

2. Paranoid Schizophrenia. This type of schizophrenic believes that hostile forces are seeking to injure them, and, because everyone is judged to be either an enemy or a potential enemy, they are extremely suspicious and will be testing for signs of threat.

The hallucinations of paranoid schizophrenics may include terrible visions and certainly tend to be of a negative nature, such as hearing abusive language directed at themselves, or experiencing the taste and smell of sulfur.

You tend to develop personality types that are either timid, keeping a low profile, with your head down and back to wall, or you'll be megalomaniacal, believing you're being persecuted because of your special qualities and powers, and you may carry yourself as if royalty.

This type of chronic schizophrenia is by far the most dangerous, and if you suffer from this form you're likely to be institutionalized because you tend to strike out, taking preemptive measures against perceived threats.

3. Hebephrenic Schizophrenia. This type of schizophrenia is marked by silly, infantile behaviors, as if you were actively avoiding reality. Especially given to vivid hallucinations, this form typically starts when someone is young and has a very poor prognosis for improvement.

4. Catatonic Schizophrenia. If you're catatonic, you're completely in your own world, often in a stupor, with an immobile and unresponsive, mask-like face. You may be moldable so that if an arm is lifted it remains there, or you may be resistant to movement, perhaps so obstinate you do the opposite of what is directed.

It's also possible you're in an excited state, with impulsivity and arbitrary movements or vocalizations, or perhaps simple, repetitive movements such as rocking. You also may indulge in mimicry and mirror a person's movements and echo them mindlessly.

Catatonics may have either the worst prognosis, with hopeless neural damage, or the best, in that it may be the result of what's called a "nervous breakdown," and, as such, it has a sudden onset and relatively rapid recovery.

MANIA

Unlike schizophrenia, which is by definition psychosis, what's called mania may or may not reach a level so profound that it qualifies as psychosis. Also, unlike schizophrenia where it is an absolute that you will be traumatized and feel on some level that what is happening to you is bad, with Mania you can have the experience that it's all good.

Phases of Mania

1. Simple Mania. With simple mania the affected person is in an elated emotional state, probably filled with a sense of well-being and power, making them outgoing and celebratory and creating a megalomaniacal condition that can be authoritarian or benevolent. You are the master of all you survey.

With simple mania the person has abundant energy and may be given to sudden starts and quick movements, tapping or fiddling. There will be increased eye movement with increased blinking.

The mentality in this state results in rapid thoughts and speech with frequent changes of topic; you're easily distracted and absentminded. There will be an increased sense of the significant and you'll have imagined profound insights. This state of mind can create overestimations of your mental capacities and dangerous overestimations of your physical capabilities.

2. Acute Mania. Acute mania is an intensification of Simple Mania symptoms with an increasing underlying anxiety. The good spirits begin to become forced, as if in an attempt to stave off a welling panic, and there becomes an increasing potential for paranoia and suspicion.

3. Delirious Mania. Delirious Mania has delusions; *see* Schizophrenia. These delusions can be fixations that are maintained over an extended period of time, and may be grand projects that include the fantasy involvement of important people. Speech may deteriorate into gibberish that is thought to be a secret language. There will be extreme impulsiveness and probably ill-advised actions that require intervention by law enforcement, perhaps even homicidal behavior.

4. Manic Stupor. The ultimate stage of mania is total overwhelm. You become speechless from too many thoughts and the eyes move about or are fixed. You become Catatonic (*see* Schizophrenia, Chronic States), but, as with all Mania, there are no hallucinations. At last, you may settle into sleep.

Mania may be part of bipolar syndrome. It's possible that the condition of mania might be part of a condition wherein you swing between degrees of mania and depression (*see* Depression), with some periods of normalcy.

Mania may be brought on by a substance or an association. It's possible that you become activated in your mania by a chemical reaction to alcohol or a stimulant; perhaps an exciting event charges you with adrenaline and stimulates an episode.

DEPRESSION

Like Mania, depression may or may not reach the level where it would be categorized as psychosis.

Phases of Depression

1. Simple Depression. This is a condition marked by grief, a feeling everything is bleak and without meaning or interest, and includes low self esteem. Unable to love, the person feels dejected and becomes isolated and inactive. There is pronounced despair, helpless and hopeless feelings, and suicidal thoughts are possible.

2. Acute Depression. This is an intensification of the symptoms of Simple Depression, with a marked feeling of dread and increasing anxiety that could lead to suicide or homicide. Delusions and hallucinations are also possible; *see* Paranoid Schizophrenia.

3. Depressive Stupor. This is a kind of shock state with a fixed stare and Catatonia. It may involve hours of extended sleep.

Possibly part of a bipolar condition. As with Mania, depression may be part of a syndrome that swings from mania to depression; perhaps the swing is so great that it ends in catatonia.

ANTI-PSYCHOTIC MEDICATIONS

Mentally dulled. Anti-psychotic drugs cause an overall flattening of the personality, an emotional disconnection, along with drowsiness and difficulties concentrating.

Agitation. If you take anti-psychotics you will often experience an agitated response and underneath the heavy, dulled sensation you have restlessness. This can cause insomnia and the resultant symptoms of sleep deprivation.

Tremors. Anti-psychotic drugs can cause symptoms identical to Parkinson's disease. Involuntary movement may either be only slight trembling or go to extremes with graphic gaping of the mouth and tension-filled gyrating.

Dry mouth. These types of medications can cause dry mouth and its natural companions, a coated tongue and residue that gathers on the lips and in the corners of the mouth. You can create this in the way you swallow and in wiping at your mouth.

Blurred vision. A typical symptom of anti-psychotic medication is blurred vision and you can create this through excessive blinking and difficulties in focusing on smaller details such as writing or photographs.

ANXIETY CONDITION

Anxiety conditions, by themselves, do not qualify as psychosis because there are no true hallucinations, and the delusions rarely get more extreme than the typical oddball things all of us supposedly normal people believe. If you have an extreme anxiety condition, however, you'll often have a feeling that you're in danger of going psychotic and hurting yourself or others.

Fear. An anxiety condition is really about an excess of fear in your system that leads to dread, a feeling of impending death or injury, anguish, the feeling of an inability to change what is fated. Panic is common, and a desperate desire to take preemptive measures against the coming injury.

Free-floating anxiety that attaches to an issue. With massive anxiety comes an exaggeration of potential threats, and histrionic associations. You may have fear of bad health, such as fear of a heart attack, or an inability to breathe, or an inability to swallow, or perhaps there's a fear of germs and exposure to harmful agents.

It could be the fear becomes paranoiac and attaches to a certain group of people that is felt to be particularly dangerous, such as terrorists or state authorities or neighbors, perhaps an entire ethnic group. This makes for constant evaluation of what and who is dangerous, and close attention to the movements of people of whom you are suspicious. It may cause you to test for threats.

Physical manifestations of anxiety. The pathology of anxiety has a wide range, from jitters to, more rarely, drowsiness. It might include a racing heart, hyperventilating, vertigo, tingling, dry mouth, itchy eyes, itchy nose, crawling skin, blurred vision, ringing in the ears, nausea, diarrhea, sweating, urinary frequency, and hunger.

A panic attack. A panic attack is an acute eruption of anxiety that can be brought about by an event, or it will simply occur out of nowhere on its own. A panic attack will bring everything to a halt. You might make sudden irrational movements or scream. A panic attack is self-perpetuating in that it often centers on a fear of attracting attention in public or of having a heart attack or an asthma attack. The very fear of these things will produce odd, noteworthy behavior that attracts the feared attention, or a rapid heart rate and problems breathing that validate the fear for your health.

Phobias. An anxiety condition may be entirely or partially attached to a particular phobia. It's possible to have a phobia about practically anything, but the common phobias are fear of heights, closed spaces, open spaces, germs, and animals such as snakes, spiders, and rodents.

Obsessive/Compulsive Disorder. Having an Obsessive/Compulsive Disorder (OCD) is a particular kind of anxiety condition. It might be that your obsessions are generated by a fear that has some basis in reality, such as a fear of germs that causes you to perform cleaning behaviors that would not be out of the norm if you were in an operating room; but these can then become irrational to the point where you're re-cleaning surfaces you know have not been re-contaminated. Someone with OCD can be extremely superstitious, and not just of the knocking-on-wood variety. With this condition you'll develop your own incredibly elaborate rituals for keeping at bay the cloud of bad luck and terror that is forever following you. It may be the rituals are based on a particular number so that everything has to be done in threes, like turning the light on and off three times, then three turns of the doorknob, then swallowing three times each time before you can leave the house. If you actually believe these behaviors have an effect the condition is then termed Obsessive Compulsive Personality Disorder, but more likely, you know they almost certainly have no basis in reality and resent having gotten stuck doing them in order to feel less frightened. Akin to this kind of superstition are hoarding behaviors, where you feel compelled to keep all kinds of junk.

Just about everybody indulges in ritual behaviors and hoarding to some degree, it's just that when it gets to the point of being extremely obstructive to one's life and causing so much fear we have this label for it called Obsessive Compulsive Disorder.

Obsessions can be totally fanciful ideas that get a grip on your imagination, such as the notion that you've told a co-worker you hate them or that you've run someone over with your car even though you can't specifically remember doing this. Now, again, I think a lot of us, if not most of us, have some capacity for this. My wife often feels the need to drive back to see if she's closed the garage. I'll go back to make sure I've locked my car. We space out and when we can't remember for that period of time what we were doing, we worry that we were not functioning properly. It's just that if you're an OCD sufferer you fill in that blank space with something wild and especially anxiety provoking, and, while you aren't psychotic and really know that the thought that's bothering you is kooky (unless it's that OCPD syndrome), you can't shake the idea that you've done this awful thing.

As with many Character Additions you can take on so that you better play your part even though they're not spoken of directly in the text, you could use the condition of OCD in the portrayal of someone who is intense or what is referred to as "tightly wrapped." I was once interviewing a prospective student who told me he had OCD, and I said to him: "You seem perfectly normal to me." to which he responded: "Yes, but while you weren't looking, I've counted every one of the ceiling tiles in this room."

With Pruit Taylor Vince
In Northwood.

Alcohol Use

MOTOR SKILL DYSFUNCTION

Alcohol is a very difficult condition to do well as an actor because it's hard to maintain consistency with the many aspects that have to be kept in play at the same time and at the same level of intoxication. It takes real, tough-minded concentration, combined with looseness and panache. There are times when the broad style of the material allows people to forgive a caricature of drunkenness (not for me, I'm afraid, and I have on occasion found myself in an audience of people laughing at the high jinks of a performer acting drunk in the manner of a silly child, while I cringe and grind my teeth), but to do a realistic version of the condition requires tremendous skill and practice.

Start by being relaxed. The fact that alcohol is a central nervous system depressant makes it difficult for you to fake as a condition. You have to first try to relax yourself as profoundly as possibly. Sit in a chair and let go of all tension in your body, flop around a bit, shake off all tightness, move your jaw around, tense and release the muscles of your face, roll your neck. Go "Blah, blah, blah." Relate it to a time when you've been extremely sleepy.

In working on being under the effect of alcohol, you can perhaps start by feeling as if you've been given a heavy tranquilizer.

Try not to be drunk. This is the classic advice on playing drunk you get from an old timer, and, of course, it really applies to many, many conditions, physical and emotional. Try not to slip into unconsciousness, try not to give in to the cough, try not to show how upset you are. And so it is that people in life try not to act drunk.

Your primitive, animal self doesn't like being intoxicated. It's a bad state to be in if you're attacked by a pack of wolves. Even as you throw back another shooter with gusto, another part of your nature is trying like hell to sober up. Watch the struggles of a cat or a dog recovering from anesthesia.

It is your job to recreate this experience. To do this you need to represent your character's rigorous attempts to behave as if sober, and struggle against your lack of coordination brought on by the drink. Of course, you have to create the disturbances of your motor skills first in order to struggle against them.

Concentrate too much on what is easy. A clear way to create the reality of a person having a problem functioning is to demonstrate an excessive amount of concentration on what the audience knows should be a simple task. You can give great focus to buttoning your coat or putting a napkin in your lap or counting out money, for example.

Slur. A slur is probably the single most distinctive quality in creating the condition of alcohol intoxication. The slur requires looseness of the mouth and jaw. Imagine how it might be to have had Novocain injected directly into your tongue. In keeping with that ongoing effort to be sober, you should usually set off your slur by over-enunciating around it.

Be continually adjusting your balance. Alcohol impairs the balance mechanism. This is typified by the drunken state wherein, even while laying still on a bed, the room seems to be spinning. I'm sure you've never experienced anything like this, but you can ask one of your debauched friends about it. This situation requires that you create a condition of instability so that it's necessary to always be correcting your balance. It's as if you're on the deck of a boat, and the seas are as rough as you are drunk.

It requires diligence to maintain the necessary constant movement of adjusting your balance and I catch actors all the time having all the other elements of their drunkenness working, and yet, untruthfully, standing stock still.

Spot and slant. A very clear way to demonstrate that your character is impaired is to violate the norm and not move in the direction that your eyes are looking. In this way, if you simply look at one spot and move in a line not directly towards that, it appears something must be wrong with your motor skills. If you're in this condition, you then have to correct and tack to your destination.

IMPAIRED JUDGMENT

The reason people drink, beyond the chemical addiction, is because it dulls pain, specifically emotional pain, and this comes, as much as anything, from its power to silence the judgmental part of your brain.

Be gregarious. People who are drunk tend to be more outgoing and loud and are unaware of the spectacle they're making of themselves. They will tend to be inappropriate in their boundaries, making them overly familiar with strangers and overly confidential with acquaintances.

Be reckless. Someone who is drunk will tend to be less concerned with consequences and will tend to overestimate their capabilities.

Be sloppy. Drunkenness causes people to concern themselves less with propriety and this tends to make them messy and have poor grooming.

CHALLENGED

There is a quality that very intoxicated people can have that they're beset by their condition, that they are undergoing an onslaught by the intoxication. This particular feeling of being beleaguered is consistent with many slang terms for being drunk, such as smashed, bombed, wasted, etc.

Have a sense that effort is required. You can take pauses to center yourself with deep concentration, and give a sense that you are making preparations, resting up or steeling yourself, to once again take on the pressure of dealing with a specific chore or reality in general. There may be behaviors almost as if a strong wind is hitting you in the face, squinting your eyes and taking heavy breaths blown out through puffed cheeks.

Get exasperated that it's all too much. Some drunks will act as if even the smallest of inconveniences are more than they can bear, given how much they've already had to deal with. Because the alcohol is impairing their ability to function and every little thing is now a chore to accomplish, they will strike the stance that it's unfair and just mind-blowing that they should have to cope with anything else.

THE EMOTIONAL LINE

One of the clearest ways for you to create the impression of a character who is drunk is to have a clear, conspicuous emotional life. It's as if the alcohol either put more emotion into your system or impaired the normal mechanism for filtering emotion, but in any case, your emotional life will tend to appear more pronounced.

Feelings are dulled. While the emotions experienced are more pronounced, they will not be as vivid as when sober and lack sharpness. In this way, alcohol is an emotional pain killer because the sharp edges of grief and anger are softened.

Emotional Types

1. The aloof drunk. It's been said, "You know you're drunk when you feel sophisticated, but you can't pronounce it." Aloofness is by far the most common emotional line, and, in keeping with your effort to be sober, it is an effort to rise above the effects of having a sloppy emotional life. You adopt a stance of detachment, acting as if you're royalty. You might do this through attempting elegance or flamboyance or how confidently forthcoming you are.

It can cause those excessively deliberate behaviors, mentioned earlier, in an attempt to belie the fact that you're stupid and ungraceful.

This aloof stance of superiority is the one usually taken by someone in an absolute stupor.

2. The happy drunk. This is where you've surrendered any pretense that you're sober and are celebrating in your freedom from inhibitions. You'll probably be given to much laughter and camaraderie and an enthusiasm to jump into whatever will bring more good cheer and fun.

3. The angry drunk. This is a mood of bitterness and smoldering hostility, sinister and sneering. Everything is grim, contemptible and probably deserves annihilation. This type of condition creates volatility. You're on the look-out for trouble and eager to insert yourself in it.

274

4. The maudlin drunk. This type of emotional line is characterized by general upset, over things both good and bad. It may be sentimental and weepy, getting nostalgic, or depressed and crestfallen. This state gives you a right to be intoxicated because the world is so painful and hard to take.

Maintain emotional lines. The emotional condition will remain consistent, much in the way that a person who is in a good mood looks for the bright side of things and someone in a bad mood the negative side (you can grouse that roses have thorns or celebrate that thorn bushes have roses). Every event will be registered with the same general emotional coloration that is presently being experienced. Everything is a reason to celebrate if you're a happy drunk; everything is a reason to be foul if you're an angry drunk.

Aloof, happy, or angry emotional lines may run on top of grief. It's possible that the emotional condition of the drunken person is graphically of one kind, while underneath, on a deeper level, grief is being experienced. You can have a life-of-the-party drunk who is desperately covering with celebration that they have lost the love of their life.

This deeper emotional state of grief may or may not erupt through the surface, changing your emotional line into that of a maudlin drunk.

Change emotional lines deliberately. If there is a change of an emotional line for your drunken condition, it has to be done with finesse so you don't confuse the audience as to what the current condition is. The transition should happen smoothly and fairly quickly, something like turning a dial.

Change for a reason or no reason. A change of emotional line may come as the result of an event, whether it's a banged elbow or a discovered photograph; or it can change purely on its own without any apparent cause.

Remember, though, as with all areas of acting, unless there is valid artistic purpose, there's no reason to change, just for the sake of change. One true thing done consistently is artistically preferable.

OTHER PHYSICAL EFFECTS

Numbness. Alcohol dulls the sensation of pain and causes a feeling of heaviness.

Sleepiness. Excessive drinking typically leads to drowsiness.

Blurring vision. Drunkenness causes visual disturbances of blurring and eventually, with enough drink, seeing double.

Flushed and sweating. Excessive drink can cause a red flushing of the skin and excessive perspiration.

Gas and sickness. There can be a feeling of fullness and belching, also gassy hiccups.

Drinking too much makes you sick (*see* Nausea). Unlike a flu type or typical poisoning sickness, however, there is no fever or diarrhea, little cramping, and the uneasy feeling is usually very brief before vomiting. Also, there may actually be an improved sense of well being after vomiting.

Passing out. Eventually, after enough alcohol, you'll go unconscious. As with all fainting, this can be represented by losing consciousness in a smooth, but rapid way, like a dial turning off a light, perhaps with your eyes rolling up in the head, showing white.

CHOREOGRAPH THE BEHAVIORS

It might add theatricality to your presentation of a drunk if you plan certain specific behaviors.

Create miscalculations. Poor coordination and poor judgment will make you prone to mishaps. It may be that an accident happens because you're absentminded or, in being overconfident of your capabilities, you're carelessly offhand. You can even make a mess of something even while trying to be especially vigilant in how well you execute the maneuver, and your blunders can be made worse by hurried and unskilled attempts to remedy them that only lead to further disaster. You could, for instance, have difficulty putting a phone back in its cradle, and the botched attempt to set it right knocks the phone off the table, and you then lunge to recover the phone and wipe out the entire table.

This is why drunk driving is so bad because in particular it leads someone to over-steer.

Make the normal difficult. Just as it can show a dysfunction to concentrate too much on what should be easy, you can demonstrate drunkenness by having troubles doing the most ordinary of things — like standing. Knees can buckle suddenly, ankles turn, your head snaps on the neck in the same way it does when someone falls asleep accidentally. Any ordinary thing can be turned into a fiasco.

Pass out. It can be effective to have your character pass out in the middle of some task, like ordering another drink, or perhaps even as you're about to make some grand statement. You don't have to have any written dialog to do this, just orient yourself as if to hold forth, open your mouth to speak, then pass out.

SYMPTOMS OF LONG-TERM USE

Increasingly dulled emotional lines. The emotional life created by intoxication will tend to become less pronounced with long-term use.

Greater ability to function with an equal degree of drunkenness. Not only does it require more alcohol to achieve intoxication after years of drinking, even when equally intoxicated, since you've had more experience with the condition, you get better at dealing with the motor skill dysfunction. It's the same as with a flight attendant who's better experienced walking down the aisle of a plane during turbulence.

Tricks used to cover drunkenness. If you're an alcoholic, you develop techniques to mask your condition; such as making sure you're anchored in place so as not to sway noticeably. This is done by adopting a wide stance or wedging yourself against objects. You'll use mints or gum to cover the smell of alcohol on your breath, and you may be attentive to correct any sloppiness.

Another ploy is to present yourself as a thoughtful person so you can justify affecting a deliberateness of speech. In this way you act like what you're saying is profound, so you can measure it out and the avoid obvious slurring that makes you sound like a dolt.

Pathology: The flushing of your face becomes permanent from broken capillaries and can appear as clusters of red marks on the face known as "gin blossoms."

The vocal cords can become damaged and make your voice raspy.

There can be liver damage that causes pain in the right, upper-mid chest; liver failure then causes jaundice, which makes you appear yellow or brownish and sallow with dark circles under your eyes.

Long-term use seems to sometimes damage you in such a way that women become more masculine, with husky voices and authoritative stances, and men become more feminine, expressed as a kind of loose squirreliness.

Brain damage is possible (*see* Nervous System Impairment), but death will occur prior to extreme symptoms of brain damage.

ALCOHOL WITHDRAWAL

Withdrawal from alcohol addiction causes a condition known as the DTs and the physical impact can be so severe you can die from it.

Deep sickness. All the symptoms of poisoning are possible (*see* Poisoning), with the fever rarely being very high and exhaustion replaced with great agitation. Convulsions are possible (*see* Attacks), and these may be brought about by over-stimulation.

Delirium. If you're a severe alcoholic, after a few days without alcohol you'll start to have delirium, and delusions may take place, typically paranoid. Oddly enough, they might specifically involve an imagined, hostile group of the same gender as yourself.

Hallucinations might occur that give the feeling that something is crawling on your skin and the hallucinations often feature hostile animals. If there are auditory hallucinations it indicates that the withdrawal will be prolonged.

Poor concentration and memory. Someone undergoing the DTs has a difficult time focusing and may be in a state of near total confusion. There can be memory loss to the extent that it is very common to have amnesia for the entire delirium episode.

It is also possible for a person who has undergone withdrawal to have what's called "confabulation," a detailed memory of what took place during the episode that is totally false.

Withdrawal usually lasts three to six days.

Nick Stahl
In Northwood.

Heroin Use

(morphine, opium)

THE EMOTIONAL LINE

Euphoria. The chemical in heroin goes to the part of the brain that tells you that what you're doing is perfect. Full, profound and constant while high, it is akin to a religious experience. If you're going to create this condition you have to strive for the deepest state of bliss possible, with a knowing quiet smile and a feeling of having perfect peace: no pain. Many addicts will say that, far beyond the physical addiction, the powerful alluring quality of the drug's high is what makes it so difficult to quit.

One of my students was wounded in Viet Nam and lying among his dead friends, terrified, waiting to be finished off by the snipers in the trees. He said a medic crawled up to him and gave him a shot of morphine and, suddenly, he was just fine with everything. The drug is that profound.

Aloof. With the heroin high, the separation from the material world is extreme. This state is absolute, and, unlike alcohol and other intoxicants, adrenaline will not sober you up.

NODDING

Immediately after taking a significant dose of heroin you'll go into a trance-like state. This is not like losing consciousness in the normal sense and has different features, in that it may still allow you to have some physical control. From this trance you'll then return to consciousness for a time, and then another wave may rise up and you'll go back into the trance state. This pattern will taper off as the heroin metabolizes out of your system.

In a fixed physical position. When you nod out, you may fall back into a comfortable, reclined position, or you may remain oddly fixed, even in a standing position, although with head down and bent, as if using just enough effort to remain standing. I watched a guy on heroin for about five minutes as he was standing and nodding off; over and over he'd go to the very brink of falling, then boost himself with just enough energy to correct his stance.

Still, when nodding off, falling over is a real possibility.

Nod off in mid-action. Nodding off offers a theatrical opportunity for you to demonstrate the condition by being in mid-activity when the trance overtakes you, as with reaching for something, or being in mid sentence, or going to stand or sit, etc.

PHYSICAL EFFECTS

A relaxed condition. You should work at being like a rag doll, as if giving in to an intense and welcome drowsiness. With heavy eyelids and slack mouth, using only the bare minimum effort to move.

Remain coordinated. For all the looseness, you must not confuse this with the motor skill impairment you get with alcohol because, apart from the special concerns when nodding out, your coordination will be normal.

Touch the tingling. In the full rush of the drug there is a tingling sensation in the skin that makes you prone to touching yourself, specifically around the neck and head and especially the tip of the nose.

Nausea. Immediately following taking the drug, especially if it is of a pure quality, there can be nausea and vomiting. Given that it comes along with the high, this retching is not experienced as unpleasant.

SYMPTOMS OF LONG-TERM USE

All-encompassing. It's hard to separate how much of the physical ravages of heroin are caused by the drug itself, and how much are caused by the monumentally unhealthy lifestyle of a heroin addict. Heroin, perhaps beyond all other addictive substances, inclines users to center their world around the maintenance of the habit. In this way, beyond cutting off all relationships not related to the addiction, there will be a near complete disregard for normal creature comforts, unless these are necessary to provide a decent appearance in order to get more money to get more heroin.

Ravaged. The physical qualities of a typical heroin addict might be thought of as similar to someone who has been kept in a dungeon: bad hair, bad teeth, sallow and broken out skin, bad body odor, weakness and frailty.

Mental toughness for the challenge. As much as heroin is an escape, it requires true strength to sustain a heroin habit. What are normally considered admirable qualities are turned to maintaining the addiction. In this way, courage is needed to enter into all manner of dangerous situations, cleverness and ingenuity is required to lie and manipulate, the ability to endure is harnessed to endure the demanding hardships of the lifestyle.

HEROIN ADDICTION WITHDRAWAL

Deep sickness. Heroin withdrawal causes violent illness (*see* Poisoning), muscle cramping is common, with chills, hot flashes, watery eyes and runny nose, although a high temperature is rare. Insomnia is common.

Strong emotions. The emotional condition during withdrawal is consistent with having all of this sickness happening as well as a separation from the love of your life, which means depression, fear, and anger, with irritation and volatility.

*Olivia Wilde on the
set of* In Northwood.

Cocaine and Meth Use

The high attained from cocaine and meth intoxication is nearly identical to the state produced by the mental illness Mania (*see* Mental Illness — Mania). With increasing dosage over time you can move from Simple Mania to Acute Mania to Delirious Mania. To achieve this progression it is necessary to spread the amount of the drug ingested over time because too much too quickly will give you a heart attack; in this way, a Manic Stupor will not be reached before death occurs from overdose.

THE EMOTIONAL LINE

Euphoria. An energized sense of well-being. Not soaring ecstasy, not warm comfort, but invigorated good spirits.

A feeling of power. The feeling of megalomania cocaine and meth engender are their chief attraction. Even after continued long-term usage, when any euphoria is minimal, the feeling of power you get from these drugs remains.

PHYSICAL EFFECTS

Muscle tension. These stimulants give you the jitters and excess energy causing such behaviors as fidgeting, clenching and grinding your teeth, shrugging, flexing fingers, or cranking your neck. There may be the feeling that there's a band around your temples.

Raised blood pressure. Using cocaine or meth gives you a raised blood pressure that can cause excessive sweating and flushing.

If snorted there is numbness. These drugs can be injected, but are much more commonly ingested by being smoked as rock crystals or taken in powder form, snorted up into the nose. Sometimes, more as ritual, cocaine powder is rubbed into the gums. Cocaine is a numbing agent and will cause a feeling of numbness in the nose, mouth and the back of the throat where the nose drains. You can show this condition of a numb throat by swallowing with difficulty.

There can be numbness of the teeth, as if they were loose, and this might incline you to champ your teeth together, or rap at them with your fingers.

Soreness and bleeding. Cocaine is abrasive to the inside membrane of the nose and can cause pain and rupturing of the capillaries in the nose.

Psychedelic Use

(LSD, ecstasy, peyote, marijuana)

THE EMOTIONAL LINE

Excited elation or quiet bliss. Psychedelic use typically gives you a joyous feeling. It might be a tickled feeling, where everything seems funny and you enjoy playing with yourself as a being and within this new condition, or it might be a quiet, rapturous feeling.

Fear and anxiety. It's possible if you take a psychedelic, especially for the first time, or if you're given to anxiety, that you can have a panic attack; *see* Anxiety Condition.

PSYCHOLOGY

Profound insights. A key indicator that you're on a psychedelic, and probably the best way to demonstrate the condition, is to take a deep interest in something that normally isn't thought of as particularly significant. You might fixate on the workings of your own hand, the texture of a table or a wall, or become intrigued by someone else's thought process.

Increased regard for the sensual. In the same way that things can take on an extra importance, interest in the five senses is increased, and there is a feeling that your sensual life has been enhanced.

Absentmindedness. Another clear indicator that you're on a psychedelic is to be engrossed by some detail and then abandon it easily and without a second thought, whether through an impaired short-term memory or because the onslaught of stimulation is so distracting, and, after all, everything is equally fascinating.

Challenged. With a psychedelic it's called "rushing," but it's the same situation that can appear when extremely drunk; *see* Alcohol Use — Challenged. You feel beset by your condition. This feeling can be especially strong with the psychedelic experience, and you may feel as if you're going to be overwhelmed. This impending overwhelm may either cause panic or a thrill that it will take you somewhere awesome.

HALLUCINATIONS

Unlike psychotic hallucinations, psychedelic hallucinations are in the vast majority of cases distortions of things seen, and not visions appearing out of thin air. Also, unlike psychosis, hallucinated smells or tactile sensations are extremely rare. If something is ever seen that is not in any way present, it means that you are so profoundly under the influence that you would be glassy eyed and unable to walk or speak.

Auras. Objects may seem as if they are surrounded by a glow of their own coloration, vibrant and with a softening blur to the contours.

Appearance of movement in still objects. Fixed objects may appear to be melting and have a kind of shimmering movement that includes an aura; patterns may seem to be in movement and changing, the distance and size of objects may be seen to rapidly change.

Trailing. When you're under the influence of a powerful hallucinogenic drug and you see an object moving through space, it will sometimes appear to leave a trail of its own images behind it that then catch up with it when it stops; this is especially the case with moving lights. An actor can create this by waving something, even their own hand, across their field of vision with fascination.

A slight buzz or echo. There can be a type of buzzing sound heard that easily becomes an echo effect with actual sounds. A garbled quality and unusual pitch changes are perceived in sounds.

SPECIFIC CHEMICALS

A. LSD

Racing. LSD is the most likely of the psychedelics to give an amphetamine-type high, with clenching of the jaw, and a feeling of a band around the head. The onset of an LSD high is typically the most intense psychedelic experience.

Vivid hallucinations. LSD will tend to give strong distortion hallucinations.

B. Ecstasy

Very euphoric, less hallucinogenic. The mood alteration is intense, while the hallucinations from ecstasy are generally mild.

Very sensual. The clearest way to delineate that a character is on ecstasy is to demonstrate extreme sensuality, especially to touch. In this way it has been thought of as an aphrodisiac.

C. Peyote Cactus and Mushrooms

Mellow. These substances are generally more subdued and mellow in their effect.

Nausea. Nausea is possible with psychedelic mushrooms, and with peyote it is likely, so there can be stomach upset and vomiting, and this would be the best way for you to delineate that it is one of these substances, as opposed to another psychedelic.

D. Marijuana

Very mild distortions. Marijuana is the most mild of the psychedelics and hallucinations are so mild as to be nearly nonexistent.

Dry mouth and eyes. Having a dry mouth and dry eyes makes clear that the psychedelic is marijuana and you can show this by licking your lips, squinting, and rubbing your eyes.

Increased appetite. Marijuana increases the desire for food and the enjoyment of food.

Drowsiness. Unlike other psychedelics, which all tend to discourage sleepiness, marijuana typically encourages, and rarely inhibits, sleep.

Different types of marijuana cause different reactions. The mental state produced from marijuana can vary in its nature depending on the type of marijuana or hashish. Hashish and types of marijuana that are dark in color or sticky to the touch, tend to give more of a heavy affect, and make you drowsier and your eyes can become squinted because of the strong drying effect. Seedless, greener types of marijuana tend to create more of a lightheaded high.

Well, there are my tips on how to approach a few possible Character Additions. It is, of course, a far from exhaustive inventory I've offered here. Not only does there remain unaddressed a vast array of conditions that exist in life (from bunions to cutting onions), but there's that extensive menu of fictional Character Additions you might face, as well. Just think of all the ways you can play zombies and androids. Include with that the possible rsg of their senses and their basic faculties, and the variety is endless.

Again, your intent with regards to Character Additions should be to study, determine what will work best, drill, execute, and allow it to flower.

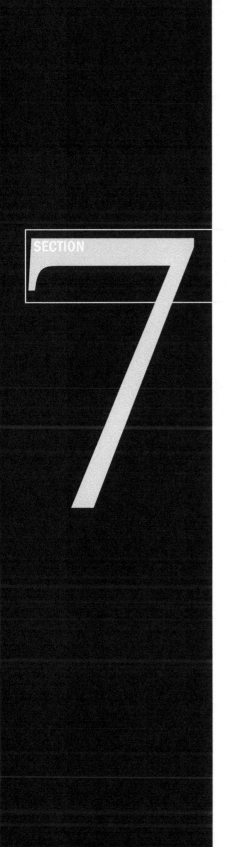

ADVICE FOR COMMENTATORS

We move now from the art of acting and an immersion into the imaginary to a completely different kind of show. It won't be a performance for an audience participating in a fantasy, willingly suspending their disbelief for "a conceit." Instead, as a commentator, you're taking part in an event that deals with non-fiction material, whether historical or current, and you're doing it as you yourself in real life, for people as themselves in real life. This means, I'm sorry, you can't be considered an artist.

I'll still speak to you commentators, stepchildren though you may be, because along the way I've acquired certain translatable skills in this area, given that both acting and commentary work have in common a requirement that you be in the moment while under pressure from people watching with an expectation, and both are more effectively done if you're unguarded and conveying a passion for the truth.

▶▶ *Note:* While stand up comedians often work as commentators, commentary work is, philosophically, profoundly different from the art of stand up. Doing a stand up routine, as opposed to dropping quips during a conversation, is a craft for presenting a character and asking the audience to join in on the conceit that the point of view being promoted is legitimate, when everyone knows in reality that it's slanting to the ridiculous.

chapter 1

Before the Event

THE SETUP

What is the reason for watching this? Before the event begins you should get a sense for the overall thrust of the program you're going to do: the reason this presentation should take place. The audience is going to have an expectation, either one they've brought to it, or one they'll rapidly take on once they start watching.

While there's probably going to be an understood precedent for how this setup has been done in the past, and there may be explicit instructions you'll have to take into account, you should nonetheless bring your own creativity and invention to the show. It may be that the program is meant to aid the functioning of society or a specific business, or it may be to improve the healthy lifestyles or the general betterment of the viewer, but, unless the information issues from an emergency, it should certainly include some entertainment value.

SOME APPROACHES

- To enlighten.
- To lay bare.
- To let unfold naturally.
- To provide a particular slant on a subject.
- To amuse through the irreverent, the goofy or the silly.

You can ask yourself: If I was watching this, what would work for me? You can imagine what would be the best thing that could happen if this event comes off right. Having an idealized achievement in mind, you can prioritize what's to be attended to and aspire to a full event.

What is the style of the Presentation? Style can be difficult to define very precisely, and maybe it really doesn't have to be defined as long as you have a feeling for it. But even if it isn't articulated, you'll want to have a sense for the overall quality, the accent, the spirit and character of the program. This sense for the appropriate tone, by itself, can govern the effectiveness of your work. Again, precedence, instruction you receive, and your creativity will help in arriving at the right flavor for the show.

The topic of discussion is a major factor in determining what style you should adopt.

THE RANGE OF POSSIBLE STYLES

▶ Light Fun (as silly and irreverent as possible): *pure entertainment subjects, games of small monetary worth.*

▶ Good Fun (mature, free spiritedness): *subjects of interest without large impact, works of artistic merit, sports, weather that does not threaten life or extensive property, games of large financial reward.*

▶ Real Purpose (dedicated and efficient business): *events of historical importance, subjects of immediate or future impact related to injury or significant financial loss.*

▶ Severe Purpose (as essential and to the point as possible): *subjects of crucial impact, events that relate to the deaths of large numbers.*

Who is your audience? It's important for you to know who you're talking to and ask: What is my relationship with the audience? They're the reason this is taking place, after all. It probably has a lot to do with the particular expectations this presentation brings as it relates to the topic, and in this way, the relationship can conceivably change from program to program, although this isn't terribly likely.

It's not wrong for you to feel a sense of pressure from the audience to deliver for them what's useful or fun.

There are many possible relationships, but as part of the purpose and expectations of the program, the emotional relationship with the audience should be clear to you. You might be expected to lead the way into this forest of a subject, or maybe you're just expected to be the most vocal member of your adventurous group.

SOME POSSIBLE RELATIONSHIPS WITH AN AUDIENCE

▸ They're well-wishers joining in for an entertainment.

▸ They're important people relying on you for help in making an important decision.

▸ They're average folks who, along with you, are being made aware of a topic.

▸ They're people with a special interest, who understand they're outside the norm. If this is the case, they might enjoy being kidded about being special; you will then either assume the role of a fellow insider, or as someone from the average population appreciating their uniqueness.

If it's a television program, you probably do well to remember that, in spite of the size and placement of the studio audience, if there is one, the broadcast is probably going to be watched by small groups of people sitting in the comfort of their homes. In this way, intimacy is usually called for and speaking into the camera is to seek a connection with someone who is located spatially very near.

There are exceptions to this, of course (there are always an exceptions, Cricket). Maybe you want to play big and loud as if to a large crowd to be goofy or assume the flamboyance of a carnival atmosphere.

There may be a consideration for what time of day your presentation will most likely be viewed. The convention for early morning shows is a soft, reassuring quality that's directed at earthy, reasonable people, while the slant tends to be more and more quirky the later at night it is seen.

Who are the guests? Just as you want to know your relationship to the audience, you'll want to know what your relationship is to the guests. This is also naturally dependent on the basic thrust of the show. It may be silly or serious, collaborative or antagonistic. In all likelihood, even if the guests are hostile to your position, you should relate to them as comrades in a search for truth. Even if their opinions are foolish, these people are here representing all such foolishly held beliefs and, because of this person's contribution, these misguided views can now be exposed for the nonsense they are. It is a rare event, and a rare stance that a guest could take, that should not be encouraged, even if combatively, by you in the spirit of a healthy adversarial process.

How will you go about getting what you want? The methodology you use to achieve your purpose may be one that comes most naturally to you and the way you normally operate. It's also possible you may want to have a conscious idea of what your approach is going to be for achieving your Objective. This approach dictates how you will carry yourself, and perhaps even affects costume.

The Most Common Methods for Commentary
▶ Direct, straightforward, plain speaking, matter of fact.
▶ Open, honest, innocent, flip.
▶ Heartfelt, frank, assuring, expressive of your deepest feelings.

Other Specialized Approaches
▶ Elegant, proper, flamboyant, uninhibited, uplifting, harsh, scary, silly.
▶ Imitative of a type of person or a specific person, a folksy lawyer: *Johnny Carson*.

Whatever the method, you should constantly be striving for the perfect version of that quality, a more relaxed, quintessential realization of that specific approach.

Believe you can get what you want. You should operate with a belief that, through the effective use of your methodology, the Objective is attainable. Even if there is a tacit understanding and embrace of the fact that Ultimate Truth is unattainable, a deeper understanding *is* possible. Even if the chance of finding common ground among the guests is remote, a chance is a chance.

You will engender faith in your audience because you have it.

What will be the Environment? You should know the basic physical layout of the program. That would include the furniture and its placement, props, if any, and the physical relationship to a live audience. It will also include the placement of cameras and lights. The necessity for concern about the whereabouts of microphones is rare, but you may want to be aware of your volume levels.

Where is information coming from? You will want to be familiar with how, during the show, you're going to be receiving information that is necessary for the smooth running of the production, whether it's by an earphone, a teleprompter, someone's hand signals, or note cards.

TECHNICAL PREPARATION

Learn the Material. You should understand how informed you're expected to be, and in this way, know what you're supposed to know. This will involve learning the definite or probable words that will come up, both pronunciations and meanings. If there are combinations of words or specialized words or names that tend to get botched, you should make sure to drill these. If these problematic words are going to be read, a notation can be made, perhaps using a highlighter of a special color, so as to be mindful of the danger when you read these. You might have peccadillo words you tend to trip on or mispronounce (I personally like to drop a syllable from *authoritative* and just pronounce it *authorative*), or perhaps you're prone to one of the classic fiasco pronunciations, when saying *nuclear, aluminum*, or *frustration*. If you're trying to cover or tame an accent, you'll of course want to watch out for those particular word sounds that bite the average ear.

Names of people should be drilled because if someone's name is misspoken it will break your rhythm and risk you coming off as incompetent, rude or both.

It's possibly good to have a few prepared witticisms, as long as it's understood that you'll want to make them seem off-the-cuff and that they'll have to be abandoned if it's not possible to insert them naturally. Forcing a witty remark artificially will tend to make your audience feel used and indicate to them that you don't have an authentic sense of humor. Unless it's part of a deadpan stance, if you tell a prepared joke you can, and probably should, freely laugh at it yourself. It's a misconception that to laugh at your own jokes is in bad taste. If done in the right spirit it communicates your appreciation for humor, not your own cleverness.

Get familiar with the set, the props, wardrobe, hair, and makeup. A professional commentator learns about their physical stuff. You should move around the physical space, handling any props that you need to be proficient with and getting wise to any issues with wardrobe, hair, and makeup. There is a whole variety of potential problems that can arise from clothing and movement. These might include bagging, awkward wrinkling, revealing skin, perspiration staining, and itching. If the troublesome clothing cannot be replaced or fixed with tape, clips, pins or by some other means, you'll want to know which movements to avoid and what postures are best to strike.

Deal with it. It's good to be as free as possible of physical encumbrances, and whatever time is available should be used for avoiding technical problems or practicing the necessary compensating behaviors, but those things that cannot be remedied must be accommodated with good cheer. Continuing to fret and be irritated about something that cannot be fixed, wishing it were some other idealized way, is pointless and potentially self-sabotaging.

THE PSYCH

Be confident. Confidence is key — and difficult to manufacture. It shouldn't be self-important and top-heavy, not a tense and forced gregariousness, grasping for an image of how great it's all supposed to go. If you take a precious stance like that, it can often turn to panic or despondency when something doesn't fit your fragile ideal. Real confidence has humor and grace and welcomes the unknown, including all the mistakes.

People with the winning mentality accentuate the positive; they play to their strengths while improving upon their weaknesses; they love details, but possess vision; they have patience, but yearn for what's better; they don't dread failures, they embrace them as lessons; they feel lucky to be of any service; and they use intense preparation to increase the likelihood of successes that will then build confidence naturally.

Get your ego out of it. An extremely useful path to getting a sense of ease for you is to understand: Either this event is bigger than you, or it's just fun. If the topic being addressed has significant impact on people's lives, then everyone involved in conveying the topic, including you, should feel humbled. In this situation you worrying about your image is shamefully egocentric. If this isn't the case and the event is just fun, as with sports or most entertainment topics, then you're in a state of silliness, as you would be if you were playing a game with a child. Having grave concerns about how you're coming across while doing this type of activity is absurd and makes you a horse's ass.

Don't fear, deny, or entertain stage nerves. Even accomplished performers at the top of their field have been known to have terrible stage nerves. But hey, it's not supposed to be about you having a cozy time of it. Once the event gets underway all that energy can be put to use toward the work. Stage nerves are something like racing your engine while the car is in park; uncomfortable perhaps, but the car only needs to be put in gear for all that energy to become useful in propelling you down the road.

Emotionally prepare. It may be good for you to get temperamentally ready for the event before it begins and to get yourself open and ready to be all of yourself and available for whatever happens.

This elevating preparation can be done by visualizing something desirable. You can visualize the event itself going well, although, again, I would warn against being too rigid in your expectations so that these don't become fixed and brittle. You can simply have a free fantasy visualization that the event is colored by optimism and good cheer and allowed to go however it wants.

You can also prepare using a visualization that has nothing to do with the actual upcoming event other than you operating in the same way you would like to for the show: *skillfully taking the game-winning shot to win a championship, confidently seducing someone sexy, being a riotous hit at a child's birthday party.*

RELAXATION AND WARM-UP

There is undoubtedly merit to warming up the mechanism and having an intention to be relaxed, but the truth is, much of the value of this work is actually just as a way to ease your stress of waiting to go on.

Practice the Alexander Technique. The basic approach of the Alexander Technique is to lengthen the neck and allow the head to float freely on top of the spinal column. It's really all about the neck. A good Alexander Technique can be achieved by tilting the chin down and then, with the same neck extension, the eyes are raised to the horizon line, and the shoulders allowed to lower. Breathing deeply, there should be a widening of the back and a filling of the stomach with air on the inhale.

Practice muscle relaxation. A tried and true means of relaxation is to tense and then relax muscles: make a fist, then release, clamp legs together, then release, lift shoulders, then drop, and so forth. The face muscles can be relaxed by making the face large, eyes wide, mouth gapping, then releasing, making the face small, scrunching tightly, and then releasing.

Having done the tense and then relax method throughout the body, you can then shake it all out. Rolling the head on the neck (caution: the head should not be pushed too far back doing neck rolls), rattling the jaw around, lolling about like a rag doll, as if you have no bones.

Practice vocal exercises. Vocal exercises typically involve warming up the mechanism by vocalizing vowel sounds using a strong diaphragm, having the sound issue freely from the center of the body, and practicing diction by precisely enunciating different word combinations: tongue twisters, especially those that give you problems.

Some Standard Tongue Twisters
   ▶ The big black bug bit the little bitty baby.
   ▶ Around the rugged rocks the ragged rascal ran.
   ▶ Peter Piper picked a pack of pickled peppers.
   ▶ The Sixth Sheik's sixth sheep is sick.
   ▶ Every elegant elephant enters Ethiopia edgewise.
   ▶ Unique New York.

chapter 2

During the Event

LIVE THROUGH THE EXPERIENCE

Beyond preparation, the most important thing for you is to really live through the experience of the show. If you do that, everything else will pretty much take care of itself. I can further specify stuff here, but it all can become organic and unconscious if you just leave yourself alone and become part of the happening.

Improvise. Usually, the only real reason to have a program is for this to be a spontaneous, living event. Whatever the aspirations for the show, it must be allowed to be what it wants to be at this moment, and, apart from hard-core news, uncertainty is almost always its most precious ingredient. That may be tough on your terrified and controlling, mathematical and cowardly mind, but if it was just information, it would probably be better from a book or a magazine.

Relate to everything that happens on the stage. It's your job to relate to everything that the audience will see and hear, and not to selectively choose what you're going to relate to and what does not fit with your idea of what was supposed to take place. If something awkward happens, you should be the first one responding to it. Pretending something didn't happen when it did then throws a contaminant into the program that is more damaging than any unpleasant incident could possibly be. Being disoriented is okay, being inhuman is not.

Furthermore, you should know that it's never too late to admit anything. If you have been living a lie by acting as if something didn't happen, whenever you catch yourself doing this you can come clean, both about the thing itself and the fact that you've been pretending it didn't happen. An audience will forgive and, beyond this, revel in such honesty.

If something's wrong, fix it.

Of course, all of this only pertains to what is happening on stage. You need to disengage from whatever madness might be going on off-stage; you are only meant to be about what the audience is experiencing.

It's possible to make reference to offstage activity, but this should probably be very limited so the impression isn't given that what's taking place is more about your world than what the audience is there for.

Keep responding. Every event demands a response equal to its specialness, and you should be continuously processing all events. Everything should be included, even the subtlest of gestures, and your response should be as free and spontaneous as possible. Of course the response needn't be verbal, or in any way meant to draw attention to itself; often the mark of amateur work is "acted," inauthentic responses.

Even if you are taking a more severe approach with a topic that demands that you be dignified or solemn, there's not a cutting off or a censoring of the moments; they are simply shaped by this particular context. Your responses to a given thing may be wildly different depending upon the thrust of what's taking place, and during a light program a given incident that brings a full laugh may, in something more grave, elicit only a wry smile, but the incident itself should nonetheless be fully responded to for what it is.

Allow the build. It is your responsibility to provide for the audience a sense of the program as it has been lived up to this moment. You shouldn't compartmentalize small segments of the show into dead ends as a particular topic is finished, or disengage from a sense of the whole because of the need to take and then return from breaks. It may be a gradual build, a succession of events bringing the program a steady development, or there might be quick escalations, caused by a single, remarkable event, but there should be an overall appreciation for the fullness of the presentation.

DIRECT YOUR ATTENTION

Stay with what's taking place now. The most fundamental, crucial advice that can be given to anyone doing just about anything is to be in the moment. That means you shouldn't be fretting over what's already happened or thinking too much about what's coming up, but instead have your attention on what's happening in front of you. Your attention should be on all of the behaviors and the sense of what's being said, and it should include the specific nature of your own response to the pertinent events.

People make the mistake of thinking that being in the moment is just observing and cataloging what's going on, something like the notations of a dispassionate scientist. Being in the moment means your full self is engaged, not just the intellect, but that you are constantly emotionally relating.

Accept self-consciousness. Self-consciousness is never a problem of any kind unless it is indulged. If it's given supremacy, it can distract and demoralize you. Just as with stage nerves, the most accomplished of performers can experience tremendous self-consciousness; they just don't let it get the best of them. You should simply ignore whatever thoughts do not pertain to your effective participation in the event. What you should not do is directly battle self-consciousness by trying to drive away any extraneous thoughts — this will only extend the process and lead to self-punishment at your failure.

Know that any thought you don't indulge doesn't produce discernible behavior, so you needn't worry about a thousand thoughts that flit through your mind, no matter how often, as long as you don't obsess over them. No one will ever know you weren't rock-solid present.

Be curious. Curiosity is a tremendous life force responsible for much of what is thought of as worthwhile about human beings. If you cultivate your curiosity, you will be pulled into the topic of discussion, the better to serve its purpose, and you will become less concerned for how you're personally coming across.

It doesn't matter if the topic is huge or small. Goethe said: "Seize life where you will, it is interesting."

COMPLETE TRANSITIONAL MOMENTS

It is your responsibility to lead the audience and the guests through the structure of the event. That may include moving from one guest to another, one topic to another, or moving into a break. To maintain continuity, these transitions should be fluid and the feeling of the event as a whole kept intact.

Recognize a transition is taking place. A transition is an event and, like all events, you need to respond to it happening. Undue emphasis needn't be placed on the transitions — most of the time they can be done behaviorally — but, whether said or implied, the message is conveyed: "*We need to hold that thought, so that we can add a different slant*" or "*I know I'm cutting this off, but reality dictates that I move on to something new.*"

Execute. As with all quality work, you must be patient and go through the steps, yet endeavor to compress as much as possible. Without rushing, jumping ahead, and cutting off any necessary moments, you at the same time move things along at the proper speed for a dynamic social interchange. You must seek maximum efficiency and command.

LEAVE YOURSELF ALONE

Allow spontaneity. You should put all of the responsibility on the situation to make you respond, and simply do as it makes you do. You should be as open a medium as possible. Allow the event to play upon and through you.

Don't hide. Stage nerves can make a person want to hide when they feel the focus of attention is on them. You have to know that there is nowhere to hide and any attempt you make to do so demonstrates obvious awkwardness.

The best approach is to face that which is most feared. For instance, if there is a part of your body that you're particularly shy about, once you've done what you can before the event to deal with this quality through makeup or costume, you should now, in front of your audience, have a mindset that you are going to freely display that thing. Sounds crazy? Still, this technique has been proven in its effectiveness. Something like turning into a skid with your car. Worried about your big nose? Show off that beautiful schnoz with lots of profile shots. Concerned you've got too much stomach? Thrust out that big belly. Frightened of sweating too much? Sweat more!

It's highly unlikely these maneuvers will in any way exacerbate whatever reality there may be to this quality you consider so unattractive, and the wonderful liberating freedom it provides is more than worth the trade off.

Don't fear fear. What is known as "choking" is not fear; everyone gets frightened. It is the fear of fear. It is a sinking feeling of doom when you become aware that you are afraid; it is an anticipation of defeat.

Fear is just an energy. It prepares a person to do what's needed for an important situation. Because in life it often indicates something is present that should be avoided, there can be a mistaken association with dread when you feel fear. While performing you should instead relate yourself to the more appropriate and truthful reality of the situation and turn that fear into invigorating thrill.

Use fear for good work.

Teaching class.

THOUGHTS ON ACTING AND ART

307

chapter 1

Acting Definitions and Advice

The audience should get the impression not of a play composed and finished by an author, but rather a series of real events taking shape before them.

— Leone di Somi

The function of the actor is to make the audience imagine for the moment that real things are happening to real people.

— George Bernard Shaw

Acting is doing things truthfully under imaginary circumstances.

— Sanford Meisner

Acting is the art of saying a thing on stage as if you believed every word you must utter to be as true as the eternal truths of life; it is the art of doing a thing on stage as if the logic of the event demanded that precise act and no other; and of doing and saying the thing as spontaneously as if you were confronted with the situation in which you were acting for the first time.

— John Barrymore

An actor should make you forget the existence of author and director and even forget the actor.

— Paul Scofield

While we look to the dramatist to give romance to realism, we ask of the actor to give realism to romance.

— Oscar Wilde

To enter physically and morally into the image of the character being portrayed on stage: mastering their thoughts, feelings, passions, defects and virtues, and making the transfiguration so complete as to make it live fully.

— Ernesto Rossi

To fathom the depths of character and to trace its latent motives, to feel its finest quiverings of emotion, to comprehend the thoughts that are hidden under the words, and thus possess oneself of the actual mind of the individual.

— William Charles Macready

Speak easily and naturally; don't adopt a false, oratorical way of speaking. Don't gesture excessively; be graceful, even when full of emotion. Don't be too tame either, but use your sense of proportion. Do as the dialog suggests and make the dialog serve what you are doing. Don't do more than what is truthful because this goes against the very purpose of acting, which is to hold a mirror up to nature: to show virtue and vice what they look like; and the zeitgeist its context and impression. If someone overacts, even though they may get a response, it will offend an honest and sensitive person, and the judgment of one such person has to count for more than a whole theater full of others.

— William Shakespeare
("Advice to the Players" paraphrased)

Keep a warm heart and a cool head. In the acting of a part, little should be left to chance, and for the reason that spontaneity, inspiration, or whatever this strange and delightful quality might be called, it is not to be commanded, or we should give it some other name. It is therefore better that a clear and unmistakable outline of the character should be drawn before an actor undertakes a new part. If the performer has a well-ordered and artistic mind it is likely that they will give at least a symmetrical and effective performance, but should they make no definite arrangement, and depend upon our ghostly friends Spontaneity and Inspiration to pay them a visit, and should these decline to call, the actor will be in a maze and their audience in a muddle.

— Joseph Jefferson

Nobody can, eight times a week, lay their whole soul on the stage and have it fully express the play. You can't do it, no matter what kind of nut you are. Therefore, I think it's best to know how to do it the other way. But at the same time, don't paint yourself into a corner; leave enough space so that when things come to take you, you're free to let all the props fall on the floor and go. And then, when the spirit's left you, keep the technical stuff there and make it send the messages to the audience.

— Geraldine Page

The actor must guard against a search for perfect solutions. When you go on the stage, giving yourself to a problem, the audience will often see you creating exactly the right degree of experience. An actor need not do a thing 100 percent in order to do it. A little coffee is coffee. A drop of blood contains all of the elements of blood.

— Lee Strasberg

You must create a character that is entirely different from the one created by the author and when those two characters, the author's and the actor's, merge into one, you will get a work of art.

— Anton Chekhov

The character is a box you build. Then you go crazy in the box.

— Sean Penn

It is an invariable characteristic of good actors that they don't seem to be conscious of the audience, but always absorbed in the world of the part which they represent; whereas it is not less an invariable characteristic of bad actors that they cannot forget themselves and the audience.

— George Henry Lewes

The audience must feel it is there because of the actor and not the other way around.

— Gotthold Lessing

The greatest performances are those that are most free from cliché, those in which every detail has been freshly conceived and which retain at each performance enough of that freshness.

— Michael Redgrave

The fault generally lies less in the bad imitation of a good model, than in the successful imitation of a bad model.

— George Henry Lewes

In every scene there is a cliché. I try to find the cliché and get as far away from it as I can.

— Marlon Brando

Do not a great many audiences prefer to see an actor "performing," which allows them to feel they safely know where they are, rather than living through the part without concession to convention. But for an actor to give themselves over to conventional acting will in time dry up whatever imaginative powers they possess.

— Michael Redgrave

We could set up attractive reading rooms in which cultured critics with good looks and good speaking voices give readings of plays after explaining them in advance; but we don't because the theater is flesh and blood: living, vibrant, luminous life. Real life illuminated by the ideas of the people who have written the words and by the art of those who speak them.

— Ermete Zacconi

When you start rehearsing, what you do is build and eliminate. You keep refining, purifying, so that you end up doing as little as possible to get an effect.

— Constance Cummings

In the art of imitation there is the level of no imitation. When the act of imitation is perfectly accomplished and the actor becomes the thing itself, the actor will no longer have a desire to imitate.

— Zeami Motokyito

Acting is not about dressing up. Acting is about stripping bare. The whole essence of learning lines is to forget them so you can make them sound like you thought of them that instant.

— Glenda Jackson

I don't know exactly where I'm going, I just know, whatever happens, I'm available.

— Sally Field

Nobody "becomes" a character. You can't act unless you are who you are.

— Marlon Brando

I work from the best qualities I see in myself, and also the worst. I always ask myself the same question: "How am I like the character? And how am I unlike him?"

— Gene Hackman

Never think less of the character. Unless, of course, he's a character who likes to think less of himself.

— Robert De Niro

The test of a real comedian is whether you laugh at him before he opens his mouth.

— George Jean Nathan

The actor invokes, lays bare what lies in every person and what daily life covers up.

— Peter Brook

In life we make excuses for ourselves. In acting you try to admit to the greater crime. You want to get down to the deeper crime in yourself.

— Dustin Hoffman

Surprise your mother. She never knew you had it in you.

— Michael Caine

The actor's job is to set themselves on fire amidst the stage and wave at the audience through the flames.

— Antonin Artaud

An actor is total carnality—all they can use to get at you is their body, their flesh, their voice, and their sense of self.

— Athol Fugard

You have fun. They have fun. It's kind of dirty.

— Garland Wright

Acting is half shame, half glory. Shame at exhibiting yourself, glory when you can forget yourself.

— John Gielgud

I think the most difficult equation to solve in acting is the union of two things that are absolutely necessary. One is confidence, absolute confidence, and the other an equal amount of humility towards the work. That's a very hard equation.

— Laurence Olivier

The poet, the actor, the artist, the tailor, the stagehand serve one goal, which is placed by the poet in the very basis of their play.

— Konstantin Stanislavsky

Stanislavsky always sought the essence of the play in the times and events described; and this he expected the actor to understand. This is what he called the core, and it is the core which must stir the actor, which must be part of them.

— Vladimir I. Nemirovich-Danchenko

It's about understanding the requirements of the story, the potential of the story, and then staying as open as you can to inspiration.

— Ron Howard

Look at your character through the lead character's eyes. How much you mean to them and in what way. Find those beats. Then, when the lead comes anywhere near your character and the beats come… crush them.
— Sean Penn

You have character and the situation the character is in. That's all.
— Martin Scorsese

There's only one real question: What is it really like when this happens? — when somebody seduces someone, when somebody kills someone, when somebody loves someone. What is it really like?
— Mike Nichols

Consciousness never creates what the subconscious does; for the subconscious has an independent faculty for gathering material without the knowledge of the consciousness.

In life our feelings come to us by themselves regardless our will. Our willing gives birth to action that is directed towards the gratification of desire. If we succeed in gratifying it, an elated feeling is born spontaneously. If an obstacle stands in the way of gratifying it, an unpleasant feeling is born — "suffering." Every action directed towards the gratification of our desires is continuously accompanied by a series of spontaneous emotions, either anticipation of the coming gratification or the fear of failure.

Thus, every feeling is the result of either a gratified or non-gratified intention. At first, a desire arises that ignites the will, then it begins to act consciously aiming towards its gratification. Only then, altogether spontaneously, and sometimes against our will, do the feelings come. Thus, emotion is a product of will and the conscious (and sometime subconscious) things that are done to achieve its gratification.

Therefore the actor, Stanislavsky taught, must think first of all about what they want to obtain at a particular moment and what they are to do to get it, but not about what they are going to feel. The emotion, as well as the means of its expression, is being generated subconsciously, spontaneously, in the process of executing actions directed towards the gratification of a desire. The actor must therefore come on the stage not in order to feel or experience emotions, but in order to do something. "Don't wait for emotions — act immediately," Stanislavsky said.

Every true action differs from simply feeling by the presence of the will element. To comfort, to implore, to scorn, to seduce, to reassure, to wait, to chase away — these are verbs expressing "will" action. These verbs denote the task that the actor places before themselves when working upon a character. The verbs: to pity, to weep, to laugh, to be impatient, to hate, to love — express feeling, and therefore cannot and must not figure as tasks in the analysis of a role. Feelings denoted by these later verbs must be born spontaneously and subconsciously as a result of the actions executed by the first series of verbs.

Desire is the motive for action. Therefore, the fundamental thing an actor must learn is to wish for whatever is given to the character to wish for. They must wish by order. An actor who is unskilled does the opposite of what nature demands of them and what the school of Stanislavsky teaches. They grasp for feelings and try to give a definite form to their expression. They always begin from the end; that is, from the final ends of their part.

In life a man who weeps is often concerned about restraining his tears — but the unskilled actor does just the opposite. Having read the remark of the author (He weeps), he tries with all his might to squeeze out tears, and since nothing comes of it, he is forced to grasp at the straw of the stereotyped theatrical cry. The same is true of laughter. Who does not know the unpleasant sound of counterfeit laughter? The same takes place with the expression of other feelings.

Thus we can say that Stanislavsky did not invent anything. He teaches us to follow the road pointed out by nature itself.

— Eugene Vaktangov

The word "art" should be written everywhere, in the auditorium and in the dressing rooms, before the word "business" gets written there.

— Federico Garcia Lorca

Private conflicts, quarrels, sentiments, animosities are unavoidable in any human group. It is our duty to a creation to keep these in check in so far as they might deform and wreck the work process.

— Jerzy Growtowski

Never come into the theatre with mud on your feet. Leave your dust and dirt outside. Check your little worries, squabbles, petty difficulties with your outside clothing — all the things that ruin your life and draw your attention away from your art — at the door.

— Konstantin Stanislavsky

There are impositions: the dread of criticism, money madness, stage fright, star-dreaming, character clichés — to be an artist you most overcome these obstacles.

— Stella Adler

In most cases success equals prison... An artist should never be: prisoner of himself, prisoner of a manner, prisoner of a reputation, prisoner of success.

— Henri Matisse

The actor who lets the dust accumulate on their Shakespeare and on their Ibsen, but pores greedily over every little column of the theatrical news, is getting lost. A club arranged where actors can get together and talk, talk, talk about themselves might actually be dangerous to an actor in the making. Be wary of it. Go instead into the streets, into the slums, into fashionable quarters. Go into the day courts and the night courts. Become acquainted with sorrow, with many kinds of sorrow. Learn of the wonderful heroism of the poor, of the incredible generosity of the very poor — a generosity of which the rich and well-to-do have, for the most part, not the faintest conception. Go into modest homes, into out-of-the-way corners, into open country. Go where you can find something fresh to bring to the stage. It is as valuable as youth unspoiled, as better than a healthy complexion is better than anything a rouge-pot can achieve.

There should be, there must be, a window open somewhere, a current of new air ever blowing through the theater. I remember how earnestly I wanted to play Hedda Gabler, as though she had just driven up to the stage door and had swept in not from the dressing room, but from out of the frosty night onto the stage. This you cannot do if you are forever jostling in the theatrical crowd where you lose the blush of youth, the bloom of character. If as author, producer, director or actor you become theatricalized, you are lost. The chance to do the fine thing may come your way, but it is not for you. You cannot do it. You have been spoiled. You have spoiled yourself.

— Minnie Maddern Fiske

Let the actor study nature in all her spiritual fullness: thus will they avoid banality and triviality. Let them study her outside themselves and within themselves, in the world and within their own breast. Then the more purely and richly they develop their personality, the stronger their temperament through which they observe nature, the more deeply too will they grasp life and reproduce life. As for the ideal, the truly beautiful, they can only feel that within themselves, not outside themselves in precepts that have been handed down. Let them find beauty in fidelity to the artistic whole of which they are a part, in the integrated character they portray and in the play in which they act.

— Otto Brahm

chapter 2

Robert Henri

(1865-1929) from *The Art Spirit*

Technique is merely a language, and as I see life more and more clearly, growing older, I have but one intention and that is to make my language as clear and simple and sincere as is humanly possible. I believe one should study ways and means all the while to express one's idea of life more clearly.

Technique must be solid, positive, but elastic, must not fall into formula, must adapt itself to the idea. And for each new idea there must be new invention special to the expression of that idea and no other. And the idea must be valuable, worth the effort of expression, must come of the artist's understanding of life and the thing he greatly desires to say.

If you want to know how to do a thing you must first have a complete desire to do that thing. Then go to kindred spirits — others who have wanted to do that thing — and study their ways and means, learn from their successes and failures and add your quota. Thus you may acquire from the experience of the race. And with the technical knowledge you may go forward, expressing through the play of forms the music that is in you and which is very personal to you.

Everything that is beautiful is orderly, and there can be no order unless things are in their right relation to each other. Of this right relation throughout the world beauty is born. This orderliness must exist or the world could not hold together, and it is a vision of orderliness that enables the artist along any line whatsoever to capture and present through their imagination the wonder that stimulates life.

Most people, either by training or inheritance, count themselves at the start as "No good," or "second rate" or "just like anyone else," whereas in everyone there is the great mystery; every single person in the world has evidence to give of their own individuality, providing they have acquired the full power to make clear this evidence.

All the past up to a moment ago is your legacy. You have a right to it. The works of ancient masters, those of the student next to you, the remark let drop a moment ago; all is experience.

To study art is to study order, relative values, to get at fundamental constructive principles. It is the great study of the inside, not the outside of nature. Such a pursuit evokes justice, simplicity, and good health.

You have to make up your mind to be alone in many ways. We like sympathy and we like company. It's easier than going it alone. But alone one gets acquainted with themselves, grows up and on, not stopping with the crowd. It costs to do this. If you succeed somewhat you may have to pay for it as well as enjoy it all of your life.

Make great things — as great as you are. Work always as if you were a master; expect from yourself a masterpiece. It is a wrong idea that a master is a finished person. Masters are faulty, they haven't learned everything and they know it. Finished persons are very common — people who are closed up, quite satisfied that there is little or nothing more to learn. A small boy can be a master. I have met masters now and again, some in studios, others anywhere, working on a railroad, running a boat, playing a game, selling things. Masters of such as they had. They are wonderful people to meet. Have you never felt yourself "in the presence" when with a carpenter or a gardener? When they are the right kind they do not say, "I am only a carpenter or a gardener, therefore not much can be expected from me." They say, or mean to say, "I am a carpenter!" These are masters, what more could anyone be!

The man who becomes a master starts out by being master of such as he has, and the man who is a master at any time of such as he has is at that time straining every faculty. What he learns then from his experience is fundamental, constructive, to the point. His wits are being used and being formed into the habit of usage.

Keep up the work. Try to reduce everything you see to the utmost simplicity. That is, let nothing but the things that are of the utmost importance to you have any place.

I think your only salvation is in finding yourself, and you will never find yourself unless you quit preconceiving what you will be when you have found yourself. What, after all, are your greatest, deepest, and all-possessing interests? What you need is to free yourself from your own preconceived ideas about yourself. It will take a revolution to do it, and many times you will think yourself on the road only to find that the old habit has possessed you again with a new preconception. But if you can at least to a degree free yourself, take your head off your heart and give the latter a chance, something may come of it. The results will not be what you expect, but they will be like you and will be the best that can come from you. There will be a lot more pleasure in the doing. No work of art is ever really finished. They only stop at good places.

Art is simply a result of expression during right feeling. It is a result of a grip on the fundamentals of nature, the spirit of life, the constructive force, the secret of growth, a real understanding of the relative importance of things, order, balance. After all, the object is not to make art, but to be in the wonderful state that makes art inevitable.

Directing Joanne Baron.

chapter 3

Art

Art is a celebration of life.

— Herbert Read

Art heightens the sense of humanity. It gives an elevation to feeling that is supernatural. A million sunsets will not spur people towards civilization. It requires Art to evoke into consciousness the finite perfections that lie ready for human achievement.

Art is more than a transient refreshment. It is something that adds to the permanent richness of the soul's self-attainment. It justifies itself both by its immediate enjoyment, and also by its discipline of the inmost being. Its discipline is not distinct from enjoyment, but by reason of it. It transforms the soul into permanent realization of values extending beyond its former self.

Truth matters because of Beauty.

— Alfred North Whitehead

Art transforms perception into feeling and feeling into perception.

— Leo Tolstoy

It is not an escape from life, but an expression of the significance of life, a stimulation to greater effort in living.

— Henry Moore

When power corrupts, art cleanses. Art establishes the basic human truths that must serve as the touchstones of our judgment.

— John F. Kennedy

Art is exalted above religion and race. Not a single solitary soul these days believes in the religions of the Assyrians, the Egyptians and the Greeks... Only their art, wherever it was beautiful, stands proud and exalted, rising above all time.

— Emil Nolde

Beauty is a primeval phenomenon, which itself never makes its appearance, but the reflection of which is visible in a thousand different utterances of the creative mind, and is as various as nature herself. Beauty is a manifestation of secret natural laws, which otherwise would have been hidden from us forever.

Even at moments of both highest bliss and highest distress we still need art.

— Goethe

In the dark times
Will there be singing?
Yes, there will also be singing
About the dark times.

— Bertolt Brecht

Art is always unexpected and always as faithful and honest as dreams.
— Alice Walker

The role of the artist is basic because, while the world's horizons have been extended, the human heart is as small as ever.
— Mark Chagall

Art bids us touch and taste and hear and see the world, and shrinks from "mathematic form," from abstract thinking, from all that is of the brain only, from all that is not a fountain jetting from the entire hopes, memories and sensations of the body.
— William Butler Yeats

All art is concerned with coming into being.
— Aristotle

Art

All true art is an expression of the soul. The outward forms have value only in so far as they are expressions of the inner spirit of human beings. All true art must help the soul to realize its inner self.

— Gandhi

There is not a single true work of art that has not in the end added to the inner freedom of each person who has known and loved it.

— Albert Camus

Art has the power to awaken us to the truth; something equivalent to the actual density of the real, that density which life offers us every day but which we are unable to grasp because we are amusing ourselves with lies.

— Simone Weil

Creativity comes from awakening and directing our higher natures, which originate in the primal depths of the universe and are appointed by Heaven.

— *I Ching*

Art should be great and unobtrusive; a thing which enters into a person's soul and does not surprise or amaze with itself, but with its subject. It should surprise by a fine excess, and not by singularity. It should strike the audience as a working of their own higher thoughts, and appear almost as a remembrance.

— John Keats

In every work of genius we recognize our own rejected thoughts; they come back to us with a certain alienated majesty.

— Ralph Waldo Emerson

You select a pattern and with that you mix your essence. This spirit is the beginning and end, the sum total of your art.

— Goethe

A work of art is a corner of creation seen through a temperament.

— Émile Zola

There is a vitality, a life force, an energy that is translated through you into action, and, because there is only one of you in all time, this expression is unique. If you block it, it will never exist through any other medium and be lost. Keep the channel open.

— Martha Graham

Make visible what, without you, might never be seen.

— Robert Bresson

Originality doesn't come from expressing what nobody has ever expressed before, it comes from being oneself.

— Anonymous

I wrote the books I couldn't find in the library.

— George Orwell

Art is made up of strength, exactitude, and will. In order to express life, to render nature, one must will with all the strength of heart and brain. Nature exceeds, and greatly, human genius; she is superior in everything. When we give ourselves wholly to her, without reserve, she lends unknown forces to us; she shows us these forms, which our watching eyes do not see, which our intelligence does not understand or suspect.

— Auguste Rodin

Art is in love with luck, and luck with art.

— Agathon

In art, truth and reality begin when the artist no longer understands what they are doing or what they know, and when there remains an energy that is all the stronger for being constrained, controlled and compressed. It is therefore necessary to present oneself with the greatest humility: white, pure and candid and with a mind as if empty, in a spiritual state analogous to that of a communicant approaching the Lord's Table. Obviously it is necessary to have all of one's experience behind oneself, but also to preserve the freshness of the instincts.

— Suzuki

Living is a form of not being sure, not knowing what next or how. The moment you know how, you begin to die a little. The artist never entirely knows. We guess. We may be wrong, but we take leap after leap in the dark.

— Agnes de Mille

Perhaps I'm unable to see things in my work that others do because if I did see them I'd be too frightened to continue. I've always insisted that there is a fine grain of stupidity required in the creative process.

— Flannery O'Connor

Because of their courage, artists are willing to make silly mistakes. The truly creative person is one who can think crazy; such a person knows full well that many of his great ideas will prove to be worthless. The creative person is flexible, able to change as the situation changes, to break habits, to face indecision and changes in conditions without undue stress. They are not threatened by the unexpected.

— Frank Goble

Exuberance is beauty.

— William James

The passions are the gates of the soul.

— Baltasar Gracian

Art has something to do with the achievement of stillness in the midst of chaos. A stillness which characterizes prayer, too, and the eye of the storm... an arrest of the attention in the midst of distraction.

— Saul Bellow

Don't play the saxophone. Let it play you.

— Charlie Parker

If a person really wishes to master an art, technical knowledge is not enough. One has to transcend technique so that the art is an "artless art" growing out of the unconscious.

— Henri Matisse

327

Willfulness must give way to willingness; mastery must give way to mystery.
— Gerald G. May

Everything in the labor of art amounts to one thing: the difficult should become easy, and the easy beautiful.
— Konstantin Stanislavsky

Clay is molded to make a vessel, but the utility of the vessel lies in the space where there is nothing. Thus, taking advantage of what is, we recognize the utility of what is not.
— Lao Tzu

It's not what you see that is art, art is the gap.
— Marcel Duchamp

Don't play what you know. Play what you don't know about what you know.
— Miles Davis

Do not finish your work too much.
— Paul Gauguin

Industry in art is a necessity, not a virtue, and any evidence of the same in the production is a blemish, not a quality.
— James Whistler

A line will take us hours maybe; yet if it does not seem a moment's thought, our stitching and unstinting has been naught.
— William Butler Yeats

Reveal Art and conceal the artist.
— Oscar Wilde

As soon as someone cherishes the thought of winning the contest or displaying their skill in technique, craftsmanship is doomed.
— Takano Shigeyoshi

The highest condition of art is artlessness.

— Henry David Thoreau

Do it as straight as you can, just like you walk as straight as you can, because it's the best way to get there.

— H. G. Wells

A true poet does not bother to be poetical. Nor does a nursery gardener scent his roses.

— Jean Cocteau

Take eloquence and wring its neck.

— Paul Verlaine

Murder your darlings.

— G. K. Chesterton

The progress of an artist is a continual self-sacrifice, a continual extinction of personality. It is not a turning loose of emotion, but an escape from emotion; it is not the expression of personality, but an escape from personality. But, of course, only those who have personality and emotions know what it is to want to escape from these things.

— T. S. Eliot

A work should contain its total meaning within itself and should impress it on the spectator before he even knows the subject.

— Henri Matisse

Genuine art can communicate before it is understood.

— T. S. Eliot

The ultimate justification for a work of art is to help the spectator become a work of art themselves.

— Bernard Berenson

Art is in itself noble; that is why the artist has no fear of what is common.
— Goethe

To an artist, nothing can be useless.
— Samuel Johnson

The greatest masterpieces were once only pigments on a palette.
— Henry S. Haskins

All art is selected detail.
— Paul Cézanne

The art of art, the glory of expression is simplicity.
— Walt Whitman

Simplicity, carried to an extreme, becomes elegance.
— Jon Franklin

It is far more difficult to be simple than to be complicated; far more difficult to sacrifice skill and easy execution in the proper place, than to expand both indiscriminately.
— John Ruskin

All my life I have struggled to make one authentic gesture.
— Isadora Duncan

One day while I was drawing a young girl something struck me: that is to say, all of a sudden I noticed the only thing that remained alive was the gaze… In a living person there is no doubt that what makes them alive is their gaze.
— Alberto Giacometti

Art has no other object than to set aside the symbols of practical utility, the general ties that are conventionally and socially accepted, everything in fact which masks reality from us, in order to set us face to face with reality itself.

— Henri Bergson

The wisest keeps something of the vision of a child. Though he may understand a thousand things that a child could not understand, he is always a beginner, close to the original meaning of life.

— John Macy

Simplicity is the seal of truth.

— Proverb

That simplicity which cost everything.

— Martha Graham

Holy simplicity!

— John Huss
(last words before being burned at the stake)

Don't let your simplicity be imposed upon.

— Brinsley

Be regular and orderly in your life like a bourgeois, so that you can be violent and original in your work.

— Gustave Flaubert

One never paints violently enough.

— Eugene Delacroix

Everyone has talent. What is rare is the courage to follow that "talent" to the dark place where it leads.

— Erica Jong

Whatever the next thing is that you create, it's got to be even more naked than the last.

— Harold Pinter

We nearly always live through screens — a screened existence. And I sometimes think, when people say my work looks violent, that perhaps I have from time to time been able to clear away one or two of the veils or screens.

— Francis Bacon

If you practice an art, be proud of it and make it proud of you. It may break your heart, but it will fill your heart before it breaks it: it will make you a person in your own right.

— Sherwood Anderson

The artist's life cannot be otherwise than full of conflicts, for two forces are at war within them. On the one hand the common human longing for happiness, satisfaction and security in life, and on the other a ruthless passion for creation that may go so far as to override every personal desire. It not only demands all you can give, but also all you can get others to give.

— Edmund Wilson

From things that have happened and from things as they exist and from all things that you know and all those you cannot know, you make something through your invention that is not a representation, but a whole new thing truer than anything true and alive, and you make it alive.

— Ernest Hemingway

Works of art can only be produced where the person is either in affluence or above care of it.

— William Blake

Being an artist means, not reckoning and counting, but ripening like the tree which does not force its sap and stands confident in the storms of Spring without the fear that after them may come no Summer. It does come. I learn it daily, learn it with pain to which I am grateful.

— Rainer Maria Rilke

The artist is not someone endowed with free will who seeks their own ends, but they who allow art to realize its purpose through them. The unborn work in the psyche of the artist is a force of nature that achieves its end either with tyrannical might or with the subtle cunning of nature herself, quite regardless of the personal fate of the one who is its vehicle.

— C. G. Jung

No one creates from reason, but from necessity.

— Romain Rolland

We work in the dark. We do what we can. We give what we have. Our doubt is our passion. Our passion is our task. The rest is the madness of art.

— Henry James

If you hear a voice within you saying: "You are not a painter," then by all means paint, boy, and the voice will be silenced.

— Vincent van Gogh

The muses do not lead; they open the door and point to the tightrope.

— Jean Cocteau

It is a horrible, exhausting struggle. A person would never undertake such a thing if not driven by some demon which can be neither resisted nor understood.

— George Orwell

It is almost as if you were frantically constructing another world while the world that you live in dissolves beneath your feet, and that your survival depends on completing this construction at least one second before the old habitation collapses.

— Tennessee Williams

If people knew how hard I had to work to gain my mastery, it wouldn't seem wonderful at all.

— Michelangelo

True artists scorn nothing.

— Albert Camus

That which is beautiful is moral, that is all, nothing more.

— Gustave Flaubert

The moment you cheat for the sake of beauty, you know you're an artist.

— Max Jacob

I think we ought to seek only that art that would wound and stab us. We need art that affects us like a disaster, that grieves us deeply, like the death of someone we loved more than ourselves, like being banished into forests far from everyone, like a suicide. A piece of art should be an ax for the frozen sea inside us.

— Franz Kafka

There is no point in asserting and reasserting what the heart cannot believe.

— Anonymous

The truth of a thing is the feel of it, not the think of it.

— Stanley Kubrick

The final test for a work of art will be our affection for it, as it is the test of our friends, and of anything else which we cannot define.

— E. M. Forster

The mind cannot act the role of the heart.

— François La Rochefoucauld

Critics, mathematicians, scientists and busybodies want to classify everything, marking the boundaries and limits… In art, there is room for possibilities.

— Pablo Picasso

Not everything has a name. Some things lead us into a realm beyond words. By means of art we are sometimes sent, dimly, briefly, to revelations unattainable by reason.

— Alexander Solzhenitsyn

Of which Beauty will you speak? There are many: there is one for every look, for every spirit, adapted to each taste, to each particular constitution.

— Eugene Delacroix

The dream reveals the reality where conception lags behind. That's the horror of life, the terror of art.

— Franz Kafka

Art is our chief means of breaking bread with the dead.

— W. H. Auden

The end of art is to figure the hidden meaning of things and not their appearance; for in this profound truth lies their true reality, which does not appear in their external outlines.

— Aristotle

A portrait, as close as it is to reality, is a paraphrase of the greatest mystery and, in the last analysis, it does not represent a single personality but a part of that spirituality or feeling which pervades the whole world.

— Ernst Ludwig Kirchner

Art itself may be defined as a single-minded attempt to render the highest kind of justice to the visible universe, by bringing to light the truth, manifold and one, underlying its every aspect.

— Joseph Conrad

Any work of art, provided it springs from a sincere motivation to further understanding between people, is an act of faith and therefore is an act of love.

— Truman Capote

The artist's struggle to transcend their pain can become the seed for many others' hope, transforming a personal journey into a vision for us all.
— Diane Cole

The essence of all beautiful art, all great art, is gratitude.
— Nietzsche

Art is a mold in which to imprison for a moment the shining elusive element that is life itself, life hurtling past us and running away, too strong to stop, too sweet to lose.
— Willa Cather

Great art is an instant arrested in eternity.
— James Gibbon Huneker

Today, like every other day, we wake up empty and frightened. Don't open the door to the study and begin reading. Take down a musical instrument. Let the beauty we love be what we do. There are hundreds of ways to kneel and kiss the ground.
— Rumi

We are all but fellow-travelers
Along Life's weary way;
If anyone can play the pipes,
In God's name, let them play.

— John Bennett

Be with me, Beauty, for the fire is dying.
— James Masefield

Conclusion

So, that's it. That's what I know about acting a role. If I've missed something, let me know. I will say, if you're going to get better at acting, like anything else, you have to do a lot of it. Theater will always be the best training ground because it's the actor's domain where you can work on a richness of parts, with, typically, good rehearsal time and an opportunity to learn from an audience's response. To begin your training, however, the best way won't necessarily be to do bunch of different scenes. Scene work can get you in the habit of putting a mask over your own mask. Better is doing improvisations where you play yourself, using your own name, and putting yourself through a lot of different circumstances; not directly from your own life, but dramatic situations you nonetheless can relate to. Before anything, you need to get okay being yourself, exposing how you would really operate under stressful, imaginary conditions, willfully playing the moments. There is no better conditioning for an actor than the first year of The Meisner System training, beautifully described by William Esper in his book: *The Actor's Art and Craft*.

Sculpt yourself. Remove all that is unnecessary, balance what is out of balance and bring to light what is beautiful; the purest version of yourself. Start now and do it wildly. You may have to risk a lot, face your fear and open your eyes to the way things really are; but before you can paint, you have to have good colors to paint with. And you study, forever, art and the human condition. If you have the courage, if you put in the work, if you allow for the Mystery and embrace disappointment and victory both, you just may find: You can act!

.

About the Author

As co-artistic head of The Joanne Baron/D.W. Brown Studio (*www.baronbrown.com*), D. W. BROWN has trained, directed and coached hundreds of actors and led seminars on acting with Sean Penn, Benicio Del Toro, Anthony Hopkins, Dustin Hoffman, Susan Sarandon and Sidney Pollack; other notables who have spoken at the studio include Robert De Niro, Jim Caviezel, Jeff Goldblum, Martin Sheen, Richard Dreyfuss, John Singleton, Martha Coolidge, Robert Towne, Mark Rydell, and David Mamet.

D.W. has personally coached and taught Robin Wright Penn, Leslie Mann, Keanu Reeves, Michael Richards, Jamie Kennedy, Nicollette Sheridan, Michael Vartan, Jenny Garth, directors Sam Raimi and Tom Shadyac, and many other great talents. He has just finished writing and directing the feature film *In Northwood* starring Nick Stahl, Olivia Wilde, Dash Mihok, Pruit Taylor Vince, Shoreh Aghdashloo, and Joanne Baron.

D.W. Brown is a lover of dogs, has a purple belt in Gracie Jiu-Jitsu (from Rickson Gracie) and feels most himself when acting, directing, or walking through a museum at night with Joanne.

DIRECTING ACTORS
CREATING MEMORABLE PERFORMANCES
FOR FILM AND TELEVISION

JUDITH WESTON

BEST SELLER
OVER 45,000 COPIES SOLD!

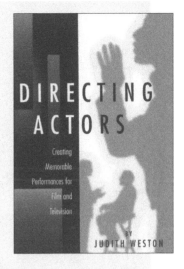

Directing film or television is a high-stakes occupation. It captures your full attention at every moment, calling on you to commit every resource and stretch yourself to the limit. It's the white-water rafting of entertainment jobs. But for many directors, the excitement they feel about a new project tightens into anxiety when it comes to working with actors.

This book provides a method for establishing creative, collaborative relationships with actors, getting the most out of rehearsals, troubleshooting poor performances, giving briefer directions, and much more. It addresses what actors want from a director, what directors do wrong, and constructively analyzes the director-actor relationship.

"Judith Weston is an extraordinarily gifted teacher."
> — David Chase, Emmy® Award-Winning Writer,
> Director, and Producer *The Sopranos,*
> *Northern Exposure, I'll Fly Away*

"I believe that working with Judith's ideas and principles has been the most useful time I've spent preparing for my work. I think that if Judith's book were mandatory reading for all directors, the quality of the director-actor process would be transformed, and better drama would result."
> — John Patterson, Director
> *Six Feet Under, CSI: Crime Scene Investigation,*
> *The Practice, Law and Order*

"I know a great teacher when I find one! Everything in this book is brilliant and original and true."
> — Polly Platt, Producer, *Bottle Rocket*
> Executive Producer, *Broadcast News, The War of the Roses*

JUDITH WESTON was a professional actor for 20 years and has taught Acting for Directors for over a decade.

$26.95 · 314 PAGES · ORDER NUMBER 4RLS · ISBN: 0941188248

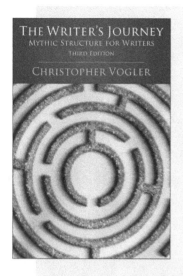

FILM & VIDEO BOOKS

SCREENWRITING | WRITING

And the Best Screenplay Goes to... | Dr. Linda Seger | $26.95

Archetypes for Writers | Jennifer Van Bergen | $22.95

Cinematic Storytelling | Jennifer Van Sijll | $24.95

Could It Be a Movie? | Christina Hamlett | $26.95

Creating Characters | Marisa D'Vari | $26.95

Crime Writer's Reference Guide, The | Martin Roth | $20.95

Deep Cinema | Mary Trainor-Brigham | $19.95

Elephant Bucks | Sheldon Bull | $24.95

Fast, Cheap & Written That Way | John Gaspard | $26.95

Hollywood Standard, The | Christopher Riley | $18.95

I Could've Written a Better Movie than That! | Derek Rydall | $26.95

Inner Drives | Pamela Jaye Smith | $26.95

Joe Leydon's Guide to Essential Movies You Must See | Joe Leydon | $24.95

Moral Premise, The | Stanley D. Williams, Ph.D. | $24.95

Myth and the Movies | Stuart Voytilla | $26.95

Power of the Dark Side, The | Pamela Jaye Smith | $22.95

Psychology for Screenwriters | William Indick, Ph.D. | $26.95

Rewrite | Paul Chitlik | $16.95

Romancing the A-List | Christopher Keane | $18.95

Save the Cat! | Blake Snyder | $19.95

Save the Cat! Goes to the Movies | Blake Snyder | $24.95

Screenwriting 101 | Neill D. Hicks | $16.95

Screenwriting for Teens | Christina Hamlett | $18.95

Script-Selling Game, The | Kathie Fong Yoneda | $16.95

Stealing Fire From the Gods, 2nd Edition | James Bonnet | $26.95

Way of Story, The | Catherine Ann Jones | $22.95

What Are You Laughing At? | Brad Schreiber | $19.95

Writer's Journey, – 3rd Edition, The | Christopher Vogler | $26.95

Writer's Partner, The | Martin Roth | $24.95

Writing the Action Adventure Film | Neill D. Hicks | $14.95

Writing the Comedy Film | Stuart Voytilla & Scott Petri | $14.95

Writing the Killer Treatment | Michael Halperin | $14.95

Writing the Second Act | Michael Halperin | $19.95

Writing the Thriller Film | Neill D. Hicks | $14.95

Writing the TV Drama Series – 2nd Edition | Pamela Douglas | $26.95

Your Screenplay Sucks! | William M. Akers | $19.95

FILMMAKING

Film School | Richard D. Pepperman | $24.95

Power of Film, The | Howard Suber | $27.95

PITCHING

Perfect Pitch – 2nd Edition, The | Ken Rotcop | $19.95

Selling Your Story in 60 Seconds | Michael Hauge | $12.95

SHORTS

Filmmaking for Teens | Troy Lanier & Clay Nichols | $18.95

Ultimate Filmmaker's Guide to Short Films, The | Kim Adelman | $16.95

BUDGET | PRODUCTION MGMT

Film & Video Budgets, 4th Updated Edition | Deke Simon & Michael Wiese | $26.95

Film Production Management 101 | Deborah S. Patz | $39.95

DIRECTING | VISUALIZATION

Animation Unleashed | Ellen Besen | $26.95

Citizen Kane Crash Course in Cinematography | David Worth | $19.95

Directing Actors | Judith Weston | $26.95

Directing Feature Films | Mark Travis | $26.95

Fast, Cheap & Under Control | John Gaspard | $26.95

Film Directing: Cinematic Motion, 2nd Edition | Steven D. Katz | $27.95

Film Directing: Shot by Shot | Steven D. Katz | $27.95

Film Director's Intuition, The | Judith Weston | $26.95

First Time Director | Gil Bettman | $27.95

From Word to Image | Marcie Begleiter | $26.95

I'll Be in My Trailer! | John Badham & Craig Modderno | $26.95

Master Shots | Christopher Kenworthy | $24.95

Setting Up Your Scenes | Richard D. Pepperman | $24.95

Setting Up Your Shots, 2nd Edition | Jeremy Vineyard | $22.95

Working Director, The | Charles Wilkinson | $22.95

DIGITAL | DOCUMENTARY | SPECIAL

Digital Filmmaking 101, 2nd Edition | Dale Newton & John Gaspard | $26.95

Digital Moviemaking 3.0 | Scott Billups | $24.95

Digital Video Secrets | Tony Levelle | $26.95

Greenscreen Made Easy | Jeremy Hanke & Michele Yamazaki | $19.95

Producing with Passion | Dorothy Fadiman & Tony Levelle | $22.95

Special Effects | Michael Slone | $31.95

EDITING

Cut by Cut | Gael Chandler | $35.95

Cut to the Chase | Bobbie O'Steen | $24.95

Eye is Quicker, The | Richard D. Pepperman | $27.95

Invisible Cut, The | Bobbie O'Steen | $28.95

SOUND | DVD | CAREER

Complete DVD Book, The | Chris Gore & Paul J. Salamoff | $26.95

Costume Design 101 | Richard La Motte | $19.95

Hitting Your Mark – 2nd Edition | Steve Carlson | $22.95

Sound Design | David Sonnenschein | $19.95

Sound Effects Bible, The | Ric Viers | $26.95

Storyboarding 101 | James Fraioli | $19.95

There's No Business Like Soul Business | Derek Rydall | $22.95

FINANCE | MARKETING | FUNDING

Art of Film Funding, The | Carole Lee Dean | $26.95

Complete Independent Movie Marketing Handbook, The | Mark Steven Bosko | $39.95

Independent Film and Videomakers Guide – 2nd Edition, The | Michael Wiese | $29.95

Independent Film Distribution | Phil Hall | $26.95

Shaking the Money Tree, 2nd Edition | Morrie Warshawski | $26.95

OUR FILMS

Dolphin Adventures: DVD | Michael Wiese and Hardy Jones | $24.95

On the Edge of a Dream | Michael Wiese | $16.95

Sacred Sites of the Dalai Lamas– DVD, The | Documentary by Michael Wiese | $24.95

Hardware Wars: DVD | Written and Directed by Ernie Fosselius | $14.95